Tidal Life

Tidal Life

A Natural History of the Bay of Fundy

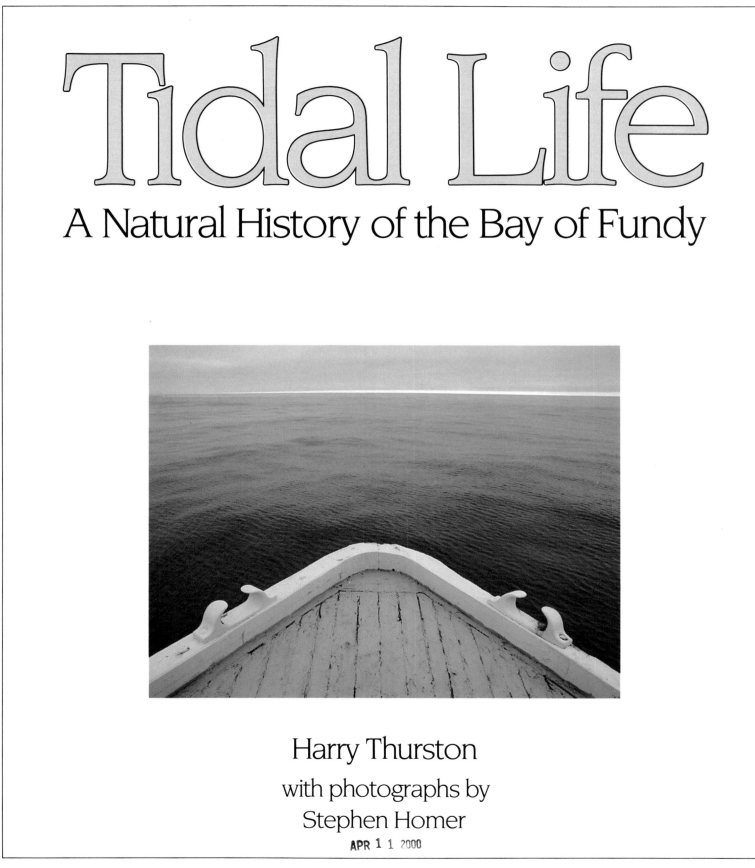

Harry Thurston

with photographs by

Stephen Homer

Nimbus Publishing Ltd.
3731 Mackintosh Street
P.O. Box 9301, Station A
Halifax, Nova Scotia B3K 5N5
(902) 455-4286

Canadian Cataloguing in Publication Data
Thurston, Harry, 1950-
    Tidal Life
    Includes index
    ISBN 1-55109-272-7
1. Natural history — Fundy, Bay of.   2. Tidal Flat ecology —
Fundy, Bay of.   3. Fundy; Bay of, Region — Social life and
customs.   I. Title

QH106.2.F85T48 1998   508.3163'45   C97-950240-3

Other Books by Harry Thurston

PROSE
Atlantic Outposts
Against Darkness and Storm
Dawning of the Dinosaurs
The Nature of Shorebirds

POETRY
Barefaced Stone
Clouds Flying Before The Eye

Design by
Linda J. Menyes

Colour separations by
Hadwen Graphics
Ottawa, Ontario

Printed and bound in Canada by
D.W. Friesen & Sons
Altona, Manitoba

Printed on acid-free paper

Preface
to
Second Edition

The ebb and flow of the tides are the very heartbeat of Fundy that sustains this remarkably productive ecosystem —home to whales, seabirds, shorebirds, and fishes. The life-giving tides keep up their steady pulse, come what may.

I began work on this book a decade ago for fear that governments would build tidal power dams across the Bay of Fundy, harnessing its natural rhythm for electrical generation and, in the process, short-circuiting its true power to nurture a diverse profusion of marine life. In making my plea for the preservation of Fundy, intact and unfettered, I wanted, more than anything, to share my wonder at the intricate workings of this tidally driven environment. Only by doing so could others learn to care for it as I did and see why it must be protected.

Fundy is not only important to those, like myself, who have been lucky enough to grow up beside the bay, it is a globally significant ecosystem. Maintaining its ecological integrity is vital to the future of a number of migratory species, including the most endangered of the world's whales, the North Atlantic right whale, and the world population of semipalmated sandpipers. Despite a four hundred-year-old history of European settlement, it is one of the last great natural places.

Recognition of this fact has been growing as more and more ecotourists visit Fundy to marvel at its natural wonders. It is reassuring that, in the few short years since this book first appeared, people throughout the Bay of Fundy-Gulf of Maine region—fishers, shore-dwellers, scientists, and politicians on both sides of the Canada-U.S. border—have banded together in a concerted effort to safeguard, restore and enhance their shared natural heritage. I am glad that the recurrent dream of tidal power now lies dormant, though I know that it awaits only the next energy crunch for a revival. In the meantime, a number of new and incipient environmental dangers have emerged to threaten the life of Fundy.

Fished for decades to the brink of sustainability, in the 1990s groundfish stocks finally collapsed throughout the Northwest Atlantic. Having decimated the upper trophic levels of the marine food web, we now seem intent on scraping clean the ocean floor by harvesting so-called "underutilized species," such as sea urchins, periwinkles, baitworms, and rockweeds. The uncontrolled stripping of seaweed is particularly worrisome, as these underwater forests are the nursery areas for many species of fish as well as a vital feeding ground for seaducks. Equally troubling are recent observations of widespread changes to mud flats—those shorebird meccas of the Upper Bay. These cumulative changes may well be due to the construction of causeways during the last forty years across virtually all rivers emptying into the bay.

By nature ecosystems are dynamic. This is especially true of the Bay of Fundy dominated as it is by great tides. Once an ecosystem is fundamentally altered, however, there are simply no guarantees that it will ever recover its former vitality and character. If we have learned anything from past mistakes, it should be to look at ecosystems broadly, not simply as a well of resources. That is what I have tried to do here for Fundy, to appreciate the intricacies of the whole, beginning and ending with its life-giving tides.

Contents

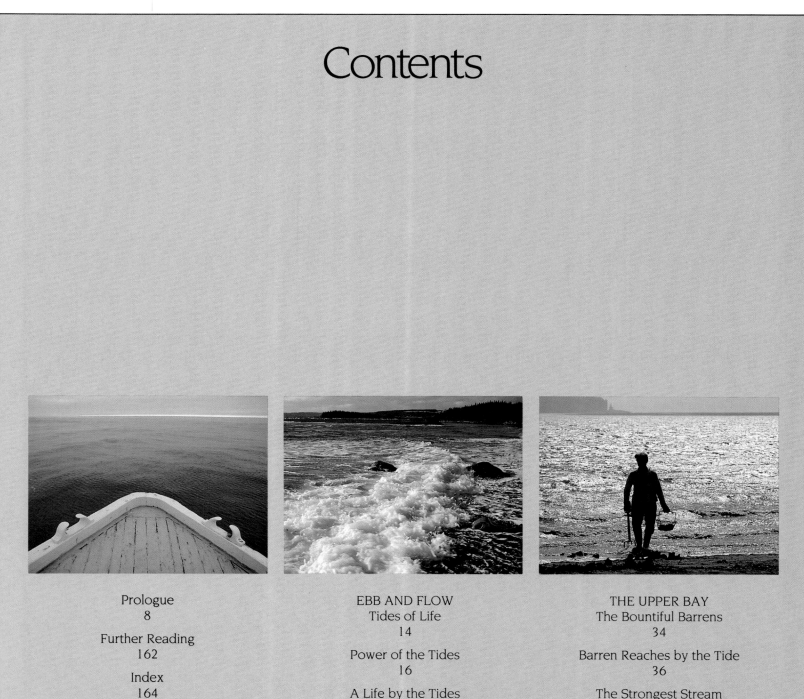

Prologue

"It is very difficult to determine at all accurately
how much life is produced in any part of the
ocean, and yet it is quite evident that there
are great differences from place to place in
the amounts produced . . . . An understanding of
the mechanism in this bay should show what
conditions are required for high production
of life in the ocean."

–A.G. Huntsman
"The Production of Life in the Bay of Fundy"

A whorl of marsh grass,
above, mimics the turbulent energies
of tide and wind. Facing page: The
placid face of a marsh creek masks its
vitality as a place where fresh and salt
water productively mix. The marsh is
home to mammals, breeding place for
birds and feeding ground for estuarine
fish, schools of which swarm across the
marsh at high tide like the shadows of
clouds ghosting over the land.

The tides of Fundy first entered my life along the umbilical loops of the Chebogue, a tidal river at the southwestern tip of Nova Scotia. Twice daily, seawater brimmed the riverbanks, overflowing on spring tides to deposit loads of North Atlantic salt at the very foot of our market garden. This invasion of the sea was my first link with the drama and rhythm of the Bay of Fundy tides.

The tidal creek and salt marsh that bordered my father's farm also introduced me to the rich and varied natural life of Fundy. In the tidal river, fresh water and salt water productively mixed, providing a home, a feeding ground and a breeding area for many creatures. As the spear-shaped cord grass rasped my feet, willet—which we called "pitawees" for the sound of their rapid, frantic song—circled overhead, chastising me for venturing near their nests. Great blue herons, like prehistoric pterodactyls, flew low over the farm twice daily, once on the way to their riverine feeding ground and again at night on their return to the salt-lapped islands. My brothers and I caught mink and muskrat, setting our traps on the muddy banks of the creek, and I fished with my bare hands for mummichogs in the tide-marsh pools. In spring, the tides brought thick schools of spawning smelt into the brook that emptied into the creek, and speckled sea trout couched their tiny packets of ripe milt and spawn in bellies pink as sunsets.

The year I turned 10, my family moved to the fogbound historical seaport of Yarmouth. The following summer, I returned to fish the brook on our farm, only to find the pristine creek of my childhood sullied by a foul-smelling effluent. Trout floated belly-up in their woodland spawning pools. A noxious runoff had spilled into the headwaters of the brook from the regional airport, which had lengthened its runway to accommodate jet flights. (More than 25 years have passed, and the brook is still pol-

luted and fishless.) It was my first disillusioning experience with the environmental consequences of technological progress.

Eight years later, after my first year at university, I returned home to Yarmouth and took a summer job at the Fundy-area laboratory of the federal Department of Fisheries and Oceans. I was assigned to a special research project to assess the feasibility of recovering usable protein from herring-meal effluent. At the time, there were 10 large processing plants in the immediate area, each reducing herring to fish meal and providing me with daily samples of its offal. My task as a technician was an unenviable one: every morning, I had to suck a sickly green, putrid slurry into a pipette for protein analysis. The herring (the protein source) were supplied to the processors by a fleet of some 60 seiners that had come to the East Coast in search of unexploited herring stocks after the collapse of the Pacific stocks from overfishing. On summer nights,

people lined the approaches to Yarmouth harbour with their cars to watch the departure of the fleet. For many, it was a welcome sight. Herring, until then an underutilized species, had become the source of an economic boom in the area.

In retrospect, there was little cause for optimism. At the height of the fishery, in the late 1960s, the Bay of Fundy herring-meal industry had a gross capacity of some 12,000 tonnes a day, enough to grind into bits every herring on both sides of the Atlantic in 200 days. The outcome was predictable. As the summer wore on, herring-meal plants began to close for lack of fish, and by August, all the plants had been shut down. So was my research project. Its aim of recovering a minuscule amount of protein from the plant "waste" in the name of conservation now seems transparently naïve. No one had considered the real waste of overfishing the herring stocks in the first place. The Department of Fisher-

ies and Oceans had, literally and figuratively, focused its concern on the wrong end of resource management.

These two experiences made me an environmentalist before I had ever heard the word. They alerted me to the consequences of habitat destruction through pollution and overexploitation of renewable resources—issues that have exploded into public consciousness during the past two decades. I realized that our place in nature, our earth home and the living things we share it with, can be destroyed with alarming speed through carelessness and avarice. I recount these experiences here because they were the background to my involvement in another long-standing threat to the Bay of Fundy environment—the development of Fundy tidal power.

In 1978, I was living at the head of the Bay near Joggins, Nova Scotia, a worked-out coal-mining town known to palaeontologists for its 300-million-year-old fossil reptiles found entombed in the fossil trees that still figure the coastline of Cumberland Basin like a bas-relief. After 60 years of talk about Fundy tidal power, it was inevitable that Joggins would soon become the site of a 2.5-kilometre power dam that would exploit the enormous tidal energy of the Bay of Fundy. The social and environmental impact of such a massive development concerned many of us in the community. Life on the Fundy shore was then, and still is, firmly rooted in the traditional pursuits of lumbering, farming and fishing. Tidal power posed a threat to the marine and terrestrial habitats of basin, marsh and coastal forest that supported the largely rural life style by the Bay.

The prospect of a megaproject in their own backyard galvanized a coalition of groups to examine a wide range of ecological and socioeconomic questions raised by tidal-power development. The Coalition for Tidal Power Education represented labour, agriculture, church and social-service groups and the environmental movement. It helped to organize committees from each of the coastal communities that would be affected by the development. I joined the Joggins committee, an eclectic collection of concerned citizens which included a fisherman (who was also a former Maritime boxing champion), a dyke-land farmer, a housewife and local activist and myself, a poet and, now that I had a name for it, an environmentalist.

In February 1978, the coalition brought together proponents of the project, representing the major Maritime electrical utilities, as well as scientists and government officials charged with overseeing an environmental review process. The list of questions we posed to this panel of experts was exhaustive, and I include only a few examples here: What would be done about dyke lands flooded through modification of river and tide levels? What were the numbers and concentrations of shorebirds near the proposed dam sites? What would happen to the shad feeding grounds in the

Cumberland Basin? What effect would siltation have on the commercial clam fishery? What would happen to local communities after the construction phase? The discussion was a stimulating and daunting introduction to the complexities of tidal power and its consequences.

One of the panel members was a senior scientist who had studied tidal-power scenarios for England's Severn Estuary. Near the end of the day, he stood up, pushed his glasses down to the tip of his nose and described to us his first impressions of the Bay of Fundy when he flew over by helicopter. Although the coast of the Bay of Fundy had in fact cradled the continent, he said, 375 years after Champlain established the Habitation at Port Royal, the Fundy coastline was still sparsely settled; and the scattering of tiny villages suggested to him that there would be very little social impact from the dam. I allowed that he was accustomed to thinking in terms of millions of people, but his lofty view did seem to ignore the people in his audience. At the same time, he noted that the Bay of Fundy was practically unknown to biologists.

As I listened, I realized that even though I had lived by the Bay of Fundy most of my life – had even studied biology at Acadia University, in Wolfville, Nova Scotia, overlooking the world's highest tides in the Minas Basin – I, too, knew very little about the life of Fundy. I also had taken a long-distance view – in my case, from the shore –

A marsh road, facing page, leads from Fundy to farm and fort. Fort Beausejour still guards the fertile marshland that, under Acadian tillage, yielded everything from flax to turnips. Even now, it produces bumper crops of salt hay. Tides of 15 metres float a lobster boat, above, as it draws a wrinkle across Parrsboro harbour; at ebb tide, a shallow creek will divide a virtually dry seabed.

and, since my childhood, had only occasionally ventured onto Fundy's waters, salt marshes and mud flats. It was at that moment that I consciously committed myself to finding out as much as possible about the natural history of the Bay of Fundy. This book is the result of that commitment.

The undertaking occupied me for the next decade. Fortunately, my curiosity was fuelled by an exponential upsurge in research: a multidisciplinary community of scientists conducted studies of everything from the movement of mud to the migration of shorebirds, in anticipation of tidal-dam construction across one of Fundy's inner basins. Much of what I have come to know and feel about the Bay of Fundy, however, has been garnered from firsthand experience as I travelled from one end of the Bay to the other.

I have drifted on the red tide to the very headwaters of the Bay, as did the region's first explorers; I have taken a joyride on the back of a tidal bore as the high-tide wave reversed the flow of a river, turning it from a peaceful stream into a menacing roller coaster; I have ridden on a horse-drawn wagon across the sea bottom, which six hours before had been covered by 12 metres of water; I have gone "mud-larking" across the intertidal barrens of the Fundy mud flats to dig clams; and I have dug into the soft red sandstone which clasps the Bay for the fossil record it contains of life that vanished here 200 million years ago.

I have watched blizzards of shorebirds

gather—hundreds, thousands, tens of thousands—whirling above their vast mud-flat feeding grounds. I have stood in the middle of the maritime prairie of the Tantramar Marshes, transfixed by the solitary flight of the marsh hawk as it patrolled its precinct of dyke land at the head of the Bay. And I have foot-raced the advancing tide to shore in a deadly serious encounter with Fundy's deceptive waters.

At the other end of the Bay, where Fundy merges with the Gulf of Maine, I have hailed the world's rarest cetacean, the North Atlantic right whale, as it returned to its nursery ground with its calf, and marvelled at the acrobatics of the humpback whales as they gorged themselves on shoals of herring. I have stripped ruddy ribbons of dulse from the rocky shores of Grand Manan and shared a fogbound island in the middle of the Bay with protesting colonies of breeding puffins, auks and terns. I have witnessed great red rivers of krill and schools of herring so thick, it seemed possible to step over the side of the boat and walk on water. And, no less memorable, I have endured the violent pitching of a Cape Island lobster boat buffeted by snow squalls on a December sea—making me pray for the sight of land.

The aim of this book is to share the insights I have gained into the Bay of Fundy's many natural wonders: its tides, geology and fossils and its myriad living things, from single-celled phytoplankton to shrimp, fish,

Weathered wharf pylons are a stark reminder of bygone (and better) days when Fundy sea captains traversed the world's oceans in wooden ships fashioned from the Acadian forest. The pylons, at mid-tide, now serve as a convenient measuring stick for the world's highest tides, which surge into the Minas Basin twice daily.

birds and marine mammals. Also, it will introduce you to the people of Fundy: the scientists who study the Bay, the fishermen who ply its dangerous waters, the naturalists who want to conserve and enjoy its natural beauty and the people who live simply by the Bay as their ancestors have done for nearly four centuries. It is also my purpose to deal with the destructive forces, such as pollution and overfishing, that now threaten the Bay's natural resources and to point to developments—tidal power, in particular—that might ruin it in the future.

Although North America's first tidal-power plant, a single-turbine pilot project, was commissioned in 1984 at the head of the Annapolis Basin, large-scale Fundy tidal power is still a dream on a drawing board. However, in sharp contrast to the situation in the 1970s, we now understand a great deal about the biology of the Bay and, as a result, have a good idea of the environmental effects tidal power would have if it ever were developed. One of the speakers at the 1978 seminar who addressed the effects of tidal power was its chief proponent, George Baker, then chairman of the Tidal Power Corporation. "It is my suspicion," he said, "that many matters in the socioeconomic and environmental sphere are not quantified for the simple reason that society does not have the necessary skills or techniques to find definitive answers. On such questions, I think we can huff and puff until we are blue in the face, and all we will get for our time and money is opinion, not fact."

Today, we have at least some of the facts. Ecology is infinitely more complex than economics or engineering. But in the past decade, scientists, along with the people of the Bay, have gained many insights into the intricacies of the Bay of Fundy ecosystem. They have found answers to many of the questions we posed that day in 1978. Through this book, I endeavour to share the search and to suggest some answers. Naturally, some opinions remain, and for these I accept full responsibility.

EBB AND FLOW
Tides of Life

The power of the Bay of Fundy surges ashore. Since the turn of the century, schemes have been proposed to harness this vast reservoir of energy. Recent studies have shown, however, that the tides also power Fundy's diverse and abundant life forms, and any interruption of their ebb and flow could harm the Bay's fragile ecosystem.

Power of the Tides

"The tides are said to be the highest in the world.
They often come up at first with a lofty
wave called the Bore, of which I saw a fine
example in the largest river of Nova Scotia, the
Shubenacadie, where the waters seemed to be
rushing down a much steeper slope than the
St. Lawrence at its rapids."

– Sir Charles Lyell
"Travels in North America," 1842

At 12:38 p.m., two minutes before the bore is due to arrive, I am sitting with six other passengers on the inflated gunwales of a 16-foot Zodiac. Henry Knoll, proprietor of Tidal Bore Park, motors the craft to midstream and turns its blunt bow, on which I am perched, toward the mouth of the Shubenacadie River. We wait. To port, a reddish sandbar extends to the far shore and covers perhaps one-third of the streambed. Astern, the river wends around a shale ledge, then cuts toward the steep shore under the viewing platform Knoll has constructed for tourists. Ahead of us, it disappears around a point of white limestone that juts into the peaceful stream.

"You are going to be surprised how this river turns into a monster," Knoll declares with sinister pleasure.

We don't have to wait long. The bore arrives at precisely 12:40, announcing itself first by a faint hissing sound. Then, around the point, comes the apparition: a brown

A gale drives waves ashore at Cape Split, above. As the tide meets the resistance of the Minas Channel, the swelling water piles up and pushes through, creating a maelstrom at the base of the headland. A barrier spit at Fox River, facing page, is the tide's work. Glacial deposits and driftwood protect one of the many salt marshes that form ribbons of green around the Fundy shore.

wave frothing white at the top and gaining height as it curls up the channel and scours the sides of the riverbank. Knoll powers downstream to meet the wall of water, which is approaching us, like a runaway beach wave, at 13 kilometres per hour.

From shore, I have heard the tide roar with the sound of an oncoming train engine, but today, the scene before me seems to take place in eerie silence. The Zodiac rears up and crests the two-metre wave that breaks over it and dumps water down our backs. As we ride over the top, Knoll steers to avoid a flotilla of driftwood and deadheads carried upriver by the force of the bore, then quickly turns the craft in a tight circle and guns its 40-horsepower motor until he catches up to the tide's advancing front, whereupon he nuzzles the nose of the inflatable over the cascading edge. We balance there like a surfer atop an ever-breaking wave crest, riding upriver on the edge of the tide that leaves a roller coaster of

rapids and whirlpools writhing in our wake.

"A tidal bore is a remarkable hydrographic phenomenon," wrote David K. Lynch in *Scientific American*. "It is the incoming tide in the form of a wave going up a river which empties into the sea." For a tidal bore to exist, tides in the adjoining body of water must be exceptionally high and the estuary must be shaped like a funnel. These conditions are easily met in the Bay of Fundy, a 280-kilometre-long arm of the North Atlantic wedged between the Maritime Provinces of Nova Scotia and New Brunswick and host to the highest tides in the world.

Fundy's waters ebb and flow within a 200-million-year-old rift valley, splayed at its head to form two major embayments. In shape, it closely resembles another rift valley, the Red Sea, with the Minas Basin as the counterpart of the Gulf of Aqaba and Chignecto Bay mirroring the Gulf of Suez. In turn, the Minas Basin cuts into the heartland of Nova Scotia, then divides into Cobequid

Bay and the Southern Bight. Chignecto Bay branches to the northeast, between New Brunswick and Nova Scotia, then likewise divides into Shepody Bay and the Cumberland Basin. These branchings make Fundy look like the body and arms of a squid, but for the purpose of understanding its giant tides, it can be said to be funnel-shaped, narrowing from a width of 120 kilometres between Yarmouth, Nova Scotia, and Cutler, Maine, to a mere 45 kilometres at Cape Chignecto.

In effect, tides act like global waves— one under the moon, another on the opposite side of the Earth. The moon's orbit places it over the same position every 24 hours and 50 minutes, thus producing twice daily, or semidiurnal, tides. Fundy's high waters are given their impetus on the outer edge of Georges Bank, where the nascent tide can be felt but not seen, a force pushing against a scallop drag signalling the captain to use more throttle or more wire to

settle the gear on bottom. Here, the tide may rise a mere metre, but by the time it sweeps by the corner of southwestern Nova Scotia and begins pushing into the Bay of Fundy proper, it reaches a height of 3.5 metres. Inch by inch, it drowns shaggy, seaweed-draped coastline, changing its shape like a compulsive cartographer constantly redrawing his charts. At North Head on Grand Manan Island, at the mouth of the Bay, the tide creeps under the keels of boats, lifting them off their wharf-side cribs, past tide-marked pylons, until their cabins bob above the wharf deck. Half an hour later, the tide streams by the lighthouse at Cape d'Or, creating the white-capped rips which local fishermen fear but which are the playground of harbour porpoises. Here, the tide reaches a height of eight metres.

As it meets the resistance of the narrow Minas Channel, the swelling water piles up and pushes through under protest, creating a maelstrom at the base of the imperious headland at Cape Split. Once by Blomidon, it floods freely, inundating plains of brick-red mud impressed at ebb tide with the tortuous meanderings of creeks. The basin becomes a red sea of muddy boils and gyres. Near the head of the Bay, the tide attains a height of 12 metres and begins to run out of room. In its final advance, it submerges emerald fringes of spiked marsh and presses against the bulwarks of 300-year-old Acadian dykes, like the breath of a surfacing diver pushing against near-bursting lungs. It looks desperately for a place to go. It leaps up at the mouths of the Fundy rivers, and for the first time, the tide becomes a visible standing wave, a foaming, hissing wall that reverses the seaward flow of the rivers and bores at their soft-lipped clay banks. Finally, far inland and out of sight of the sea, it swirls its salt with the fresh waters of the salmon pools. Its energy dissipated, the tide is briefly at rest before it begins again to ebb toward the sea.

Tides in the Minas Basin, into which the Shubenacadie River flows, rise and fall 13 metres on average and more than 16 metres during spring tides, when the sun and moon are aligned to exert a maximum pull on the waters of the Earth. These are the highest tides in the world. They are fed by 100 billion tonnes of water, a flow equal in volume to that of the Gulf Stream, or 2,000 times the discharge of the St. Lawrence River. How a one-metre-high tide on the ocean is amplified by a factor of 12 or more on its six-hour journey to the head of the Bay has been a matter of speculation for most of this century.

Laws of physics tell us that every basin has a characteristic period of oscillation, which means that once set in motion, waters within it will slosh back and forth with a regular rhythm. However, where an open bay communicates with the sea, the influence of the lunar-dominated tides must also be taken into account. If the period of the basin is similar to the period of the ocean tides—if they are rocking back and forth in harmony with one another—then a

phenomenon known as resonance occurs.

David Greenberg, a soft-spoken mathematician with a salt-and-pepper beard and gentle humour, has become the guru of the Bay of Fundy's tides by dint of his sophisticated computer models that accurately describe and predict their rise and fall. I usually find him surrounded by a cascading pile of printouts in his office at the Bedford Institute of Oceanography, in Halifax. "The high tides in the Bay seem to be related to resonance. The easiest analogy is the wine glass," he told me on our first meeting. "A crystal goblet, because of its shape and substance, rings at a certain tone if you strike it. Now if you sing at the same pitch, the glass begins to vibrate, and if you keep hitting it at the right time, the glass will start to ring. Eventually, it will break."

A more common analogy is the oscillation of water in a bathtub, which is why resonance is often called the bathtub effect.

Glistening mud banks of the tidal Shubenacadie River, facing page, loom through mist that bathes the sleepy farms. The tidal bore, above, turns the peaceful stream into "a monster," according to Henry Knoll of Tidal Bore Park. Joyriders crest the wall of water, advancing upriver at 13 kilometres per hour. The bore leaves a roller coaster of rapids and whirlpools writhing in its wake.

Greenberg himself has used this model. "If a standard bathtub is filled to a depth of 20 centimetres, a wave of water sloshes back and forth about once every two seconds. Now, if one were to help the wave by giving it a push every time it went by, the wave would quickly increase in size and threaten to overflow the sides of the tub."

For 50 years, this is what scientists thought was happening on a grand scale in the Bay of Fundy. But when they made precise measurements of the resonant period of the Bay, they found it was nine hours—too short to support the theory. Subsequently, however, it was shown that it is not just the Bay of Fundy but the Bay and the Gulf of Maine acting together as a single oceanographic system, as one big bathtub, which produces the resonant effect. The Bay-Gulf system has a period of 13.3 hours, close enough to be in resonance with the 12.42-hour moon-forced ocean system.

Resonance alone does not explain the extreme tidal ranges observed in the upper reaches of the Bay. Fundy's shape and bottom topography significantly enhance the effect once the tide enters the Bay itself. Toward its upper reaches, the Bay becomes progressively shallower, shelving from 130 metres at the mouth to 40 metres at Cape Chignecto. Therefore, as the high-tide wave enters the more constricted upper reaches, the water has nowhere to go but up. The geography of the system more than doubles the resonant effect and gives rise to such peculiar Fundy phenomena as the tidal bore—the last hurrah of the flood tide.

Like Sir Charles Lyell, most first-time travellers to Fundy are impressed by the power of the tides, which transforms a meandering, peaceful stream into a gorged, rapid-filled river or floats a boat to the top of a wharf and then, six hours later, settles it onto the sea bottom 12 metres below. Many have not been content merely to marvel at this power but have been inspired by a desire to exploit it. This century has spawned a number of ambitious schemes

to harness the vast repository of potential power, equal to the output of 250 large nuclear-power plants.

Neither the idea nor the technology of tidal power belongs to this century. Records exist of tide mills along the Atlantic coast of Europe during the 12th century, and a tidal-power construction handbook was published in the 15th century. In its simplest form, tidal water is held behind a dam at high tide, then released on the ebb tide when a sufficient difference in water level is created between the landward and seaward sides of the dam. Most of the mills used tidal waters (or a mixture of tidal and fresh water) to turn a waterwheel that provided power for grinding grain. The first such mill in the New World was probably built in 1607 by Samuel de Champlain's cohorts in the Order of Good Cheer on the Lequille River, not far from Annapolis Royal, where North America's first modern tidal-power plant was designed in 1984 to provide electricity for 5,000 households. The chief difference between the traditional and present-day uses of power from the tides is that the tides are now seen as a means to turn turbines for generating electricity rather than as a source of mechanical energy to turn millstones.

W.R. Turnbull, an inventor in Rothesay, New Brunswick, first proposed harnessing the energy of the great tides of Fundy for electrical generation in 1910. In 1919, he and an American engineer named Dexter P. Cooper designed a double-basin scheme, utilizing both Passamaquoddy and Cobscook bays, that would cross the international boundary between New Brunswick and Maine. Franklin D. Roosevelt, who summered on the Canadian island of Campobello in Passamaquoddy, gave his blessing to the project, and in 1935, preliminary construction of a dyke was begun. However, the project quickly ran into financial and political trouble. One Republican governor dubbed the scheme "a moondoggle," and subsequently, it was abandoned

S un gilds the Minas Basin, which at high tide creates a moat around the Five Islands, above. Myth holds that they were clods of earth thrown after a fleeing tormentor by the Micmac man-god Glooscap. As if by magic, the ebbing tide exposes the tidal plain, facing page, and maroons a lobster boat, high and dry, in the muddy landscape.

for lack of funds. The Army Corps of Engineers reevaluated the scheme during the 1950s, 1960s and 1970s but each time rejected it for economic reasons.

Canadians, too, have a long history of on-again, off-again Fundy tidal-power development. In 1915, Ralph P. Clarkson, an Acadia University physics professor, designed a current generator that he planned to install in the tide race at Cape Split, at the entrance to the Minas Basin, where eight cubic kilometres of water muscles its way through the constricted passage of the Minas Channel with a force equal to that of 8,000 locomotives or 25 million horses. The device consisted of a propeller encased in a tube providing intake and draft; on testing in the Gaspereau River, it proved to be highly efficient. Confident investors formed the Cape Split Development Corporation, but the scheme went up in smoke when Clarkson's prototype was destroyed by fire on December 2, 1920. Two decades later, the Canadian government assessed options for blocking off one of Fundy's inner basins with a tidal-power dam. A more ambitious survey was undertaken in the 1960s; of 27 sites identified, the most promising were at the mouths of Shepody Bay, Cumberland Basin and Cobequid Bay. Although in each case the project was thought to be technically feasible, tidal power was still not competitive with conventional hydroelectric and thermal sources.

As the Canadians and Americans procrastinated, the French proceeded to build the first full-scale tidal-power electrical generation station in the estuary of La Rance, near the Bay of Mont-Saint-Michel, which boasts 13-metre tides. The dam, almost a kilometre long, is 29 metres high and contains 24 bulb turbines with 6-metre blades. Built in 1967 at a cost of $100 million, the computer-controlled power plant, with a capacity of 240 megawatts (MW), is considered a glowing technological achievement and produces the cheapest electricity available to Électricité de France.

In Canada, the OPEC (Organization of

Petroleum Exporting Countries) oil crisis of the early 1970s revived the 60-year-old dream of Fundy tidal power. As oil prices soared, the Bay of Fundy Tidal Power Review Board reassessed earlier studies and this time recommended construction of a plant in either the Minas Basin or the Cumberland Basin. On paper, both plants dwarfed the La Rance facility. The Cumberland Basin scheme would generate 1,085 megawatts, nearly five times as much as the La Rance facility and fully one-half of the entire electrical demand of the province of Nova Scotia. The monumental Minas Basin scheme, at 4,560 megawatts, would produce more than twice as much electricity as is now generated in Nova Scotia from all sources – coal, oil and hydro – and would

rank as the largest water-driven electric-power plant in the world. It would produce more power than Newfoundland's Churchill Falls (1,900 MW) and Ontario Hydro's Pickering nuclear-power plant (2,160 MW) combined. Ninety percent of this energy was slated for export to the Eastern Seaboard of the United States.

The Tidal Power Corporation, a Nova Scotia Crown corporation, gave the nod to the Minas Basin site in 1982. The proposal was to build an eight-kilometre-long dam, or barrage, between Economy Point and Tennycape, thus impounding the entire Cobequid Bay area. The barrage would consist of more than 100 concrete caissons, each weighing 50,000 tonnes and measuring 59 by 40 metres – comparable in size to

two Scotia Square towers, the province's largest buildings, which dominate the skyline of Halifax. These mammoth support towers would be constructed off-site, installed with sluice gates and turbines, then towed to the barrage site, sunk, ballasted and secured on the seabed – all while the tides of Fundy surged to and fro with ever-increasing velocity as each new caisson was put into place. Closure dykes of rock and fill would be built at low tide to finish blocking the basin. On completion, a road would cross the causeway, and a rail line would be installed for a mobile derrick to replace out-of-commission turbines. It was a daunting engineering challenge, with a daunting price tag of $25 billion for a plant expected to last 75 years.

The Minas Basin scheme was the grandiose culmination of 70 years of economic and engineering planning. During that time, however, there had been very little study of the possible impact of tidal power. In the 1970s, the scientific community realized that if such a massive engineering project ever did proceed, there would be significant environmental effects arising from changes to the tidal regime brought about by impairing the free flow of Fundy's tides. All the Fundy schemes were to operate as single-effect ebb-generation systems; that is, power would be generated only on the ebb cycle of the tide. (La Rance is a double-effect system in which electricity is generated on both flood and ebb cycles.) Two-way turbines were considered for Fundy but rejected as too costly.

In the single-effect system, sluiceways are opened to allow the incoming tide to fill the headpond, then closed when the water levels on both sides of the barrier equalize. Two hours after high tide, when the water on the seaward side of the barrage has dropped, water is released from the head-

pond to the sea through the turbines. Power can be generated for about six hours, until the flooding tide rises to within a few metres of the water level in the headpond, and the cycle begins again.

The barrage would change the tidal regime by shortening the length of the Bay, thereby bringing it closer to resonance. David Greenberg's computer model has shown that seaward of the Minas Basin barrage, the amplitude of the tide would increase by as much as 20 centimetres within

T he ebbing tide beats a hasty retreat from an estuary, above, and exposes barnacle-encrusted beach stone, facing page, which seems to spill from the sloped back of Spencer's Island. The basaltic island, a reminder of the Bay's violent volcanic origin, 200 million years ago, is now protected as an important nesting site for blue herons.

the Bay itself and 15 centimetres 480 kilometres away, in Massachusetts Bay. Within the headpond, there would be a general dampening of tidal ranges because the barrage sluiceways could not accommodate as much of the tidal flow as the original estuary did. The water level behind the barrage would only fall to the midtide level before the tide turned again and began to refill the headpond. As a result, within the headpond, the high-water mark would be lower and the low-water mark much higher than is now the case. Tidal energies within the headpond would also diminish, but conversely, they would increase seaward of the barrage.

Prior to the reassessment of tidal power in the mid-1970s, what little ecological work that had been done had concentrated on the oceanography and the commercial fisheries of the lower Bay. Hardly anyone had looked into the inner basins of Fundy, where the barrages were to be constructed. The muddy waters of the Minas Basin and Chignecto Bay were thought to be relatively nonproductive marine environments, hardly worthy of scrutiny. To the layperson's eye, the slick plains of mud cut by meandering creeks do look at low tide like watery deserts. At high tide, the water grades in colour from milky blue to strong tea to chocolate brown in the innermost reaches. Scientists considered these turbid waters, muddied by cliff-line erosion, too light-limited to be productive. No one had tested this theory, so the illusion persisted.

However, a conference on Fundy tidal power and the environment, held at Acadia University in November 1976, went a long way toward overturning that traditional, unflattering view. Reports pointed to an unsuspected array of animals living and feeding in the mud flats and muddy waters and warned that any large-scale engineering project in the inner reaches of the Bay could cause massive mortalities in the rich biological community of mud shrimp, shellfish and saltwater worms.

The Fundy Environmental Studies Committee of the Atlantic Provinces' Council on the Sciences, a unique organization of 20 university and government laboratories, was struck at the Acadia conference to gather baseline data on the biological systems of the Bay before the development of tidal power proceeded. The committee met in the fall of 1982 at the University of Moncton, in New Brunswick, to share the results of their research.

Our view of the Bay changed forever. The mud flats were identified as shorebird feeding areas of international significance. More than a million shorebirds, primarily sandpipers and plover, arrive in Fundy from their Arctic breeding grounds in midsummer, consume enough food to double their weight and then fly nonstop to South America. Any shrinkage of the intertidal zone— and a barrage would reduce the mud flats in the headpond by 50 percent—could greatly reduce food availability. A fisheries researcher, Michael Dadswell, demonstrated that the so-called dead bay of upper Fundy is also a prime feeding area for the entire North Atlantic shad population, which gorges on the abundant mysid shrimp found in the muddy waters. He feared high mortality rates as the shad moved in and out of the basins—and through the turbines —feeding on the tidal cycles. Oceanographic changes were also expected far from the barrage site, with unknown implications for the rich fisheries of the lower Bay of Fundy.

The intensive period of study shifted the focus from the mechanical power of the tides to the biological power inherent in the Bay's comings and goings. This work shaped my own understanding of how the tides rule life in Fundy. Since then, no matter what aspect of life in the Bay I have examined, whether it is the timing of a fisherman's departure and landfall or the complex behaviour of seabirds and whales, I have come to the conclusion that the influence of the tides is the dominant factor. The tides of Fundy dictate the daily rhythms and life cycles of all those who dwell along its

shores, underneath or upon its waters—creatures and people alike.

Today, much of the biological modelling of the Fundy ecosystem is being carried out by the Acadia Centre for Estuarine Research, which uses the Minas Basin as a backyard field laboratory as well as a model for other estuarine systems around the world. Graham Daborn, the centre's founding director, has been a driving force in Fundy research since he organized the Acadia conference in the mid-1970s. With his black hair and goatee, he reminds me of the Black Mountain poet, Robert Creeley. Daborn, too, has dived into dark waters. Fundy's innermost reaches have proved much more productive than he or anyone else had guessed. "It is a progressively more fascinating environment," he says.

As Daborn has observed, the Bay of Fundy is "a system with a biological pump at both ends." In the lower Bay, the strong tides pump nutrients from the seafloor up into the light, or photic, zone, which sets in motion the marine food chain: phytoplankton, copepods, herring, seabirds and whales. In the shallower upper Bay of Fundy, huge expanses of mud flat and salt marsh are the biological factories. Slicks of single-celled algae (each a tiny solar greenhouse) flourish at ebb tide on the mud flats, and lush ribbons of salt marsh supply carbon-based food to the marine environment, which is then churned by the action of the tides into a nutrient soup for a variety of bottom dwellers, fish and birds.

Fundy's food-production system, which

is fuelled by the tides, attracts large numbers of species from faraway hemispheres and oceans. The Bay of Fundy, both at its lower end and in its upper reaches, is a gathering place where north meets south – a vast natural smorgasbord for marine life. "Things come here to feed," Daborn says. "Most estuaries don't have great invasions of fish. One can find some similar examples – menhaden migrate into Chesapeake Bay, for instance – but not on the scale that seems to be happening in the Bay of Fundy, either with the diversity of species, both fish and birds, or with the vast numbers of a given species, such as shad or alewives. In that sense, the Bay of Fundy seems to be unique."

A similar gathering of whale and seabird nations takes place in the lower Bay. Puffins, auks and terns return every year to their fogbound breeding islands at the mouth of the Bay in late spring and early summer, where brit (young herring) school in silvery shoals; throughout the summer and into the fall, Arctic-breeding shorebirds and nonbreeding pelagic birds arrive to take advantage of the upwelling food-delivery systems around these same isles, which pump great swarms of red krill to the surface, setting a colourful table for a marine banquet. It is to the food-rich haven of the outer Bay of Fundy that the rarest of the world's great cetaceans, the North Atlantic right whale, brings its calves in its struggle to stave off extinction. And on both sides of the Bay, spouts and flukes signal the return of fin and humpback whales, harbour porpoises and dolphins to Fundy's "sea meadows."

The experience of the past decade has taught all of us who have studied Fundy that the giant tides create life-enhancing conditions for a wide variety of creatures. The nature of Fundy's power is not only physical – it is not just potential electricity locked up in the rise and fall of water – but biological as well. It is a mistake merely to measure the value of Fundy in megawatts without also taking into account the

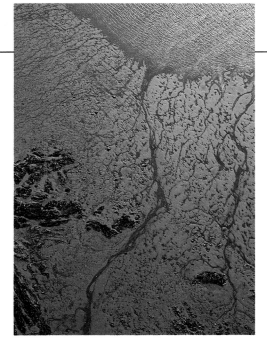

shorebirds, seabirds, whales and fish that come back to the area year after year or call the Bay home. In the end, the power of the tides and the life of the tides may be seen as the same force in different guises. And, for me at least, it is the Bay of Fundy's bounty of life, more than its physical power, that fascinates.

Still, the sheer brute force of the tides can be overwhelming, a feeling that is shared by the seven of us holding hard to the gunwales of the Zodiac as Knoll pilots us upriver on the bore's back. Having ridden the bore for half a kilometre, Knoll turns the craft once again toward the mouth of the river. Where the flooding tide is diverted by the limestone point, a muddy

The ebb and flow of Fundy's tides are an untapped source of power equal to the output of 250 nuclear-power plants. The tide pours into the historic seaport of Parrsboro, facing page, filling its harbour twice daily. When the tide withdraws, it exposes mud flats, above, which support a host of tiny creatures that feed migrating shorebirds and fish – a source of biological power.

whirlpool 30 metres across is turning like a clay bowl on a potter's wheel. Knoll manoeuvres the Zodiac over the rim of this minor maelstrom, and we slowly descend its sides. At the eye of the whirlpool, I look up the spinning walls to see the river flowing by, two metres above our heads. The Zodiac follows the counterclockwise motion of the whirling water and climbs the sides of the whirlpool until it finally spits us out.

The most exhilarating part of the ride awaits us upriver. Where the incoming tide had met the resistance of the sandbar, three-metre-high rapids undulate like a watery washboard. "This is the only upriver-rapids ride in Canada," Knoll announces as the Zodiac rears up the face of one of the river giants, then disappears into the trough to be met almost immediately by a bigger and more menacing wave hurling its brown body against the prow of the boat. We make several passes through this carnival ride, whooping it up to quell our nervousness, before the ever-rising water level restores a semblance of order to the chaotic face of the river.

For an hour, the tide pushes us upriver. Knoll points out that every year, the river becomes a thoroughfare for fish life, with alewife, shad, striped bass, sea trout and salmon following each other in season, from spring breakup to leaf fall. Like us, they hitch a ride on the tides. Even in winter, when the river is choked with ice, tomcod come in from the Bay to spawn on the undersurface of the ice, and I have seen dozens of bald eagles, which come from as far away as Cape Breton, cruising the river on the lookout for these little fish. Thinking of this movable estuarine feast as the river's currents coil about us, I am reminded that the power of Fundy's tides ultimately exists in the life they feed and maintain in their ceaseless ebb and flow. And if that natural rhythm were ever disturbed, as it would be by a tidal dam, it would affect, inevitably and fundamentally, Fundy's diverse and abundant life.

A Life by the Tides

"So far does the tide recede in this part of the
Basin that these islands may be visited on
horseback at low water, when the tide has rolled
away from their foundations and retreated
from the small rivers which wind their way into
the country beside them."

– Abraham Gesner
"Remarks on the Geology and Mineralogy
of Nova Scotia," 1836

I am standing on the brow of the Blue Sac Road, overlooking the Minas Basin in the upper reaches of the Bay of Fundy. The tide is out. Below me, a brick-red tidal plain stretches for more than a kilometre from the shore, out beyond the Five Islands that at high tide are precipitous sea-girt blocks of basalt-capped sandstone. On the plain, I can trace a serpentine two-wheeled track, a sea road that begins at the marsh-fringed mouth of the Harrington River and leads toward a V-shaped structure which is placed dead centre on the main channel, running between the Five Islands and the shore, stuck there like a herringbone in the channel's throat. I know this to be Gerald Lewis's weir. In fact, the reason I've sought this high ground is to gain a better perspective on the weir's workings, which I've inspected on many occasions but always from sea level. One thing is immediately obvious: any fish retreating with the ebb tide would follow the channel and run smack into the arms of

The rock crab, above, is one of the less remarkable curiosities Gerald Lewis has discovered stranded in his weir. Others in the past have included a six-foot harbour porpoise and a 150-pound tuna. Facing page: Together, Gerald and his horse Peter keep alive a fishing tradition that is a century and a half old. When there is a run of shad, they sometimes work 20-hour days.

the weir. As the baffled fish tried to puzzle out how to go around the obstruction, the tide would continue to ebb, eventually stranding the fish behind the trap.

Although the operation of the weir may be simplicity itself, it depends on a truly remarkable natural phenomenon for its success—the ebbing of the tide in the Minas Basin. The sea literally abandons this arm of the Bay. The waterline can recede five kilometres offshore, exposing fully one-third of the basin. This great recession makes possible the peculiar weir fishery of the region. Because the tide ebbs so far offshore here, the weirman has no need of a boat. He can tend his trap just by driving onto the flats at low tide.

Gerald Lewis is the last of the Fundy weirmen to do so with horse and wagon. He is a farmer of the sea. He tends the tide and fences in the fish. He is a man completely at home with the nature of his place and with his place in nature. He does not try to

manipulate his surroundings, nor does he ask more of the sea and the land—and here the two domains are interchangeable—than they have to offer. He accepts what the tide delivers without complaint.

As one might expect, Gerald's traditional technology has provided him with only a modest living. Often, the tide delivers little enough—no more than a few flounder or shad for his table. His one-storey house is a squat affair sheathed in unpainted particleboard and weathered shingles. There is a porch attached, with a television antenna at the corner nailed to the top of a weir stake. In the yard, the winter's hardwood is neatly piled in rain-shedding beehives.

Every year, I make a trip with Gerald to his weir at the height of the shad run in July. Tending weir with him is as much a social occasion as a business. He rarely makes a trip alone. Cottagers, local kids, tourists, scientists and writers pile aboard his rubber-tired wagon, day or night, for a jolting journey across the sea bottom to the weir.

"This is a good tide," Gerald says, cracking a grin at the bright summer sun. "There should be some shad tonight."

"Why?"

"Warm day. Shad come in heavy when you get a good spell of hot weather. It drives them down. That's when you get them." Shad avoid strong light and swim at greater depths on bright days.

At 6 p.m., the sun beats down relent-lessly upon the shadeless flats. Slanting under the bill of his baseball cap, the rays redden his already naturally high colour. Gerald squints toward the Five Islands hovering in the heat haze. From left to right, they are Moose, Diamond, Long, Egg and Pinnacle. Moose Island is the largest, perhaps 40 hectares. A century ago, it was inhabited, and now, it is said to be haunted. Diamond Island, a neatly faceted chunk of rock rising vertically some 60 metres above the tide line, was the last known peregrine falcon aerie in the Bay. Now it is the nesting site for a pair of bald eagles, which are often seen perched on one of Gerald's weir poles inspecting his catch. Long Island, a horizontal, nearly flat-topped slab, has a neat arch bored through one end by the tide. Egg Island probably got its name by being a source of gulls' eggs; every summer, it becomes a raucous breeding ground for great black-backed and herring gulls. Treeless, it is thatched with the sinister silhouettes of cormorant nests. Pinnacle Island was once called Cathedral Island for the steeplelike needles of rock at its tip.

We sit waiting for a team of fisheries researchers, who for several years have used Gerald's weir to study the migratory behaviour of shad, alewife and striped bass, all of which circulate through the Bay in summer. When the tagging crew arrives, Gerald shouts, "Get up, Peter," and the long-legged Percheron plods down the gravelly beach and out onto the flats. Each hoofbeat makes a plash followed by a sucking, gurgling release. "Paschendale, Paschendale," the hoofbeats and harness seem to say as Peter pulls the wagon in the rutted track leading across the sea bottom which, six hours before, was under 10 metres of water.

As we approach the near-shore wing, I see that stakes form the framing for the weir, as uprights do for a wall, and that the bottom is brushed in with a couple of feet of spruce bows, thus the name "brush weir." Then spindly hardwood branches are woven like basketry into an impenetrable web to shoulder height. Finally, in the centre of the weir, Gerald has strung a heavy cotton twine net to the top of the 3.6-metre stakes. From ground level, the two wings, which consist of brush and saplings, appear to branch out in straight lines like the legs of a drawing compass. But earlier, from my vantage point on Blue Sac Road, I noticed that the ends of the wings were curved slightly and gracefully back toward the middle of the weir in the shape of a heart.

I ask Gerald why the weir is fashioned this way. He raises his bushy, red-tinged eyebrows and smiles: "You noticed that, did you? Better for shad. When they swim up along the wing and hit that curve, they'll turn and go back into the middle of the weir. If

it was straight, they'd go right up and keep on going. For shad—it's better for shad."

As we near the apex of the weir, a cormorant taxis the length of the tide pool and lifts its bellyful of fish into graceless flight. Fish crows, they're called here. The greedy sound of wheeling gulls—white motes circling the eye of the weir—builds anticipation. What's going to be in the weir today? It's the question on everybody's mind.

A weir is a passive piece of fishing gear. It catches what passes by. This principle of random operation still seems to excite Gerald's sense of boyish wonder. "You never know what you're going to get when you come out here," Gerald says, bringing Peter to a stop between two hitching posts

Ruddy in the early-evening light, Gerald takes a friend to help tend the weir, facing page, which is as much a social occasion as a business. He rarely makes the journey across the sea bottom to the weir alone. Pleased with his catch, Gerald "twists" a shad, above, to remove blood from the backbone. "One just like that, just about enough to make me a lunch in the wintertime," he says.

planted firmly in the mud. "Whoa!"

Most days in midsummer, the tide pool, which remains in the centre of the weir, or "the bin," as Gerald calls it, is a reunion place for herring-family members: blueback and Atlantic herring, alewife and shad. Today, shad dorsal fins slice the water in sharklike fashion, sending the tide pool into paroxysms of silver, green and purple panic, a lightning storm of colour. Gerald and I draw the seine net, which is strung between two poles, toward the mud flat. A couple of hundred shad slap the wet flats, muddying their iridescent sides. Gerald is relieved; his sisters are home from Toronto and will want a taste of home to take back with them—salt and the sweet fat of Fundy shad.

Using an overturned bait box as a cutting board, Gerald guts and heads the fish. Then, with one sure pass of the blade, he splits the shad down the back, laying open the sweet flesh of a three-pounder fat enough to fry in its own oil. "One just like that, just about enough to make me a lunch in the wintertime," says Gerald, dousing it in the warm tidewater and flipping it into a five-gallon plastic bucket. Twenty fish and five pounds of salt to a bucket.

After processing the shad, Gerald hitches up his hip waders, takes pitchfork in hand and works down the wing of the weir, where the debouchment of the Harrington River feeds after its lazy peregrination across the flats. He stabs blindly at the sandy bottom, which provides a perfect camouflage for the flounder as they lie, clandestinely, with only their lopsided eyes periscoping out. "They come down the wing, and soon as they get into deep water, they bury themselves in the sand."

Gerald stops, puts weight on the fork, then, with a shout, sends a flounder whizzing over the top of the weir, where it bellyflops onto the bare mud flat. "No good," he says. "If I brought them in, no one would buy fish from me." It's a smooth, or witch, flounder. Locally, they're called flukes or old maids, pejorative terms in rural society, indicating the low worth accorded them.

and shad. They can reach lengths of 10 feet and weights of several hundred pounds, but much smaller ones, in the two-to-five-pound range, are more usual. I have seen a 20-pound salmon, a yard long and too big around to gird with two hands, stranded in the tide pool, where it died of heat exhaustion under a blistering July sun. Much smaller fauna abound too. Hermit crabs, with and without their borrowed homes on their backs, hobble through the shallows. Tiny shrimp, both sand shrimp and mysids, jackknife across the tide pool. In late summer, striped bass begin to show up, and in late fall, small cod, which Gerald calls rock cod, find their way into the weir.

Gerald remembers two stranded prisoners of the weir: a six-foot harbour porpoise and a 150-pound tuna, both rare in the upper Bay. Although he had no licence to catch tuna, Gerald threw the fish onto the back of his wagon and cut it into steaks for his neighbours: "What did they expect me to do," he says, referring to the fisheries department, "pick it up and throw it over the weir where it would flop and die?"

Finding the porpoise struggling for life in his weir was a different matter. At first, he admits, he didn't know what he had caught, though he realized it was not a fish. He quickly went to work to rescue the beached mammal, tying a rope around its middle and leading it into the bin, where it survived in the shallow pool until the sea returned on the flood tide.

Gerald keeps alive a tradition that dates back more than a century and a half. Abraham Gesner, best known as the inventor of kerosene, practised medicine in Parrsboro in the 1830s and often travelled the Minas Basin shoreline on horseback. Gesner tells of the inhabitants of the shore repairing with pitchforks and "other implements of husbandry" to one of the intertidal pools near Five Islands, where they caught a variety of species—cod, pollack and halibut, as well as herring so thick they could be scooped out by hand. Since then, people have exploited the tides and seasonal

The flounder's skin is spotted and quite beautiful—nebulas soft-focused through the shallow water—but its sweet fillet is extremely hard to remove. I had discovered this only the week before, when, sweating and swearing, I had taken half an hour to skin a fluke. "Ten times harder to skin," says Gerald.

I ask him how he knew he had stabbed a fluke and not a winter flounder without first seeing it. "Like anything else, you know. After you been fishing flounder this way, you can tell by the way they move—just by their

movement. Sculpin pull hard, old maids are slippery, skate tuck down and are hard to get off the bottom."

Gerald's weir can, and often does, contain a variety of curiosities. Among the more remarkable are sea sturgeons. These primitive fish, armoured with five rows of bony plates, each of which is pointed with a spike, look like ancient knights of the sea bottom. Rare elsewhere along the Eastern Seaboard, they are relatively common in the upper reaches of the Bay and probably migrate here along with the bass, herring

fish runs by erecting primitive but effective brush weirs. In the 1850s, Moses Perley, the first person to formally investigate the fisheries of the upper Bay, sought high ground as I had done and described a now vanished Minas Basin scene: ". . . the flats for about four miles were observed to have an almost unbroken continuance of these weirs, crescent-shaped, the ends of the weirs touching each other."

In Perley's time, thousands of barrels of Bay of Fundy salt shad were exported annually to "the eminent fish merchants of

Gerald displays his biggest catch, 2,000 shad, facing page; his take usually numbers in the tens of fish. In the 1850s, shad catches of 50,000 were reported on a single tide. "After you been fishing flounder this way, you can tell by the way they move. Sculpin pull hard, old maids are slippery, skate are hard to get off the bottom," says Gerald of his fishing method with a pitchfork, above.

Boston." Shad catches of 50,000 and even 100,000 on a single tide were reported. Those halcyon days are long gone. Today, scarcely half a dozen weirs are scattered along the coast. Of these, Gerald's is the largest (1.3 kilometres long) and occupies what is arguably the best site in the basin. Even so, his biggest catch in recent years is 2,000 on a tide, and catches are more often numbered in the tens of fish. He sells them fresh on the beach for table fare and salts the balance for sale as bait to local lobstermen or for his own larder.

There has been a weir registered at the site for 115 years, and no doubt it was used long before any official record existed. Weirs have a lineage that reaches back into prehistory. The word (which is pronounced like "where" by Fundy fishermen) is derived from the Anglo-Saxon *weiran*, "to dam up." Archaeological digs have demonstrated that Amerindians had weirs 1,400 years ago, and until recently, the Inuit constructed primitive weirs by damming up rivers with stones and then collected the fish trapped behind them. More elaborate "fish fences" or "fish hedges" were developed in Europe to trap fish as they migrated along the coastline. The most sophisticated examples of this type of weir are found today in the outer Bay of Fundy, around the island of Grand Manan. These heart-shaped devices are tended by boat and constructed at great expense and effort, and they can yield tens of thousands of dollars in herring in a single day.

Though less productive, brush weirs in the Minas Basin are also considerably less costly, primarily because they can be constructed on "dry land" between the tides and don't require the services of pylon drivers and scuba divers. Fifty years ago, building and maintaining a weir was a community affair.

"There was no work in the spring," says Gerald, "only they waited for a scow to come in to load lumber, or they waited for a pulp boat to come into Economy to load pulpwood. And when they was puttin' that weir in, everybody working at it, they used to have three or four teams out there. They used to say how quick it took them to put it in. They used to work out there a month. Now I only work out there six weeks with one horse," he says with a proud chuckle.

Gerald cannot begin actual construction on the weir until April, when the pack ice leaves the basin, taking with it the remains of the previous year's weir. But he begins cutting his stakes in the late fall. "If there's sap in the stakes, they don't drive as well: there's a spring to them, and they'll bounce, and they're not as tough neither." The best stake is a 7-to-10-centimetre-diameter hardwood sapling—yellow birch, white birch, maple or beech, all species common to the Cobequid Mountains that overlook Five Islands. Standing on a makeshift platform, or "horse," mounted on his wagon bed, Gerald drives a stake every metre, alternating short and long stakes. In total, he drives 1,500 stakes into the tidal mud and soft underlying sandstone.

"You've got to have your stakes down good, so they won't break off with the tide. The tide's got a lot of pressure, you know," Gerald says.

He talks a hurried "downshore" pitch, so I always find myself attending carefully to discern the many subtle degrees of meaning he can attach to a single word. Like "work," for example. Listen to the fine-tuning: "These stakes here, we put them down three and a half, four feet. They're sturdy, because if they're too handy the top, and start workin', they work up. Stakes to me, now, they have to work a little, but with the tide."

Tidal currents surge between the islands and the shore with a force that can soon make a shambles of a poorly constructed weir. Two makeshift, come-lately efforts near Gerald's weir attest to the consequences of poor materials and shoddy workmanship. At the height of the shad season, they are partly collapsed, unable to fish. Gerald's weir is a paragon—the neatest weir on the Bay, it's said, a tribute to the dancing spirit level of his eye, for the weir stands straight-backed in an unbroken line, as if a carpenter had snapped a chalk line through the air. The top of the weir is always kept level with the waterline. "I'll tell you why my weir is so straight at the top," Gerald says. "Because I want all of the weir to bare at the same time." If the water level drops below the top of the weir all at once, he explains, the fish find themselves suddenly with nowhere to go. Otherwise, the ebbing tide will pour over the lowest part of the weir, providing an escape route.

During spring tides, the retreat of the sea can be so rapid that fish may be stranded even without the contrivance of a weir. I have walked on fish that have sought sanctuary under rockweed during the ebb tide. One fish in question—an ocean pout—was a foot long, mottled red and yellow, had the body of an eel, the horned head of a sculpin and Mick Jagger's lips curled down at the corners in a most sour expression. It thrashed its tail defiantly and slithered under cover of the wet weed to await the imminent return of the tide. Many species of fish native to the Minas Basin, including skate, flounder, sea ravens and goosefish, are left high and dry on such occasions. It is not uncommon for whales—pilot, minke and fin—as well as porpoises to be stranded when they follow schooling herring into the shallows or even into tidal rivers.

In Fundy, the great tidal range dominates all living things—large and small—for good and for ill. Survival here depends on an ability to adapt to the range and rhythm of the tides. I have found that this principle can hold as true for people as it does for the animals and plants that live by and under Fundy's waters. And no person I have met lives more in tune with Fundy's tides than Gerald Lewis.

Like his well-chosen and well-placed weir stakes, Gerald "works" with the tides. From

Gerald heads home with a couple of crates of flounder, facing page. Twice daily, he and his horse follow the muddy waters as they ebb and flow across the tidal plain. One of Gerald's young helpers tentatively displays a long-horned sculpin by its fanlike pectoral fins, above. A voracious predator, the sculpin eats crustaceans, mollusks, worms and fish—all found in Gerald's weir.

a purely practical point of view, his methods might seem archaic and inefficient. But the steady measure of his movements mirrors the rhythms of his tidally ruled environment. He and his horse retrace their steps twice daily, following the muddy waters as they ebb and flow across the tidal plain and making welcome anyone who wants to come along for the ride.

"I don't think I'd be content unless I was fishin'," Gerald confided in me one time, "I don't know whether it's the job or whether it's just meeting the people. I only have one regret."

"What's that?" I asked.

"I'm sorry I didn't have everyone's name that I took to the weir. There'd be more names than there would be fish I brought in." And he threw his head back in laughter unsullied by irony.

He hopes that someone will take over his weir when he's done. But it is difficult to imagine anyone quite like Gerald, who is willing to gauge his life to the pace of a horse and wagon and the strict regimen of the tides. During the two-month shad season, he rarely misses a tide, day or night. I remember a conversation we had on a night tide at Harrington River Beach. It was the last season for his 23-year-old horse, Tom, Peter's predecessor. The yellow light from a Coleman lantern hanging at Gerald's shoulder fell across Tom's flanks, magnifying his shadow to Trojan proportions. I listened to the horse shifting in harness as Gerald talked of a life lived beside Fundy.

"You work 18 or 20 hours a day when you're into a run of shad. You're tied to it. It's like farming, I guess."

In the silences between Gerald's thoughts, I could hear the tides of Fundy shifting in the void.

"People say, 'Gerald, why do you keep fishin'? You're not making any money.'"

His answer was simple: "I love it. It is not everybody who can have a job doing what they like. You're only here for a short time. You might as well do what you like."

THE UPPER BAY
The Bountiful Barrens

Long viewed as a kind of watery desert, the upper Bay of Fundy is now recognized as a feeding ground of international importance for both fish and shorebirds. A cornucopia of bottom-dwelling organisms, such as clams and mud shrimp, is the life source for migratory species and for the people who live in isolated pockets along its dramatic, tide-sculpted shores.

Barren Reaches by the Tide

The sun goes down, and over all
These barren reaches by the tide
Such unelusive glories fall,
I almost dream they yet will bide
Until the coming of the tide.

– Bliss Carman
"Low Tide on Grand Pré"

It is easy to share Carman's sentiment when looking out over the ebb-exposed Minas Basin at sunset. The slick flats are a crazy quilt of subtle colours, reflecting all the azure hues of sky but hoarding deeper burgundies and lavenders in the creekbeds that fan out across the mud flats like capillaries.

Close up, though, the muds of Minas Basin are less inviting. In fact, it is hard to imagine them as an environment that anyone would want to toil in or inhabit. Nonetheless, in midsummer, spread out across the sun-burnished flats, Brueghel-like figures can be seen bent at the waist, arms outstretched, so that they assume the shape of human tripods. They are clam diggers. They mine for buried biological treasure: the soft-shelled clam, one of a host of creatures that do choose to make the mud their home.

For 40 seasons, April to October, one of the figures dwarfed in the intertidal land-

A basket of clams, above, is a boon to Five Islands, which otherwise might be a "ghost village," says clammer Clayton Eagles. The soft-shelled clam is but one of the creatures that live in the Fundy mud flats. Clam diggers, facing page, spread out across the seemingly limitless flats. In fact, there are only 445 hectares of productive clam flat in the intertidal zone exposed in the Minas Basin.

scape of the Five Islands' clam flats has been Clayton Eagles, the undisputed dean of Fundy's clam diggers. At 54, Eagles is a wiry, walnut-tanned knot of sinew. His extraordinary fitness might be accounted for by the fact that he hauls his day's harvest home on a makeshift two-wheeler, or "gig," an eccentric vehicle, to say the least. It resembles nothing more than a rickshaw. The chassis consists of a cut-down bed frame mounted on two 28-inch bicycle wheels, the wide-tube kind, not the 10-speed variety which, Clayton says, are "too narrow and can't stand up to a load." The shafts are fashioned from hardwood hockey sticks. Add a piece of galvanized pipe for an axle, and there you have it.

"A lot of people got these three-wheelers now," Clayton observes wryly. "I guess I'm not that advanced." He loads the tools of his clam digger's trade onto his gig – galvanized buckets, wooden washing tray, onion bags and clam hack. Then, stepping

between the shafts, he gives a tug and leads his wife Marie, son Claytie and me onto the brick-red expanse of mud flat, a vast intertidal prairie dancing in the early-morning heat.

Going out to the clam bed, he takes the path of least resistance, following a meandering stream carved into the flats by the outflow of a tidal creek. The gravel bottom makes for easier hauling than the turgid muds. The Minas Basin at low tide epitomizes muddiness. The fine silts that blanket much of the intertidal zone make for

Clammers are dwarfed in the intertidal landscape, above. Going out to the clam bed, they follow a meandering stream carved into the flats by the outflow of a tidal creek. One 19th-century visitor described a trip onto the flats as an adventure in "mud-larking." The Minas Basin flats were once considered a watery desert but are now known to be host to a rich community of invertebrates.

hard slogging. In the early days, when clams were hauled ashore by sledges, the horses had to be fitted with wooden "mudshoes"—similar in function to snowshoes—to prevent them from becoming hopelessly mired. For humans, walking is difficult at best: the mud is slippery and can fasten onto a rubber boot with a viselike grip. Better to go barefoot. One 19th-century visitor described a trip onto the flats as an adventure in "mud-larking." I have found that even if I try to avoid the mud as much as possible, I invariably return to shore so smeared and

daubed that I look like one of the region's ancestral Red Paint People.

Once onto the flats, Marie and Claytie split up to find their own digging spots. Clam beds are easy to find. We look for holes in the sand made by the clam's long "neck," its feeding apparatus for sucking up water. When we approach a clam bed, small geysers of water gush from the holes as the clams withdraw their necks.

Clayton prefers to dig alone so that he can concentrate on what he's doing and set his own rhythm. There is a craft of sorts to this clam digging and an economy to Clayton's every movement. He plants his legs as far apart as possible, bends from the waist and grips the wooden hack handle that has been moulded to his hand by use. He buries the tynes (set at a right angle to the handle) half their length into the mud, interlocks the fingers of his left hand with the tynes where they meet the handle and gives a couple of short tugs to loosen the clay. Then, pulling with both arms, he flips over a lid of flat. Most digs are just the right depth—about 10 centimetres—so that he can reach down with his left hand and grasp the necks of the exposed clams.

"Awful torture," he jokes. "You're really not liftin' that much out here. There's really a knack to it."

Clayton chuckles when he thinks of the campers at nearby Five Islands Provincial Park. He finds evidence of their novice efforts littering the flats. "A lot of people who never dug before put that shovel right down out of sight. Couple of digs, they break it. Too much leverage, you know. You see more new shovels out here on the flats. A new shovel lasts them one trip."

Although clam beds with more mud than sand are heavier and therefore harder on the arms, Clayton says they are also less abrasive to the hands and the clams are not as gritty. Also, the clams that burrow in the mud take on the blue hue of their surroundings. Clayton likes that colour of clam. "All my life I liked the mud. I'm used to it, I guess."

Although a clam digger might profess to like mud and view it as a source of both life and livelihood, most people don't fancy mud. Even biologists harbour traditional prejudices against it, thinking of mud flats as unwholesome environments. In Fundy, the biologists assumed that the mud and the muddy waters that flooded the flats twice daily constituted a watery desert.

It is easy to understand why this unflattering view of the flats prevailed for so long. Penetration of light into the water column is the basis for the marine food chain: light promotes the growth of single-celled plants, the phytoplankton, which are fed upon by zooplankton, which feed fish fry—and big fish eat little fish. In the upper reaches of Fundy, mud in the water seemed to block out much of the solar energy, drastically limiting phytoplankton growth. There was no reason to think that much was out there worth looking at. There were no major fisheries, as in the outer Bay, and the few weirs and the sprinkling of clam diggers merely seemed to confirm the notion that little was living in the muds and muddy waters.

When you first venture onto the ebb-exposed Minas Basin flats, you are presented with a vast tissue of mud and water, which has the globular contour of a jelly mould. The flats look unnourishing. A few translucent strands of sea lettuce cling to small stones; in places, slicks of diatoms lend a velvety brown sheen to the flats. On closer inspection, however, you begin to notice star-shaped and pinwheel impressions in the mud. There are also constellations of tiny holes which, when you incline close enough, you discover are the source of the popping-and-hissing music of the flats—a message from another world buried under the tonnage of mud.

Mud is no wasteland. In its unpolluted state, it can be an ideal environment for the nurturing of life. "Mud," wrote Peter Steinhart, in an *Audubon* essay entitled "Kind Words for Mud," "is a lively place. It is one of those rare edges where sun, water and earth come together, and the combination is host to whole libraries of life." However true that may be, the intertidal zone (the area between high tide and low tide) is a stressful place in which to live, and few creatures can adapt to its rigours. They must learn to cope with tidal currents and the great fluctuations in salinity that are the inevitable consequence of the coming and going of the tides. During low tide, salt can be concentrated by evaporation under a hot sun or diluted by rainfall. As well, denizens of the mud flats are subject to periodic catastrophic events, such as storm surges and ice rafting, that may physically remove mud and all the creatures harbouring in it. For example, in 1975, Hurricane Beulah roared into the Bay of Fundy and scooped up the top 20 centimetres of mud in the Minas Basin, killing 90 percent of the creatures snuggled in the flats. Those that survived were tough customers.

The few cursory surveys of the Minas Basin mud flats that had been done before 1970 revealed a specialized community of creatures that could tolerate such discouraging conditions. There is, for example, the community of *Macoma*, a tiny clam common to the Boreal coast. Windrows of this inch-long, pale pink-and-blue-shelled clam can be found washed up in many coves of upper Fundy. They look disconcertingly like tiny fingernails. The bigger, soft-shelled clam, *Mya arenaria*, which is the basis for the half-million-dollar industry in the Minas Basin, also inhabits areas where the mud has a slightly sandier consistency. A more common, if less prominent, member of the community is the tube-building amphipod *Corophium volutator*, or mud shrimp. To this select, robust group are added a few saltwater worms, the nematodes. In general, the community is characterized by low species diversity but very high numbers of individuals. In other words, the few species that can adjust to intertidal conditions usually do very well. However, until intensive study of the mud flats was carried out in the 1970s as a consequence of tidal-power environmental studies, no one guessed just how many of these bottom-dwelling creatures there really were in the Fundy "barrens."

I first became aware of the fecundity of Fundy's mud flats in 1976, when I attended a lecture by Dr. Michael Risk at the University of Guelph, in Ontario. Later that year, Risk presented the surprising results of his research to the first conference on Fundy Tidal Power and the Environment, at Acadia University. His landmark paper on the marine ecology of the Minas Basin overturned the long-held attitude that the area was unworthy of scrutiny.

Risk displays a refreshing offhandedness to match his boyish good looks. His training as both a biologist and a geologist makes him ideally suited to study the complex animal-sediment relationships in the upper Bay of Fundy. When he joined the geology department at McMaster University, in Hamilton, Ontario, in the early 1970s, he asked students who had been studying the megaripples of sand that corrugate the shores of the Minas Basin what kinds of animals they had encountered. Their answer— "None, not a damn thing"—left him incredulous. He knew there were at least soft-shelled clams on the Fundy flats. The next summer, Risk was digging into the tidal ooze to see for himself what else might be

hiding there. In the sand, true to the students' word, there was an absence of creatures, but in the mud, he uncovered an embarrassment of riches. Risk's spaghetti strainer sieved as many as 4,000 *Macoma* per square metre from the tidal muck. *Corophium* burrows dotted the flats, and he counted as many as 63,000 mud shrimp living in a single metre of Minas Basin mud, among the highest numbers ever recorded in the scientific literature.

This cornucopia of bottom-dwelling invertebrates—the source of the flats' intricate arabesques and percussive music—had to be feeding on something. There was no significant phytoplankton, so Risk looked for alternative food sources. He examined the

Τhe sun sets on the Minas Basin, facing page, and "unelusive glories fall"—to quote the poet Bliss Carman—across the "barren reaches by the tide." With an eye on the advancing tide, a grandfather shoulders his clam-digging fork, above, and follows his gambolling granddaughters as they do a clam digger's shuffle for shore.

feeding habits of the fingernail-sized clam, *Macoma*. The diminutive bivalve has a long incurrent siphon that acts as a vacuum cleaner to suck up the slurry on the surface of the mud flats, and a short excurrent siphon that expels waste. Clayton Eagles calls *Macoma* "the double-headed clam"— an accurate anatomical description. In effect, *Macoma* is an organic gardener of the flats, stripping the bacteria that cling to the mud particles, then expelling the cropped sediment, which in turn becomes a nucleus for more bacterial growth. Risk estimated that *Macoma* in the Minas Basin recycle about 85 boxcar loads of sediment in this way every day.

Another source of organic carbon—food, that is—are the benthic diatoms. These single-celled organisms sport intricate silica exoskeletons that act as tiny solar collectors or portable greenhouses, converting solar radiation into edible organic molecules. Diatoms bloom on the flats between tides, forming velvety, greenish slicks from April to August. As well, the salt marshes supply carbon in the form of dead grass, which is transported to the intertidal zone by winter ice and high tides flowing and ebbing over the marsh. The marsh clippings, or detritus, are broken down by the action of bacteria. And so the cycle goes.

Studies carried out in the late 1970s by the Marine Ecology Laboratory of the Bedford Institute of Oceanography (BIO) determined that one-half of the primary organic production in the upper Bay is due to benthic diatoms, one-quarter to phytoplankton and the remainder to salt-marsh detritus. However, BIO also determined that production is relatively low compared with other estuarine systems, again due to the presence of mud and the physical stresses of the tide. A Georgia salt marsh, for example, is 10 times more productive than a Fundy salt marsh, and even the more northerly Mackenzie River Delta is 10 times more productive than the upper Fundy. Nevertheless, the biomass of animals in the Fundy muds is very high—among the highest anywhere—because nearly all its organic production is consumed where it is produced. There is very little loss to energy storage within the system or to export of energy outside the system.

The key to the efficient functioning of such food production, according to Risk, is the flushing action of the tides. The ebb and flood currents keep the bottom slurry of bacteria, diatoms, detritus and algae—what Risk calls "nutrient soup"—in motion and therefore available to bottom feeders such as the clams. "Tides," he says, "do a good deal of the biological work, transporting nutrients, larvae and dissolved oxygen and removing waste products."

Risk makes another fundamental observation: "In the case of the Bay of Fundy, where the food is moved with the sediment and the sediment controls the distribution of animals, you can't study the biology without studying the geology." In other words, you have to understand the vital properties of mud. After a decade of inquiry, I have determined that if you talk to any scientist about Fundy long enough, the conversation will eventually turn to mud—how much, what kind, how and where it is moving.

A walk along the Bay's shoreline reveals the source of the material that reddens the waters of Fundy's upper reaches and pre-

occupies the minds of investigators. The soft, red sandstone of Triassic origin that borders much of the upper Bay is no match for strong tidal currents. Cliff-line erosion is constantly reshaping the coastline, sometimes with such whimsical results as the famous "flowerpots" at Hopewell Rocks. Millions of tonnes of sandstone are dumped into the Bay every year. Normally, the swift tides keep much of the material in suspension, but if the tide's action is slowed, such as by causeways, the mud settles out, with disturbing biological consequences.

This effect was shown dramatically by the construction of a solid-rock causeway across the mouth of the Avon estuary, near Windsor, Nova Scotia, in 1970. Almost before the last stone was put in place, sediment began to accumulate at an alarming rate—5 to 14 centimetres per month. Within seven years, a four-metre-high island of silt, which became known as the Windsor Mudflat, formed on the seaward side of the causeway; and the effects were felt up to 20 kilometres downstream, where two metres of mud impaired navigation at Hantsport. A similar impairment occurred seaward of the Moncton causeway, on the Petitcodiac estuary in New Brunswick. Large ships, which once had docked easily in Moncton, could no longer navigate the mud-choked river.

What Risk found at the Windsor Mudflat was a world gone topsy-turvy. He identified it as a "biological desert." There were no

T he soft, red sandstone of Triassic origin that borders much of the Bay is no match for strong tidal currents. Cliff-line erosion, facing page, is constantly reshaping the coastline and, in the process, dumps millions of tonnes of sandstone into the Bay every year, where it reddens the waters and settles out to form vast mud flats.

Mya, and when he tried to introduce some, they sank into "clam oblivion." On occasion, Risk and his research team would follow the clams, sinking up to their armpits in the water-saturated mud, inspiring Risk to add the term "human penetrometer" to the vocabulary of science. A penetrometer is an instrument that measures the penetrability of a substance; at Windsor, the human penetrometer measured ankle mud, knee mud and the dreaded armpit mud. The accumulation of watery sediments at Windsor also wiped out the small *Macoma* clams and the *Corophium*—the two most common creatures everywhere else in Minas. Risk estimated that the bottom-dwelling creatures at Windsor were experiencing a two-thirds mortality rate.

In fact, sediment deposition was occurring so rapidly on the Windsor Mudflat that not only were bottom-dwelling creatures being buried alive, but the nutrients normally suspended in the water column were also being precipitated and overlaid with silt. The carbon food source was fast becoming unavailable to Fundy animal life.

Normally, there is very little free carbon floating around in the upper Bay. Everything that is produced is quickly consumed at its source by bottom dwellers, birds, fish and, ultimately, humans. But at Windsor, Risk found a conspicuous absence of signs of a healthy habitat. From his work on typical healthy mud flats, he had become accustomed to seeing shorebirds scurrying across the flats, jabbing the mud for a boneless tidbit. At high tide, groundfish moved in over the flats and left feeding pits. Other bottom feeders—flounder, sturgeon, cod, skate, rays and tomcod—also frequented the flats. By contrast, at Windsor, birds and fish had quit the flats because their food sources, the clams and shrimp, were no longer there in sufficient numbers.

Risk's work on the differences between life on normal Fundy mud flats and on these human-induced death traps raised concerns over how a tidal barrage blocking a major basin in the upper reaches of the Bay of Fundy might affect the ecology of the inner Bay. If the causeway at Windsor was a reliable model, then massive siltation could be expected, with catastrophic effects on the community of creatures residing in the mud flats. This, in turn, would "domino" up to the birds and fish feeding on those creatures in the upper reaches of the Bay. Risk posed a fundamental question to the scientific community: "To what extent is tidal power already working for us?" The choice inherent in tidal-power development, he suggested, might be between two kinds of energy—electrical and biological. Electrical power could destroy the mud flats; biological power, in the form of fish and birds, depended on and sustained the mud flats.

Since Risk's pioneering work, there has been intensive study of the Fundy estuary. Recently, the research was given impetus by the establishment of the Acadia Centre for Estuarine Research, which uses the Southern Bight of the Minas Basin as a backyard field laboratory.

Estuaries are generally considered to be stressful environments, subject to constant changes in salt concentration, dissolved oxygen availability and sediment level. In the Bay, such stresses are magnified, as is everything, by the incredible strength of the tides and the ubiquitous mud.

However, the research of Dr. Graham Daborn, the centre's first director, on the turbid near-shore environment has revealed an unexpected phenomenon. Zooplankton in the extremely muddy waters of the upper Bay are more abundant and more diverse than previously thought. They appear to be able to thrive on nonliving organic matter, such as salt-marsh detritus, as well as bacteria and single-celled (benthic) diatoms associated with sediments. The tides have a mixing-bowl effect, suspending nutrients and food organisms from the seafloor, thereby making them available to zooplankton, invertebrates and fish.

Such an abundance of creatures at the lower end of the food chain suggests a considerable nursery role for the inner Bay.

Traditionally, the warm, nutrient-rich and relatively predator-free waters of estuaries have been viewed as nature's marine nurseries—that is, as especially good places to grow up in if you're a larval fish. Risk and his co-workers had observed juvenile flounder literally stacked one on top of another in the shallows. They wondered to what degree the upper Bay was acting as a nursery for commercially important species caught offshore or in the outer Bay.

The work of Dr. Sherman Bleakney, also

Dogwhelks prey on a starry colony of barnacles, above. To breach the barnacle's protective limestone shell, the whelk secretes a poisonous purple dye, which kills the animal inside, causing its muscles to relax and the trapdoor at the top of the shell to open—whereupon the dogwhelk tucks in. Facing page: Clayton Eagles pulls his day's harvest to shore on his makeshift two-wheeler, or "gig."

at Acadia University, anticipated the recent intensive scientific scrutiny of Fundy by 20 years, and his research tends to confirm the view that the upper Bay is a fish nursery. He has witnessed schools of fish moving in over the flooded marsh like the shadows of clouds ghosting over a submerged green field. At night, he has netted the creeks and found them clogged with fish. In all, he identified more than 50 fish species in the upper reaches of the Bay, including herring, smelt and flounder, which are of commercial importance to the coastal zone. Bleakney has also identified 15 species using the miniature marine worlds of marsh tide pools. "There's a constant turnover of adult fish using these pools as breeding areas and juveniles using them as nurseries," he says.

Recently, Daborn and his colleagues have teamed up with sedimentologists and geologists to study the biology-geology relationship in the mud flats. "The biophysical interactions that take place in the Minas Basin are amazingly varied," says Daborn. "The ramifications of a simple change in current velocity, and therefore in suspended sediment concentration, are mind-boggling. It influences every activity you can think of. For example, barnacles presently live in protected portions of the basin. If you change the current velocity there, you change the distribution of barnacles."

Daborn has also begun to look at the mud-animal relationship from a new perspective. He is examining the effect of biological activity on the mud, rather than the effect of mud on the biology. Ecological dogma has it that the types of sediments available determine what kinds of creatures will live in the mud flats. Daborn's research, however, suggests that in the Bay of Fundy, the reverse also holds true: the sediments are there because the animals are there. The benthic animals and the microscopic diatoms seem to control the stability of the surface sediments. Daborn showed this experimentally by poisoning a section of the flats and observing that when the creatures in the mud died, the normally stable fine surface sediments were washed away by the tidal currents.

It appears that the mud's susceptibility to erosion is decreased if there are creatures living in it. In other words, biological activity somehow holds the mud together. Such studies may ultimately lead to more reliable answers about the impact of tidal-power development on the ecology of the Bay. In any event, it is now abundantly clear that the muds of Fundy, once spurned by the scientific community, have yet to yield all of their hidden secrets.

As I stand in the midst of the encircling flats, an insignificant speck in the intertidal landscape, the clam beds seem virtually limitless. They are not, of course, and neither is the resource they support. There are some 300 square kilometres of intertidal zone exposed in the Minas Basin at ebb tide, but only 445 productive hectares of clam flat. Clams require a specific kind of substrate, one that is neither too muddy nor too sandy. Only where these conditions are met and there is available food will larvae begin burrowing to make a home and a living. Once young clams burrow into the mud, they reabsorb their foot (their digging tool), and there they must stay.

In the 1940s, when Clayton started clamming, large crews of 20 people could work a small area profitably for a month. In those days, diggers took only the larger clams because smaller ones were uneconomical to shuck. Clayton can't break the habit. On every dig, he plucks out only the choice, mature clams and leaves the rest. This learned conservation technique seems to have been abandoned by the new generation of diggers forced onto the flats by hard times. The unmanaged exploitation of the resource worries Clayton.

"They think I'm crazy, I don't like diggin' everything. I don't know, clams got to have somewhere to start. Some of them digs them little ones. Holy Moses, this clammin's made a lot of work around here. If we lose it, it would be a ghost town – or a ghost vil-

lage, I suppose. Years ago, there used to be breeding beds, we'd call them. We never used to dig them at all. They started diggin' them out. I think it made a difference. I just can't see it. You dig everything out, what's going to be left to grow? I don't know how the clams can stand it with that many clammers on them – really."

By October, the Five Islands' mud flats are so pocked and pitted by clam diggers' hacks that they look like a war zone. It seems that hardly a square metre has not been turned over. As a result, the clams are becoming fewer and farther between. So, too, are the clammers, who are frustrated by the cold and the diminishing returns for their efforts. A few have earned enough stamps to qualify for unemployment insurance and no longer see the need to work. The flats are abandoned to stalwarts like Clayton.

The digging is discouraging, the clams, elusive. "Them old clams, they're some scarce today. That's the trouble in the fall, it's hard to tell where they are. I don't know, it must be the cold weather. The clams just seem to disappear. Sunny weather, the holes just seem to show up better on nice warm days. A fellow should have radar here in the fall to find where they are."

In an hour, Clayton digs a bucket and

heads for the stream, where he empties the clams into his washing tray, a box with a slatted, slightly rounded bottom. He swishes it in the cold stream, then, holding the wet box against his stomach, tips the washed clams into an onion bag. The wind is whipping across the tidal plain. To find shelter, Clayton hunkers down in the streambed. Leaning his weight back on his haunches, he lights a cigarette. He holds his other hand, white with cold, inside the front of his faded purple plaid woods shirt. The bad digging seems to have made him meditative.

"Clam digger is the foolishest fellow there is. Ninety percent of clam diggers just spend what they make," he says.

After 40 years on the flats, Clayton is just now beginning to put a little money aside. He's never wanted luxuries but simply what most working men have aspired to – a better chance for his family than he had for himself. If his body holds out, he and Marie could get by on two or three buckets of clams a day, he figures; that is, if the clams are there to dig.

Clayton puffs on his cigarette, eyes the advancing tide, then begins to load his equipment onto his gig. Gripping the shafts, he hauls his meagre harvest home across the barren reaches by the tide.

The Strongest Stream

"You are aware that the shad taken at the head of
the Bay are, perhaps, the best in the world . . ."

—M.H. Perley, Esq.
"Reports on the Sea and River Fisheries
of New Brunswick," 1852

Two hours before high tide, the boat belonging to Marven Snowdon and his son Rick is grounded, its keel mired in the glistening, visceral mud of the sea bottom. When I arrive, Marven is standing above the creek bed, his washed-out blue eyes trained on the red waters of Cumberland Basin. The red contrasts shockingly with the emerald-green fringe of the salt marsh. Marven, presented in powerful, barrel-chested profile, is waiting for the tide to fill the creek and refloat his boat.

Marven's schedule is determined by the extreme range of tides, which reach 14 feet on a spring tide, such as the one pushing up the Bay today. Fishermen here cannot simply decide to go fishing at any hour, nor can they come home to port when they wish. The time of their departure and their eventual landfall are strictly dictated by the time of high tide. Boatmen often stay on the water for the full 12-hour diurnal cycle so that they can make it out of and back into

The American shad, above, the largest member of the herring family, ranges in length from 40 to 60 centimetres and weighs up to three kilograms. In Canada today, it is of little commercial importance, which is surprising considering its superior culinary qualities. In Fundy's Cumberland Basin, fishermen, facing page, still drift on the tide for this locally prized, delicious fish.

port without risk of grounding. If high tide comes in the middle of the night, that's when they go. Marven stands watching for the tide's coming so that he can begin the day's drift. "Won't be long now," he says, flicking a cigarette from his stubby hand.

To board the boat, I pick my way carefully down the intertidal gulch of Allen Creek on the slippery rungs of a floating dock, which is now also mired and thus more ladder than dock. As we wait, the tide makes an appearance around the bend of the creek and begins creeping up the lavender banks.

The inundation of the creek happens with subtle but inexorable force. Before long, Marven is starting up the thunderous diesel and we are powering out of the channel, which minutes ago had been a dry bed. We trail a muddy wake that sloshes up the creek walls holding us in their clasp. Three metres above us, a green horizon of marsh grass shimmers in the midday sun. The creek is narrow here, providing barely

enough room for Marven to manoeuvre. As we round a bend, he points the bow between two spindly trees stuck in the mud to serve as channel markers leading into the red waters of the open Bay.

Marven steers for the Nova Scotia shore. The tide advances more quickly on that side of the basin, and he knows that shad move with the strongest tidal currents. Rick and his crewman Billy pay out the course of gill nets as Marven steadies the wheel, giving the boat throttle when necessary to keep the two kilometres of net stringing out in a straight line. "You try to get in the strongest stream and work toward the slack water," Marven explains. "If the wind is hard, you pay out net with the wind. Otherwise, the wind's pushing the boat. If you get a tangle, you got to pull your guts out. There's always a wind up in here," he adds. "They say it's because of the cold water here and the warm water in the Northumberland Strait."

When the nets are set, Marven cuts power and the younger men go below to sleep. Now we drift on the inrushing tide, which sends ruddy boils charged with mud, detritus and various kinds of sea wrack to the surface. The tidal current is a swift four to six knots. To starboard, we pass the verdant slip of pastureland still called Elysian Fields, a reclaimed marsh that was part of the Minudie estate. In the 19th century, it belonged to Amos "King" Seaman, who amassed a fortune on the basis of salt hay, the shad fishery and grindstones cut from Cumberland's cliffs and reefs. It was at Elysian Fields that Seaman described the prosperity of the shad fishery a century before: "Sometimes may be seen in [the] Bay and around the shores of Minudie upwards of two hundred boats out at one time. The boats leave the place of rendezvous with the ebb tide, drift down the Bay until they meet the flood and return with it to the place whence they started."

The method hasn't changed much in the intervening 200 years, but the state of the fishery has deteriorated markedly. We drift

alone: the Snowdons are the last of the New Brunswick shad fishermen in the Cumberland Basin.

To the first fishermen here, the French Acadians, this arm of Fundy was Beaubassin, and it is not difficult to understand why they considered it a place of beauty. The billiard-table-green expanse of the Tantramar Marsh stretches before the bow. On one side is the sleepy university town of Sackville; on the other, a spruce-clad hill sloping toward the marsh. I can make out the patina of the 18th-century sentinel Fort Beausejour, which still looks out imposingly upon the Bay, though it has been two centuries since a menacing warship tacked toward it on the tide. We drift toward the earthen battlement of the dyke, which protects the Trans-Canada Highway connecting New Brunswick to Nova Scotia. In the hazy distance, the towers of Short Wave Canada rise high above the marsh, beaming their messages to the world from the cradle of the continent.

"It's just forgotten," says Marven. He is speaking of the official attitude of the Department of Fisheries and Oceans toward the shad fishery of Cumberland Basin. "They just don't care, don't want nothin' to do with it. You go to a meetin' and tell them how many fish you caught, how many fish is here, well, they might as well call you a liar. They say, 'They ain't there.' They don't even come out here and look for themselves."

The American shad, *Alosa sapidissima*, is the largest member of the herring family, a silvery iridescent fish with the deeply forked tail and laterally compressed, streamlined body of a fast swimmer. Shad range in length from 40 to 60 centimetres and weigh up to three kilograms. In Canada today, the shad is considered of little importance as a commercial species, which is surprising considering its superior culinary qualities. *Sapidissima* means "most delicious," praise to which most who have savoured a stuffed, baked shad will attest. The one drawback to the shad's table virtues is that, like other allosids, including the alewife, it is exceedingly bony, containing no fewer than 1,500 Y-shaped bones. Even so, for New Brunswickers living along the Saint John River Valley, shad with fiddleheads is one of the rites of spring. All along the Eastern Seaboard, shad are caught when they enter their spawning rivers, and shad roe is a highly prized delicacy.

The shad fishery in the upper Bay is unique to North America, as it is only here that nonspawning shad are caught in oceanic, if shallow, waters. Marven and Rick are the third and fourth generations of their family to be sustained by the shad fishery, which has been pursued along the New Brunswick shores since the first Europeans settled here in the mid-18th century. But true to Marven's complaint, for most of the 20th century, there seems to have been an official amnesia about the shad fishery in the upper Bay. In retrospect, it is apparent that the declining interest has gone hand in hand with a dramatic deterioration in shad stocks.

When M.H. Perley, Her Majesty's Emigration Officer at Saint John, New Brunswick, was dispatched to the upper Bay to prepare a report on the sea and river fisheries of New Brunswick in 1850, he discovered a thriving shad fishery that was carried on by "fishing-farmers" between seed time and hay making. As many as 100,000 shad were harvested in a single tide by drift net and in stationary weirs, which had to be tended with ladders at low tide. King Seaman wrote enthusiastically to Perley about the commercial potential of the shad fishery in the upper Bay: "At the present time, there is a great demand for shad caught at the head of this Bay as being of superior quality—much fatter and more delicious flavour than any found on American shores or in the markets of the United States. . . . That the supply is inexhaustible is plain to everyone; for notwithstanding the number of people employed, and the means for capture have greatly increased within the last few years, there appears not the least diminution in the quantity of fish—none complain. . . . We consider our shad fishery to be only in its infancy."

The endless bounty of nature described by Seaman in the 19th century proved short-lived. Between 1870 (when fisheries' statistics commenced) and 1900, total commercial catches for the inner Bay of Fundy were two million to six million pounds a year—two-thirds of the entire Canadian landings. Most of the fish were salted in 100-pound barrels for export to the Atlantic Seaboard. Today, Marven's market for shad is strictly local: he services a supermarket account in the nearby city of Moncton as well as a list of faithful customers, door-to-door, who buy an annual supply of shad for their freezers.

After the turn of the century, catches suddenly plummeted. The export trade pe-

Fisheries researcher Michael Dadswell, above, pulls in a shad from the turbid waters of the Cumberland Basin, once called "the dead Bay." Dadswell's tagging programme, facing page, has shown that every shad from the Eastern Seaboard comes to Fundy once during its life cycle. Dadswell now has a tag from every river on the east coast of North America with a known shad population.

tered out in the 1920s, as the shad, for mysterious reasons, no longer frequented Fundy waters in bountiful numbers. As late as the 1970s, fisheries researchers dismissed the upper Bay as having no significant fish life; they called it "the dead Bay."

Fifteen years ago, near Allen Creek, New Brunswick, two men looked out to the Cumberland Basin, watching a small boat drift seaward. Their curiosity had begun to border on concern. Several times they had seen the boat drift out with the tide after motoring ahead, and they could not decide whether the drift was intentional or if the small boat was having engine problems. Neither man wanted to interfere, but each knew that this is not a piece of water in which to be at the mercy of the tide.

The man in the boat was Michael Dadswell, a fisheries research scientist from St. Andrews Biological Station, in New Brunswick. He had come to the inner Bay on his own initiative, wondering what fish, if any, resided there. He believed that theoretically, the estuarine upper Bay could be a nursery for offshore species such as cod. But he was beginning to believe rumours that the Bay was dead. Each time he pulled his trawl, it came up empty. Persistent, he repeatedly motored against the six knots of ebb tide, set his trawl and drifted sea-

ward. Finally, Marven Snowdon, one of the two men watching from Allen Creek, said, "Suppose we better go out and see if he's all right."

It was to be a fateful meeting—a case, Dadswell says now, of "serendipity." When Dadswell came ashore, Snowdon revealed to him what another local fisherman, Mr. Buck of Dorchester, had told Perley a century and a quarter before: there were three separate runs of shad in the upper Bay of Fundy; the last run, the autumn fish, were the fattest. And the shad came to the inner Bay to feed, not to spawn.

However, Snowdon added one critical bit of topical information: the shad fishery had been showing a steady improvement so far in the 1970s. Dadswell intuitively con-

nected the local fisherman's confidence with his own knowledge of major restoration efforts on American shad rivers—in particular, the Delaware and Connecticut rivers. Dadswell was aware of the decimation of many spawning populations caused by pollution and hydroelectric dams. He also knew that concerted effort in recent years had cleaned up native waters and that fish ladders had opened up traditional spawning grounds, contributing to a dramatic revitalization of stocks.

Dadswell suspected that the nonspawning shad which frequented Cumberland Basin were, in fact, emigrants from the south and that their increasing numbers were attributable to habitat restoration on southern rivers. He asked Snowdon to assist him

in a tagging programme, and the following spring, the fluorescent orange tags that had been inserted under the dorsal fins of shad caught in Cumberland Basin began to arrive on Dadswell's desk with southern postmarks. He now has tag returns from every river on the east coast of North America with a known shad population—from Quebec's St. Lawrence to Florida's St. John's. "Every blinkin' river," he says.

The locally prized Minudie shad were actually migratory shad from the major rivers of the Eastern Seaboard: the Hudson, Connecticut, Delaware, Susquehanna and St. John's rivers. All congregate in Fundy's muddy waters. Dadswell had found the long-sought piece of the migratory puzzle of the American shad.

The life history of the shad is that of the classic anadromous fishes that spend most of their adult lives at sea, entering fresh water only to spawn when the water temperatures exceed 12 degrees C. The males are the first to arrive on the spawning ground — usually a deep, fast-flowing section of river — followed by the females, each of which lays 130,000 eggs on average. The translucent larvae spend their first summer in the river, feeding on insects and planktonic crustacea, and in the fall, when the temperature drops below 15 degrees, the 10-centimetre fry descend to the sea.

But just *where* in the sea was a long-standing mystery in fishery science. At the turn of the century, it was believed that young shad remained close to their native river mouths and reentered fresh water as soon as the temperature was suitable. However, in the late 1950s, an extensive tagging programme, undertaken by William Leggett (now dean of science at McGill University) as part of the Connecticut River Ecological Study, showed that adult shad made impressive coastal migrations, moving northward as summer advanced along the coast. Shad that spawned in the St. John's River in Florida in January were found in the Gulf of Maine. It was another 25 years before Dadswell showed that their migration continued into the Bay of Fundy, penetrating to its innermost reaches.

In the fall, shad retreat southward to the mid-Atlantic, which makes for an annual migration of more than 3,800 kilometres. Leggett believed that this predictable pattern of coastal migration came about in response to changing water temperature. Shad seemed to prefer to stay in an envelope of water (known as their isotherm) with a temperature range between 13 and 18 degrees C. Their predilection for warm water led them into the Gulf of Maine, the only place along the Atlantic Coast with that specific temperature range during August and September. Dadswell's work has revealed a more complicated picture of shad migration, which depends, among other things, on the tides once shad enter the Bay of Fundy itself.

Perhaps because staying in one place requires effort in their dynamic environment, fish, more than any other animal group, are likely to make seasonal migrations. It is easier to drift with the tide than it is to fight against it. Athough fish may be more likely to migrate, they do so for the same reasons as land animals or birds do: to find food, return to a breeding ground or seek out a suitable wintering area.

Marven Snowdon, facing page, a Fundy shad fisherman, pulls in his gill net decorated with a fat shad. The once thriving Fundy fishery deteriorated after the turn of the century when stocks were decimated by dams and pollution on American shad-spawning rivers. Shad merely open their capacious mouths, above, and let the gill-rakers filter mysid shrimp from the dark waters.

Fishes that make seasonal migrations of thousands of kilometres tend to do one of two things: either they follow the big ocean gyres offshore, as west-coast salmon do; or, like shad, they haunt coastal corridors, using a variety of external cues to guide them. Changes in temperature and photoperiod, associated with changing seasons, influence the general direction of migration along the coast. As temperatures rise and days lengthen, shad move north; when the days shorten with the onset of autumn, the fish move south again.

During the five years that shad normally spend at sea, they may travel 20,000 kilometres. They are found as far north as Nain, Labrador, in summer, and as far south as Florida during January and February. However, until Dadswell, no scientist considered looking for shad in the turbid inner basins of the Bay of Fundy.

During the past several years, Dadswell has sketched in the details of the shad's migratory pattern within the Bay itself. His tag returns show that the first shad appear on Fundy's southern shore, near Digby, Nova Scotia, in early April and May. These arrivals are spawners, destined for Fundy rivers: Annapolis, Shubenacadie and Hébert. Immigrants that have already spawned in the more northerly rivers of the Eastern Seaboard — those from Cape Hatteras, North Carolina, to the Gulf of St. Lawrence — start arriving in late May and early June, when the water temperature has risen above 10 degrees C. The more southerly fish (which are fatter and more prized for home freezers or salting) surge into the Cumberland and Minas basins in July and August. By then, the sun-soaked tidal flats have warmed the water to 15 to 20 degrees, a temperature similar to that of the southern waters of the shad's origin.

Once the shad enter Fundy, the direction of their migration is dictated by the residual current structure of the Bay. The counter-clockwise pattern of the currents within the Bay results from the so-called Coriolis, or estuary effect, created by the Earth's

rotation. In the northern hemisphere, if you stand facing the sea, the major current flow in estuaries always comes in on the left side and goes out on the right side. The effect is accentuated in the Bay of Fundy because Grand Manan Island blocks the tidal impulse from entering on the New Brunswick shore.

By following the residual currents, shad make use of a common energy-conserving strategy of fishes: tidal-stream transport. In essence, they hitch a ride on the tide. As Fundy fishermen have long known, shad swim with the strongest stream. When the tide is in flood, they surge ahead; when it ebbs, they drop back, but not quite so far. By this one-step-forward, half-a-step-back movement, they progress through the Bay at a rate of 3.5 to 4.5 kilometres per day.

The shad seem to have no choice in how they circulate through Fundy. "It's as if they're on railway tracks, and they just go wherever the residual currents guide them," says Dadswell. However, the migration does split randomly at Cape Chignecto, with half the shad run going into Minas Basin, the other half into Chignecto Bay. Those which enter Minas Basin first embark on a counterclockwise circuit of the entire Bay that takes them through Minas, into Cumberland and finally out past the city of Saint John into the Gulf of Maine—a circumnavigation that takes four months.

It is precisely this programmed behaviour of going with the strongest stream—a behaviour understood by every Fundy shad fisherman from Buck to Snowdon—that worries Dadswell. If a tidal-power plant were built across the mouth of one of Fundy's muddy inner basins, its effect on the shad runs could be devastating. Unlike a locally spawning fish, which risks passage through a turbine only once on its spawning run, a shad migrating through the Bay's inner basins risks being chopped to bits by the whirring blades of a turbine perhaps as many as 20 or 30 times as it makes its stepwise progress through the area. "The mortality rate added up, even if it's only a couple of percentage points a day, might get rather high," Dadswell points out.

Dadswell estimates that there are 10 million adult shad and many more juveniles feeding in the Bay of Fundy every summer. That number represents half the North Atlantic population. Furthermore, it is likely, he feels, that every shad from the Eastern Seaboard comes to Fundy at least once during its life cycle.

The more he has learned about the origin and behaviour of the shad, the more it seems to him an unacceptable risk to build a tidal dam in one of Fundy's turbid inner basins. Dadswell is frustrated that the degree of risk has not yet been appreciated either by conservationists in the United States or by fisheries officials in Canada. Current revitalization efforts, such as a stocking programme on the Susquehanna to restore the Chesapeake Bay population, pollution-abatement programmes on the Delaware River and the opening of traditional spawning grounds on the Connecticut River by fishways—all of these projects could be undone by a Fundy tidal-power project.

Furthermore, Dadswell now believes that shad are not the only species using the Bay's inner basins as summer feeding grounds. He suspects there is a parade of southern fish, including striped bass, alewives, sturgeon and dogfish, coming up the Eastern Seaboard and into Fundy's tidally dominated migratory circuit. As well, in season, the tides become thoroughfares of indigenous fish life, as anadromous and estuarine species such as salmon, tomcod and smelt make their spawning runs into the tidal rivers at the head of the Bay. Other deep-water species—cod, pollack, mackerel and halibut—also visit Fundy's shallow upper reaches during certain months to feed on the offerings of mud flat and salt marsh. All of these species would have to negotiate passage through a tidal barrage.

It is a warm summer day in 1984, and I am drifting the Minas Basin with Dadswell. I have come to respect the biologist for his

synthesistic, if unconventional, cast of mind—an ecologist's mind, interested in piecing together the patterns of life in the Bay. Dadswell looks the part of the iconoclast. He wears his lank black hair over his ears and looks at the world through dark-coloured glasses, a habit he acquired working long hours on the water. He and his assistant, Daphne Themelis, are making plankton tows to determine what the shad eat during their summer-long sojourn in these waters.

F rom spring breakup to leaf fall, the tidal rivers of Fundy become thoroughfares for fish life, as smelt, alewives, shad, sea trout and salmon follow each other in season. Silhouetted against a fiery Maccan River, a fisherman, facing page, prepares to dip a meal of smelts. Rod fishermen on the Shubenacadie River, above, try their luck for striped bass, which come to Fundy to feed.

At sea, shad are planktivorous fish—they feed on a variety of zooplankton, including copepods, mysids and euphausiids. In the oceans, they are usually found at depths of 50 to 200 metres, which is why they are not susceptible to a concerted commercial fishery. The preference for deep waters appears to be related to their peculiar photobiology. Shad are photonegative; that is, they appear to prefer low light intensity. "Shad are really an old fish. They've been around for 490 million years," Dadswell says. "They've evolved to exploit this kind of habitat—high turbidity, low salinity, with limited food resources. Out there, there are no other competing planktonic fish, such as mackerel. Shad somehow exploit this kind of resource when other fish cannot."

At first, Dadswell felt that it was the shad's ability to live in the extremely low-light environment of Fundy's muddy waters that accounted for their numbers in the Bay. Even though there is abundant food in the mud-laden waters—mysids and other small crustaceans—he has found that the turbidity limits feeding time to the ebb cycle, when

the water clears enough to allow the shad to find their prey. Perplexing as it seems, shad may spend as much as a month in Cobequid Basin, where visibility of less than a metre prevents effective feeding. Dadswell has collected many shad that had nothing in their guts other than marsh detritus. Under such adverse conditions, he says, some shad actually lose weight.

Nevertheless, they return to Fundy year after year and have probably been doing so since the turbid environment evolved 6,000 years ago with the onset of macrotidal conditions. I wonder aloud why they had not evolved during that time to avoid, or at least better exploit, an environment which seemed to do little to enhance their conditioning and therefore their survival.

"It seems," Dadswell says, "that they're so programmed with the currents, there's no way for them to get around it. They're on the tracks, and they can't get off because they wouldn't know where to go, they wouldn't have any cues. They have to use the directional cues they've been given. So they just go along."

We drift past the place between Tennycape and Economy Point where 110 fourteen-storey caissons are to be strung together—the proposed site for an eight-kilometre-long tidal-power barrage. Our conversation turns from the mysteries of evolution to the vagaries of politics.

"There are going to be an awful lot of fishermen affected down the east coast," says Dadswell, "and a lot of people who like

to eat shad roe down south. I would say that if we start to damage the shad population, well then the concern will come. But it's too late then."

On many rivers of the United States, the shad is a highly esteemed sport fish whose aerial acrobatics have earned it the sobriquet "poor man's salmon." On the Delaware River alone, 20,000 anglers try their luck during the annual spawning run. "A lot of Americans think we're never going to build a dam because we've been talking about it for so damn long—so they're just not that worried about it."

We drift toward the head of Cobequid Bay, which in high summer reaches 20.4 degrees C. "You know," Dadswell adds, "you feel a little bit like Don Quixote out here."

Actually, tilting at windmills is an apt metaphor. The risk to the shad from the whirring blades of a tidal-power turbine is now a partial reality. Despite decades of delay, the megaproject is a step closer to commitment, largely because of the proven technological feasibility of the low-head, straight-flow (straflo) turbine installed in North America's first tidal-power plant at Annapolis Royal in 1984. The plant operates on a so-called single-effect mode: a sluiceway allows water to flow through the dam on the flood tide. On the ebb tide, the sluice gate is closed. As the tide ebbs away in front of the dam, a head of water—the difference between the water levels on the two sides of the dam—develops, and when the head reaches five metres, the wicket gates in front of the turbine open and the generating cycle begins. A fishway was installed adjacent to the spillway, but the strongest flow is through the turbine itself, and unfortunately, that is where the shad are likely to go—with the strongest stream.

In 1985, Dadswell set out to quantify the potential problem. He tagged the shad with sonic devices, then released them at the intake of the turbine on its generating cycle. The four 7.6-metre turbine blades have an outside edge speed of 90 kilometres per hour. From what he knew of the shad's behaviour and the design of the power plant, Dadswell predicted that 10 percent of the shad would suffer a fatal direct hit. His prediction proved optimistic: 55 percent of the shad were killed, from a combination of direct hits and the equally devastating indirect effects of the turbulence created by the turbine. A diver discovered a graveyard of fish piled three deep—striped bass, mackerel, alewives and shad—on the bottom of Annapolis Basin downstream of the turbine. Some were macerated—cut in two; others had suffered shear—heads torn off; others were pressure-killed—eyes popped out, and blood haemorrhaged into the fins. Still others had been blown apart by air bubbles that had exploded inside them like tiny sticks of dynamite. Dadswell repeated

the experiment in 1986 with only slightly less discouraging results. This time, 21 percent of the shad were killed on passage through the turbine's draft.

"Still pretty bad," Dadswell observes. "For multiple passage, the mortality adds up pretty quickly, especially when 300,000 to 400,000 fish are moving on a single tide."

Marven Snowdon has seen the effects of dams on the river systems of the upper Bay of Fundy, in particular on the Petit-codiac, where a solid rock causeway built

A patient fisherman-farmer lies suspended over the Gaspereau River. When the spawning alewives, or gaspereau, as they are known locally, ascend the river and pass over his square net, he will grasp the long pole beside him and jump from his stand, levering the fish from the water so that he can dip them, above. Most of the gaspereau are salted for export to the Caribbean.

in 1970 decimated salmon stocks. The possibility of a tidal-power dam in either Minas Basin or Cumberland Basin worries him. Such a project would surely threaten the fishery that has sustained his family, despite official neglect.

As Marven talks of his frustrated attempts to keep his fishing tradition alive, the tide rests full—time to pull the nets. He shouts below, and the young men climb sleepily into their wet gear. The wind has come up, and the water is choppy. Waves slapping at the back of the boat shoot spray into the faces of the men as they pull in the nylon nets, hand over hand. It has been a good drift, a heavy September shad decorating the net every few metres.

With the deftness of basketball stars, Rick and Billy toss the fish into two plastic barrels that hold about 60 fish each. The barrels are soon overflowing, and small bait boxes begin to fill up. There are about 150 shad on this short drift and more to be taken on the ebb tide. But now that the wind is kicking up in earnest, Marven decides not to reset the nets for the return drift. We head full throttle toward shore in a race against the turning tide. The wind is churning the sea against our bow, sending veils of spray over the wheelhouse, while raucous gulls follow our stern.

Rick takes the wheel from his father. "In another hour, seas will be 10 or 12 feet high," he says. "Wind running against the tide piles it up."

It is a spring tide, and the southwest wind is pushing the water even higher up the coastline. The high marsh is flooded, with only the barest fringe of green showing around the rim of the wind-tossed basin. The seascape is so changed, in fact, that for a moment, I don't recognize where we are as Rick points the bow for shore.

"Where's that?" I ask.

Rick looks at me incredulously.

"Allen Creek," he says.

Then I see the tips of the spruce-tree markers poking above the brown waves, pointing the way to safe mooring.

Wings Over Fundy

"The value of these shorebirds for their
aesthetic appeal alone was sufficient reason for
protecting them . . ."

–Robie Tufts, "Birds and Their Ways"

An aerial dance, a grand ballet of flight performed by tens of thousands of mercurial dancers, storms my vision: the peeps have returned to Fundy. They are a flock of semipalmated sandpipers, a dark cloud of wing beats that creates its own musical wind. Their speed is startling, and the swift beating of their two-tone wings, flickering first white, then dark, produces a stroboscopic effect as unsettling as the rapid eye movements of a dream. The mist of birds grows denser, darker, then thins out like a summer storm cloud buffeted and frayed by high winds. The flock has an infinite elasticity that allows it to change shape constantly as well as a magnetic cohesion that draws it back to an ever-shifting centre. The eye delights at the constant metamorphosis. Flying low over the water, the flock abruptly spirals upward like a tornado; at the zenith of its curving climb, it seems to explode in all directions like a flowering of fireworks; then, pulled together by an

A semipalmated sandpiper, above, makes a harmless rendezvous with a mist net in the upper Bay of Fundy, the most important stopover point for migratory shorebirds along the Eastern Seaboard and an area of international importance for the sandpipers. For a few weeks every summer, thousands of sandpipers, facing page, transform Marys Point into a living, pulsing place.

inseparable bond, the birds continue their peregrination of the Bay in long, wavy banners of flight.

Flying wing to wing, each bird seems miraculously to anticipate its neighbour's next move so that none seems to lead and none to follow. Executing this impossibly intricate choreography, the flock becomes one body, supremely alive and in touch with all its parts.

Suddenly—and with uncanny precision—the sandpipers bank, revealing their white underbellies; instantly, the dark cloud becomes a silver cloud. In the strong light, the effect is of thousands of palm-sized mirrors turned to the sun in unison, then turned again to show their dark sides. It is a constantly changing light show, engineered to take advantage of every caprice of breeze.

Ornithologists have suggested that such illusory patterns of flight evolved as a protective measure, designed to decoy a raptor by imitating sea spray or wave move-

ment. But to the inexpert observer, the manoeuvres seem to be executed for the pure joy of it.

This great dancing spectacle is performed every summer, beginning in mid-July, above the drab brown stage of the upper Bay of Fundy. The gathering shorebirds may delight us with their aerial acrobatics, but their own agenda is far more practical: they have come here to get fat. Most of their hours in Fundy are spent not in the air but on the flats, pecking for mud shrimp. They follow the tide line, in and out, with dogged alacrity.

Despite the enormous area of Fundy's intertidal zone—1,052 square kilometres at ebb tide—the shorebirds show a marked preference for only a few sites along its upper coast, where extensive flats allow them to feed without crowding and where a beach above the high-tide mark provides a roost. Marys Point and Grande-Anse in Chignecto Bay and Starrs Point and Evangeline Beach in the Minas Basin constitute the most important shorebird sites in the upper Bay. At these select spots, thousands of shorebirds amass shoulder to shoulder at high tide, transforming the inanimate beach, deserted for most of the year, into a living, pulsing place. Then at ebb tide, flocks thin out across the exposed flats until they vanish from sight altogether, and it is possible to drive by without noticing the birds are there at all. Perhaps because of this inconspicuousness, it was not until the last two decades that the importance of the upper Bay as a shorebird staging area was acknowledged.

Marys Point, New Brunswick, is the single most important roost along the entire Fundy shoreline. The sickle-shaped peninsula sheltering Ha Ha Bay (an embayment of the larger Shepody Bay) is now protected as part of the Shepody National Wildlife Area under the administration of the Canadian Wildlife Service. Credit for its recognition as a major shorebird staging area for the autumn migration is due in large measure to Mary Majka, a New Brunswick nat-

uralist, and David Christie, an avid bird watcher who conducted some of the first shorebird surveys in the Bay of Fundy while he was a curator at the New Brunswick Museum in Saint John.

Today, Mary Majka's century-old farmhouse presides over her beloved Marys Point like a benign, ever vigilant sentinel. For the past 10 years, Mary has lived year-round in this isolated community which, a century ago, thrived on the export of building stone (Boston's Custom House is built of Marys Point sandstone) but now has all but reverted to nature. Mary is its unofficial warden, a protector of the vital link in the shorebirds' migratory chain. Although this sickle-shaped bay was named for another

Naturalist Mary Majka, above, unofficial warden of Marys Point, the main roosting site in the upper Bay of Fundy, plunges into the water, inspired by the sandpipers dancing above her. Facing page: The sandpipers spend most of their hours on the flats, pecking for mud shrimp in preparation for their nonstop 4,000-kilometre flight over open water to South America.

Mary, a half-Micmac, half-Acadian girl whose short, unhappy life was lived out here two centuries ago, one cannot now think of Marys Point without thinking of Mary Majka. In leading her to Marys Point, fate smiled on Mary Majka: "I never planned my life. Perhaps if you have such a love as I have, you just end up where you belong."

I remember my first meeting with Mary, when she plunged into the brown waters of Fundy Bay, clothes and all, inspired by the sandpipers dancing above her head. "It is more than a profession. It is a lifetime occupation. I feel almost like a nun," she told me, speaking of her work as a naturalist. There can be no doubt that this daughter of a Czechoslovakian countess and a Polish school principal has found her spiritual home in a place that has absorbed other waves of immigrants—Indians, French, English and Irish—and, for a few brief weeks of summer, millions of shorebirds.

Since then, I have returned every year to watch the shorebirds at Marys Point. A few summers ago, I joined Mary at her perennial observation station near the bone-grey trunk of driftwood on the beach. "This is my old friend," she said, patting the weathered trunk.

"The Bay's comings and goings are something I treasure very much," she continued, "because I don't think there could be anything more rewarding than to live with the pulse of nature, in accordance with each heartbeat, so to speak."

The shorebirds, too, live in accordance with Fundy's heartbeat. They follow the tide line as it retreats and advances across the flats, constantly feeding, bobbing in their up-and-down sewing-machine motion as they go. Only when the tide is full do they rest on the thin crescent of beach that serves as their roost. On this particular day, the inexorable lapping of brown tide packed a relatively small flock of 30,000 into a tighter and tighter clutch. Eventually, the flock occupied just a few hundred square feet, a postage-stamp corner of inundated Ha Ha Bay. The peeps huddled closely together—rank upon grey, white and buff rank—to conserve precious calories for their imminent journey south.

"They sleep here like a giant," Mary observed of this sensitive nexus of avian life pulsing with pent-up energy. "In a way, they form a solidarity that is like one body. That is how they function."

Occasionally, a menacing gull or buffet of onshore wind that was whipping the Bay into whitecaps startled the flock into flight. Then the air became a drum skin for beating wings that carried the flock in a flowing loop out over the water.

"It's interesting, I always liken their flight to festivities," Mary mused. "They are like a banner or a ribbon on a stick, waving in the wind as they descend."

The nervous birds returned to the crescent of beach 30 metres from our vantage point, and we sat for hours absorbed in their behaviour. At times, disturbed by some threat, real or imaginary, a few birds would fly up and hover momentarily before settling down again into the anonymity of the flock's midst. At the edges of the roost, there was a steady lineup of birds bathing in a tiny tide pool. There were also small groups of the more statuesque black-bellied plover and dowitchers and a few sanderlings skittering stiff-legged along the lap-

ping tide line. After their ablutions were performed, the peeps again returned, as if on a conveyor belt, to the flock. Now and then, a few couriers scurried across the flats, carrying clandestine messages from the main roost to the smaller outlying camps. But as the tide rested full, the birds became less active, their churring faded to near silence; they tucked their heads under their wings and slept, their frenetic activity, so restless with anticipation and purpose, momentarily stilled.

For 20 years, Mary has welcomed the sandpipers back to Fundy. Every year is different. Once, she remembers, the spectacle of half a million birds in one flock moved her to tears. Some years, there are what she calls "special guests": pectoral sandpipers, Hudsonian godwits, whimbrels, golden plover, willet, a Baird's sandpiper—and once, a very rare curlew sandpiper from Siberia. "I have spent many hours alone with the birds," Mary remarked in a hushed voice. "A communion exists after a while. I get lost in the whole phenomenon. I have to say to myself, 'Come on, Mary, there are other things in the world.' Just being here, just the fact of experiencing them all over again, is something that becomes a very important part of oneself. After a while, you become so immersed, you lose yourself—it almost becomes frightening."

Mary paused to regard the living beach. "You forget your name. You are part of nature. It's a tremendous experience."

Mary's sense of community with the shorebirds is one I have grown to share. I've also become increasingly fascinated with the underlying biology of this remarkable gathering. Scientists, no less appreciative of nature's mysteries than naturalists, have been digging beneath the experiential aspect of the annual phenomenon for answers to fundamental questions: Why this mass immigration into the upper Bay of Fundy? Why such large concentrations at so few select sites?

Since Audubon's time, it has been recognized that large numbers of shorebirds used the rich estuarine environment of Fundy's salt marshes and mud flats as a staging area. Beginning in mid-July, shorebirds funnel into the Bay from their wide-spread Arctic breeding areas en route to their wintering grounds in South America. The Maritimes Shorebird Survey, conducted by the Canadian Wildlife Service in

Biologists, above, painstakingly count mud shrimp (*Corophium volutator*), amphipods that live only in Fundy and are the sandpipers' prime prey. At Grande-Anse, with ideal substrate conditions, as many as 63,000 per square metre can be found. Biologist Peter Hicklin calls Fundy "a fat station," where shorebirds, such as this one being banded, facing page, double their weight in two weeks.

the mid-1970s, established that the upper Bay of Fundy was, in fact, the single most important stopover point for shorebirds along the entire Eastern Seaboard, and an area of major international importance to semipalmated sandpipers in particular.

A total of 1½ million of the 2 million shorebirds that use the Atlantic flyway stop in Fundy. Thirty-four species have been spotted in the upper Bay. The nine most common are the least sandpiper, the short-billed dowitcher, the semipalmated sandpiper, the red knot, the semipalmated plover, the black-bellied plover, the white-rumped sandpiper, the sanderling and the dunlin. Of all these, by far the most common is the semipalmated sandpiper, which makes up 95 percent of the migrant population. In a given year, one-half to three-quarters of the world's population of semipalmated sandpipers stops to feed on the intertidal offerings of Fundy's mud flats.

As Canadian Wildlife Service ornithologist R.I.G. "Guy" Morrison reported in the 1976 tidal-power conference at Acadia University, the upper Bay of Fundy plays a critical role in the shorebirds' life cycle as a feeding and resting place where the birds are able to accumulate large fat reserves, the energy source for the imminent 4,000-kilometre migration over water to the north coast of South America. However, the scientific community did not then know how the shorebirds were using the habitat or just what qualities made parts of it more attractive to them than others.

Then Peter Hicklin, a young ornithology student from Acadia University, tackled the problem. He concentrated his early work on the Southern Bight of the Minas Basin, near Wolfville, Nova Scotia, then switched his focus to Chignecto Bay in the late 1970s when he accepted a position with the Canadian Wildlife Service in Sackville, New Brunswick. Since then, his field-work has been concentrated at Grande-Anse, at the mouth of the Petitcodiac River.

Grande-Anse has provided me with some of my most memorable moments as a shorebird watcher. Often, more birds can be seen there than at Marys Point. I remember one evening, as the setting sun burst out from beneath a heavy bank of cobalt cloud, the birds' busy feeding behaviour suddenly transformed the drab mud flats into a sparkling, light-enlivened surface like that of a dancing summer lake. Later, in the dying light, the flocks spiralled like snow devils, each bird a fleck of silver whirling with ecstatic energy. On another evening, when the last light of the setting sun lay in peach and roseate pools on the great flats, I saw the unmistakable, professorial silhouette of a Hudsonian godwit, a relatively rare visitant to Fundy.

However, the day I joined Hicklin at Grande-Anse was less auspicious. A south-

west gale was whipping off the Bay, lashing with such force that it was difficult to open our eyes. When we did, we saw a homogeneous slurry of mud flats, water and stormy sky. Our bodies leaned into the weight of the wind as our feet plodded in mud that, with each step, only reluctantly loosened its hermetic grip on our rubber boots. As we neared the tide line, 2.5 kilometres from shore, the birds came into view. Everywhere we looked, the flats were overrun with them, and at our feet, the wet tablet of the sea bottom was imprinted with the infinitely repeated cuneiform of three-pronged tracks. Scattered flocks took to wing, seeming to delight in the acrobatic possibilities of the tempest. But most were possessed by a single-minded purpose—eating. At the tide line, phalanxes of the slate-backed peeps bobbed up and down, apparently oblivious to the vicissitudes of the weather, which, that day, made scientific observation impossible, and Hicklin and I repaired to the summer cottage that served as his field camp.

Hicklin is a handsome, articulate man, whose speech retains a hint of his Acadian origin. At Acadia, he switched his major from French literature to ornithology. He seems to embody the necessary characteristics of a biologist in an environmental age—impassioned curiosity tempered by circumspection. He has logged untold hours on the flats, perched unceremoniously on an aluminum lawn chair, mud oozing between his toes, a telescope to his eye, as he observes the birds that become so used to his presence that they continue to feed all around him.

He views the uninviting muds of Fundy with an intensity and an insight unshared by the casual passerby. "When you drive by the Bay," he says, "you see this wasteland of mud and ooze that looks all the same, but not all mud flats are equal." The mud flats consist of a mixture of sand and mud particles of different sizes, varying from very fine to coarse. Depending upon the relative mixture of sand and clay

particles, the Fundy flats exhibit vastly different capacities for supporting invertebrate populations.

Of the 34 invertebrates Hicklin has identified as living in Fundy's red mud flats, the most abundant creature—and the most important to the sandpiper—is the scavenging amphipod *Corophium volutator*. Commonly called the mud shrimp, *Corophium* is a tiny (five-millimetre-long), lipid-rich crustacean that feeds on the abundant detritus and benthic algae churned up by the turbulent ebb and flow of tide. Common to the European coast, it is found on this continent only in the Bay of Fundy-Gulf of Maine region. There, however, the unprepossessing mud shrimp is a vital link in the estuarine food chain, providing the main food source for a number of fish species as well as for the shorebirds.

In Fundy, the number of mud shrimp in a particular mud flat is directly related to the amount of very fine sand. *Corophium* builds its U-shaped burrow with seemingly biblical wisdom: too much fine sand and its hole collapses, too little and the mud is too thick to dig. Where substrate conditions are ideal, such as at Grande-Anse, they live in extraordinary proximity. Numbers peak at an astronomical 63,000 per square metre and average an impressive 20,000. As they process water through their burrows to extract oxygen, they make small crackling noises. "On a quiet day," says Hicklin, "they make the flats sound like a giant bowl of Rice Krispies."

Hicklin has shown that sandpipers forage in greater numbers on mud flats with the highest densities of *Corophium* and will not feed where the little amphipod is scarce, even though other prey, such as saltwater worms, may be extremely numerous. In other words, sandpipers have a critical dependence on the tiny mud shrimp as their prime source of fat for the impending journey to South America.

Hicklin becomes animated when he speaks of "the magic of the relationship" between sandpiper and mud shrimp, which results in one of nature's grander imponderables: a nonstop, unerring flight between hemispheres. The key to the successful functioning of this prey-predator relationship is the reproductive cycle of *Corophium*, which experiences a population explosion just in time for the arrival of the sandpipers from their Arctic breeding grounds.

Corophium live but a year. In the Bay of Fundy, ice scouring drastically reduces the overwintering population. The survivors produce their first young, which look and act like miniature adults, in late May. The progeny grow and mature quickly, releasing more young in mid-July. In Europe, mud shrimp produce only one generation of young; in the Bay of Fundy, two generations are produced annually. Thanks to the second generation, peak numbers of mud shrimp occur, as if by magic, just as the first sandpipers fly in from the Arctic, on or about July 18.

Females are the first arrivals. During the short Arctic breeding season, they produce a clutch of three or four eggs. The precocial chicks are capable of taking care of themselves at birth, and the females leave shortly thereafter, flying from their central and eastern Arctic breeding grounds to the west coast of James Bay, where extensive marshes and mud flats provide ideal staging conditions for the 1,500-kilometre flight to the Maritimes. The females may arrive in Fundy with a small fat reserve, whereupon they immediately begin topping up for the last leg of their journey by selectively removing the larger, overwintering mud shrimp, unhampered by the more aggressive males.

The peeps continue to build their numbers throughout July with the arrival of the males and eventually the juveniles in August, so between the third week of July and mid-August, there are often as many as 100,000 birds on the major mud flats. Hicklin's prime concern has been to determine how long the sandpipers must stay in the Bay of Fundy in order to put on enough fat to complete their over-water odyssey. This has meant painstaking counts of the number of crustaceans that a single bird ingests. The figure is mind-boggling: during a single tidal cycle of 12½ hours, each

A common eider duck guards its down-lined nest, above, on The Wolves, major eider breeding islands in the outer Bay of Fundy. Nests are well hidden for protection against the elements and predators. Eiders have made a remarkable comeback in the Bay of Fundy in the past 50 years. Facing page: Ubiquitous herring gulls hang in the air like beautiful mobiles.

bird consumes between 9,600 and 23,000 mud shrimp.

The sandpipers feed by sight, using their relatively long bills to pluck invertebrates from the mud flats. They scurry from one meal to another, pecking with an almost maniacal diligence. After very little observation, it becomes obvious that the sandpipers' strategy is to follow the retreating tide closely, where *Corophium*, which have left their burrows during high water to feed, are exposed on the surface of the mud flat. Male mud shrimp are particularly vulnerable, as they leave the safety of their own burrows at low tide in search of the burrows of females. During these amatory excursions, which last only 20 minutes after the tide retreats, many males fall prey to the ever vigilant peeps.

Hicklin refers to Fundy's flats as "mud pastures." Due to the vast area of the flats and the huge numbers of *Corophium* in them, the shorebirds enjoy the unique advantage of being able to graze without competition. From colour-marking experiments, Hicklin estimates that birds stay in the area from 10 to 14 days to accumulate sufficient fat reserves for their migration. During that time, some birds double their lean weight of 20 grams. "Nowhere else can you record this high fat content," Hicklin says. "That's the advantage of coming to Fundy, because they can put on so much fat. And since these are the highest weights recorded on the Atlantic Coast, I would guess there's a selective advantage, that there's greater fitness if they come here, because they can put on so much fat. There is so much food and so much mud flat."

Perhaps the most convincing sign that Fundy confers a selective advantage on its inhabitants is that every year, Hicklin finds birds at Grande-Anse that were banded on the Maine coastline, which means that some birds actually head north to Fundy to put on extra fat before heading south over open water to Suriname. Also every year, some western sandpipers, which breed in the Alaskan Arctic, wing all the way across the continent to Fundy en route to South America. "They need a lot of fuel," Hicklin says, "and I've always thought of Fundy as a refuelling area. It's a gas station—a fat station."

The mystery of the migratory behaviour of birds has always fascinated natural philosophers. More than 20 centuries ago, Aristotle observed that "all creatures are fatter in migrating," and recent studies confirm that birds undergo hormonal changes, inducing them to lay down fat, and that migration may only begin when birds have accumulated a critical fat reserve. In Fundy, however, Hicklin has observed sandpipers that were too fat to fly. Mary Majka tells of her horrific experience of picking up a prone sandpiper only to have it burst in her hands and ooze accumulated oils. Whether the internal mechanism goes awry in such cases or whether the birds stay for a certain amount of time in Fundy regardless of how much fat they accumulate, Hicklin does not yet know—though he suspects the latter is the case.

Whenever I watch the frenetic feeding behaviour of the sandpipers, I cannot help feeling a sense of urgency as they scurry and stab their way across the flats. Their search for food—the hapless mud shrimp—is unceasing, and time seems of the essence. The birds appear to be driven by some innate knowledge that they must lay on as much fat as they can as quickly as they can.

Whatever intrinsic forces drive and regulate such behaviour, in the past few years, a number of computer- and radar-aided studies have shown that external as well as internal factors play a role in triggering migration. Weather—in particular, the passage of cold fronts—seems to influence the shorebirds' time of departure. By means of some mysterious physiological mechanism, birds are amazingly sensitive living barometers, able to detect minor changes in atmospheric pressure and therefore to anticipate the movement of weather fronts.

In the late 1970s, shorebird movements

were tracked from four radar stations—three in Nova Scotia and one in New Brunswick. A consistent pattern of movement was detected. Birds tended to migrate over Nova Scotia in the largest numbers when the wind shifted from southwest or west to northwest, a condition that often occurs in advance of cold fronts. The shorebirds usually departed just before sunset and preferred nights when there was no precipitation and little or no crosswind. The following winds carried the birds high over Nova Scotia (at an average height of 2 kilometres, though flocks have been detected at 6.65 kilometres) so that they were above any cloud cover. Curiously, the radar indicated that the direction of their flight was so far east as they headed out to sea, they would have to change course if they were to make a landfall in the western hemisphere.

Christopher Columbus first reported large numbers of shorebirds and passerines migrating over water. Ships' crews often see, or are visited by, overflying birds. Radar studies in the 1960s showed that an estimated 100 million birds of all kinds migrated from many points along the east coast. Once over the water, the birds appeared to pay no attention to Bermuda or the Caribbean Islands while making their intercontinental nonstop leap. They merely maintained a constant compass direction —yet another innate navigational ability birds miraculously possess—and the same northeasterly trade winds that brought Columbus to the Americas eventually pushed them back to their destination on the north coast of South America.

Flying at an average airspeed of 60 kilometres per hour, shorebirds can complete the migration in 40 to 60 hours. Once they commit themselves by taking a ride on a northwesterly offshore wind, there is no looking back. Neither can they rest on the water, since they do not have the salt-clearing mechanism that seabirds do. The epic journey is a nonstop ordeal, and it exacts a tremendous toll. Birds arrive in South America with their fuel reserve of

fat nearly gone. In some cases, the birds actually deplete muscle tissue to complete their journey.

So why do birds choose the sea route rather than a seemingly less risk-fraught overland flyway? Perhaps one important factor is that the ocean route is only half as long as an overland route through Mexico and is one-third shorter than an island-hopping route from Florida through the Antilles. Shorebirds are generally capable of storing enough fat to make nonstop flights of up to 4,600 kilometres, and it is approximately 4,000 kilometres from the Bay of Fundy to Suriname, where two-thirds of the world's semipalmated sandpipers winter. If tropical storms do not blow the shorebirds disastrously off course, which rarely happens, and if they have topped up on enough fuel before setting out, most should make it. That the majority of the birds do successfully accomplish the flight makes it no less awe-inspiring. Although it has been calculated that such a flight is equivalent to a human being running continuous four-minute miles for 60 hours, such an analogy is meaningless. There is no human comparison to this feat. What makes such a migration so compelling is the simple fact that it is far beyond our realm of experience.

This amazing flight, though critical to the birds' survival, is only one event in the annual shorebird cycle. Semipalmated sandpipers have different migratory routes for their northward and southward migrations.

A dapper pair of black guillemots, better known as "pigeons," keep watch both ways from their rockweed-draped perch. The most widespread seabirds in eastern Canada, they nest from the Bay of Fundy to the high Arctic islands. These two wear their distinctive summer plumage—black with white wing patches and what appear to be garish, bright red spats.

In spring, peeps that breed in the eastern Canadian Arctic migrate by an Atlantic route, stopping by Delaware Bay in time to fill up on horseshoe-crab eggs, then turn inland and hopscotch through wetlands in the centre of the continent, bypassing Fundy.

Although the rate of adult survival is high (75 to 90 percent), the life cycle of a shorebird is precariously dependent on timing. The short Arctic summer means they get only one chance to lay a single clutch of three to four eggs. What makes the shorebirds' population so vulnerable, however, is their dependence on a few critical sites, which are like links in a chain. The breeding and wintering grounds are separated by what shorebird biologists call "ecological barriers"—vast expanses without suitable feeding sites. This habitat restriction creates bottlenecks as large portions of the shorebird population funnel into a small area such as the upper Bay of Fundy.

Whenever I see the birds, I am struck by the extreme vulnerability of their circumstance. One cannot help being aware of the potential danger when one sees tens of thousands of sandpipers packed into an area no larger than a suburban front lawn: a single untoward action could have disastrous consequences. Peter Hicklin once told me of an incident at Grande-Anse, during an extremely high tide, when the shorebirds were forced onto the road to roost. Inadvertently—or perhaps not—a car drove through the roost, killing 1,200 peeps. Even more ominous than such an isolated accident is the prospect of tidal development, which could have a permanent effect on the shorebirds' highly restricted habitat. The proposal to build a tidal dam in Cumberland Basin in the mid-1970s threatened the integrity of the feeding grounds at Marys Point and Grande-Anse and consequently the sandpipers' ability to complete their autumn migration without full access to the fat stations of the Bay of Fundy's mud flats.

It is likely that the migratory sandpipers have been exploiting the rich flats of the up-

per Bay for several thousand years, perhaps since Georges Bank sank beneath the Atlantic and the tides of Fundy began their ceaseless ebb and flow. Shorebird biologists are concerned that the birds' preference for traditional sites, like Marys Point and Evangeline Beach, could inhibit their ability to switch to other feeding habitats, such as offshore islands or salt marshes, if they were forced off the mud flats. If inundation or sedimentation damaged prime roosting sites, crowding might result in lower foraging efficiency, therefore less fat accumulation and ultimately reduced probability of migratory success.

"My gut feeling is that there are going to be problems," says ornithologist Peter Smith of Acadia University, who has been studying the effects of crowding on feeding efficiency. "It's the space, and the behaviour that ensues from trying to forage in limited space, that is really our concern."

Sandpipers are still numerous and, so far, do not seem to be suffering a decline. However, in the past 15 years, several other shorebird species have suffered reductions

of more than 75 percent through the loss or deterioration of vital wetlands. These are the largest reductions of common North American bird species reported in the 20th century, and they have spurred conservationists to mobilize a strategy to stave off future threats to shorebird populations.

The Western Hemisphere Shorebird Reserve Network has been established to protect the stopover points in the shorebirds' annual cycle. Each is a critical link in the birds' evolved system of survival. To be

Female eiders proudly lead their broods across the sea, above, having evaded the gulls that capitalize on the annual migration from land to water. A blizzard of semipalmated sandpipers, facing page, storms into flight. The roosting sites at Marys Point and Evangeline Beach, which are vital links in the shorebirds' migratory chain, have been designated as Hemispheric Shorebird Reserves.

recognized as a hemispheric site, an area must harbour more than 250,000 birds or at least 30 percent of the flyway population of a species—criteria easily met at Marys Point for semipalmated sandpipers.

On August 8, 1987, wildlife officials from Canada, the United States and Suriname, along with shorebird lovers and the press, congregated at Marys Point to dedicate the area as Canada's first Hemispheric Shorebird Reserve. (Evangeline Beach, in the Minas Basin, was added to the small group of critical sites in 1988.) At the ceremony, Stanley Malone of Suriname spoke of his country's commitment to establish 200,000 acres of a "sister reserve" at the mouth of the Coppename River—a concept devised by R.I.G. Morrison to twin efforts by nations that share natural responsibility for the shorebirds' welfare. (The Suriname government has since complied.) Malone expressed for all of us our admiration for the little birds whose travels bind together our two nations. "It is an incredible feat these small birds accomplish—4,000 kilometres in three or four days. I find it remarkable, and it still puzzles me. When I get home, we will be experiencing the first birds on our coastal mud flats."

Dr. Peter Myers, the National Audubon Society's vice president for science and co-originator of the hemispheric network, then spoke of the important work of naturalists Mary Majka, David Christie and Reid McManus and of his colleague, Morrison, in recognizing the critical role of Marys Point to the health of the semipalmated sandpiper population. And he reminded everyone present that the time to save a species is when it is still abundant.

After the official dedication, we took our sandwiches and tea to the beach to be with the birds, the real guests of honour, that had assembled in front of Mary Majka's "old friend" as if aware of the auspiciousness of the occasion. Birds and people communed quietly. Then suddenly, I heard Mary's urgent voice—"Look, look, look!" and I looked up to see the straight, deadly pass of a pere-

grine falcon as it swooped down on the roost. The flock exploded into flight, eluding the raptor's talons.

The falcon had thermed down from Fundy National Park, a few kilometres down the coast, where, since 1982, biologists have released 143 hack-box-raised young in an effort to reestablish a breeding population along the Fundy coastline. In 1989, two breeding pairs—one under the Saint John River Bridge, another in Fundy National Park—had successful nests, thus raising the hope that the birds would return to their former range. Fundy's high cliffs once provided perfect nesting sites for 15 pairs, and the arrival of the shorebirds, timed exactly to the fledging of the peregrine young, ensured ample food supply. However, pesti-

cide use in Canada and in the peregrine's southern wintering grounds extirpated the last of the natural breeding peregrines from Fundy more than three decades ago.

The peregrine's appearance was an ironic reminder of the interconnectedness of nature and how humankind's unthinking actions can undermine that delicate perfect balance. In Fundy, the *Corophium* population explosion sets the table for the sandpipers' migration; the abundant sandpipers, in turn, once provided easy prey for the inexperienced fledgling peregrines. The experiment at Fundy Park has made it painfully clear just how laborious and uncertain the task of rerighting nature's balance can be. Given the obvious mistakes of the past, it is especially disconcerting to contemplate

a prospect like tidal-power development, which could alter the life-giving tides of Fundy—thereby undermining the pyramid of life at its very foundation.

As I watched the sandpipers' wavy flight undulate above the brown waters of Shepody Bay, I remembered a conversation that I had once with Mary Majka about the ability of shorebirds to adjust to a major change to their habitat. "We know from history that many species have been extinguished because they couldn't be as flexible as human beings," she told me. "And I think that certain species are very much more dependent on special environments, and those birds definitely are. They certainly cannot survive without the Bay, its tides and its beautiful muds."

BAYSHORE
Gift of the Tides

Fertile fringes of salt marsh brighten the Fundy coastline and provide a vital link between marine and terrestrial ecosystems. Open to the sea, these tidal meadows support a complex marine food chain. As dyked land, they were the basis of the Acadian culture, which still thrives along the bayshore.

Dawn of the Dinosaurs

"It has often happened to geologists, as to other
explorers of new regions, that footprints in
the sand have guided them to the inhabitants
of unknown lands."

–Sir J. William Dawson
"Air-Breathers of the Coal Period," 1863

At the base of a 200-million-year-old cliff face, Dr. Paul Olsen of Columbia University's Lamont-Doherty Geological Observatory is sitting on the talus of a rock slide washed down by last night's torrential rains, picking through the reddish rubble for a telltale speck of white that might indicate fossilized bone. "There's a scoot right there," he says, palming a nondescript slab of mudstone. "That's a crocodile plate." To my surprise, he pops it into his mouth. After a moment, he sticks out his tongue and picks off a triangular speck of bone. "There it is, virtually completely prepared."

According to Olsen, the little crocodile lived primarily on land and had a whiplike tail and long spindly legs that made it "the cheetah of its time." I drop the scant remains into a small vial to add to the hundreds of thousands of bones—from skulls to scoots—that Olsen and his colleagues have plucked from the debris at Wasson's Bluff in recent years.

Dr. Paul Olsen (left) of Columbia University's Lamont-Doherty Geological Observatory and Robert Grantham of the Nova Scotia Museum, above, carefully extract a dinosaur footprint from Fundy's sandstone. The Fundy basin is a rich source of dinosaur footprints, bones and plant fossils, such as this perfectly preserved 300-million-year-old fern frond, facing page.

The green-grey basalt cliff behind us is the weathered remains of a lava flow 90 metres thick that spewed from the earth 200 million years ago at the beginning of the Jurassic age. Abutting the lava is a red wall of sandstone that was once a windblown dune. The basalt and sandstone cliffs, which today are washed by the tides of Fundy, were formed during a critical juncture in Earth history called the Triassic-Jurassic boundary. On the basis of the fossil record, palaeontologists have determined that nearly half of the world's creatures never made it across this threshold in time. Olsen—the world's leading expert on the Triassic-Jurassic boundary—has found, preserved in the rocks that enclose the Minas Basin, the bones and footprints of the victims and survivors of this cataclysm. These fossils offer palaeontologists the best chance there is of discovering what caused the Triassic-Jurassic extinction and perhaps others like it that have punctuated the evo-

lution of the planet and dictated the rise and fall of many of its inhabitants—including ourselves.

The little crocodile discovered at Wasson's Bluff is just one member of what Olsen characterizes as "the day-after community"—those that made it into the Jurassic. The community included lumbering, long-necked prosauropod dinosaurs; small, fleet-footed, birdlike (ornithischian) dinosaurs; lizardlike reptiles; ancestral crocodiles and mammal-like reptiles. "This is the oldest assemblage known in the western hemisphere, just after the major extinction event," says Olsen. "The major Triassic extinction occurred probably no more than a million years before this assemblage was preserved. These are the survivors, right here. Even though we have hundreds of thousands of bones, we have seen no sign whatsoever of typical groups from the late Triassic. Nothing—they're gone."

He points across the brown, choppy waters toward the red bluff of Cape Blomidon. On the face of the headland, the clearly demarcated red beds of Triassic sandstone glow brightly in the clear October air; on top, rising perpendicularly from the sloping red cliff, is a cap of dark basalt that was, as near as geologists can tell, extruded from the Earth's core around the time of the Triassic-Jurassic boundary. "This is the only place where you can see it accurately dated, the change in the animal assemblage through that critical time when the dinosaurs began to rule the Earth," Olsen declares in his New Jersey accent. "You can actually see the opening of

Coal age shales pitch in shadowy lines toward the beach at St. Martins, New Brunswick, where they deposit their fossil litter, above. Parrsboro rock and fossil collector Eldon George, facing page, drives a wedge between the upright layers of siltstone along the Parrsboro shore. He has been credited with a number of important finds, including the world's smallest dinosaur footprints.

the age of dinosaurs right here, starting off with no dinosaurs, or very few dinosaurs, in the older beds, coming up to the full blossoming of the Mesozoic dinosaur assemblage that was going to dominate the Earth for the next 100 million years.

"On the other shore," Olsen adds, "they didn't rule the Earth yet, and here, they did. What's really exciting is that sometime in between, a little event happened. About 500 kilometres northwest of here, in Manicouagan, Quebec, there is a giant crater, caused by a meteorite at least as big as the one that some palaeontologists think hit during the Cretaceous-Tertiary boundary."

Periodic extinctions of large numbers of terrestrial and marine flora and fauna have occurred throughout geological history. These "great dyings," as they have been dubbed, may have happened as many as 13 times in the past 600 million years and have accounted for the disappearance from the Earth's record of 20 percent of all terrestrial families, 17 percent of all marine-animal families and 14 percent of all freshwater families. Although palaeontologists are divided according to their belief in a gradual or a sudden great dying, the evidence supporting a series of extraterrestrial impacts has been mounting steadily for two decades.

The belief in a sudden cause for the extinctions observable in the fossil record has its root in the Catastrophism of Georges Cuvier, the French scientist who first broached the idea of extinction in 1796. Cuvier's *Discourse on the Revolutions of the Surface of the Globe* proposed that sudden changes in the physical geography of the Earth led to the periodic obliteration of existing creatures. Cuvier did not, however, propose a cause for these "revolutions."

Catastrophe as an agent of biological change lost much of its appeal in light of the subsequent theories of Charles Lyell and Charles Darwin, who proposed a more gradual change in both the Earth and its biota. Lyell's doctrine of uniformitarianism, which influenced Darwin's thinking, essen-

tially held that given infinite time, all change could be explained by reference to observable phenomena—the things going on around you. Harvard palaeontologist Stephen Jay Gould and others have pointed out that the impact theory poses a serious challenge to this long-held Lyell-Darwinian view of slow change to the Earth and its inhabitants.

Of all the seemingly sudden and synchronous extinctions of terrestrial and marine creatures, the one at the Cretaceous-Tertiary boundary—65 million years ago—has attracted the most attention because it marked the demise of the dinosaurs. The proliferation of theories to explain this extinction has divided the palaeontological community. The gradualists hold that there was no event per se but that the extinction of the dinosaurs (and other fossil species) in fact occurred over vast periods of time, up to 10 million years. They have invoked a variety of slow mechanisms, including a global warming or cooling trend, competition from mammals, the evolution of inedible plants or the lowering of sea level.

The catastrophists have argued that a sudden extinction did occur and was caused by an astronomical calamity, such as the explosion of a supernova, the planet's collision with an asteroid or an earthly upheaval such as massive volcanism.

In 1980, a group of scientists from Berkeley, California, led by geologist Walter Alvarez, swayed the argument toward the catastrophist view when they discovered an iridium-rich layer of clay in limestone beds in Italy and Denmark, exactly at the stratum separating Cretaceous and Tertiary times. The beds contained 30 to 160 times the normal levels of the rare platinum-group element, which is found only in minute quantities in the Earth's crust. Iridium occurs at relatively enriched levels only in the Earth's underlying mantle or in extraterrestrial materials, such as asteroids, which were formed at the same time as our solar system. Alvarez proposed that an asteroid or cometary impact had caused the Cretaceous-Tertiary extinctions. Such an impact would have thrown up global dust clouds, blocking out sunlight and prevent-

ing photosynthesis for months, perhaps years. Wildfires, it is thought, might have added soot to the deadly cloud cover and prolonged the wintry darkness. As a result, the food chain collapsed, causing mass extinctions—so the theory goes. One of the problems with the Alvarez theory is that no one has ever found a crater impact dated to the Cretaceous-Tertiary boundary.

What so intrigues Olsen is that there *is* a known crater impact at Manicouagan, in northern Quebec, dated to 210 million years ago, roughly the time of the extinction event recorded in the rocks along the Fundy shoreline. The Manicouagan crater is now a 72-kilometre-wide ring lake and must have been created by an asteroid at least 10 kilometres wide with a weight of 400 million tonnes. It would have hurtled into the Earth with a force of 100 million megatonnes of TNT—that is, 10,000 times the force of the world's current nuclear arsenal. The fireball might have reached Virginia as billions of tonnes of debris mushroomed into the air. The shores of Fundy are a mere 500 kilometres from the centre of the asteroid impact, close enough, Olsen feels, for him to expect to find debris of the impact. He hopes to uncover in Fundy either an iridium layer or shocked quartz crystals, which would provide more direct evidence of Alvarez's extraterrestrial-impact theory.

The Triassic-Jurassic extinction was perhaps of even greater magnitude than that at the Cretaceous-Tertiary boundary. As the latter spelled doom for the dinosaurs, the former heralded their ascendancy. The preceding Triassic age was dominated by reptiles of all kinds—the so-called archosaurs, or ruling reptiles. In fact, the Triassic was a time characterized by many bizarre forms of reptilian life. One of these, *Hypsognathus*—fossilized skeletons of which Olsen found in the red Triassic beds at Paddy's Island, near Wolfville—was the size of a large turtle with a broad head surrounded by bristling horns. Its eyes were enormous and keyhole-shaped, and it had a well-developed third eye in the middle of its forehead; to complete its overall eccentricity, it was buck-toothed. *Kuehneosaurus* was a lizard that used its expanded rib cage like the "wings" of a flying squirrel to glide through the treetops of Norfolk pine and monkey puzzle. There was a variety of large plant-eating mammal-like reptiles (which Olsen delights in comparing to Volkswagen bugs) prowling the land, then clothed in yews, ginkgoes and palmlike cycads. Preying on this unlikely bestiary were the large carnivorous thecodonts, the direct ancestors of the dinosaurs. As well, the first true dinosaurs–more mobile than their crocodilian predecessors–had begun to appear on the scene by the late Triassic.

Then, suddenly, at the close of the Triassic, all large herbivorous and carnivorous forms other than dinosaurs disappeared. Gone were the large plant-eating protomammalian reptiles. Gone, too, were the thecodont reptiles. Their disappearance seems to have paved the way for the diminutive survivors whose bones are found at Wasson's Bluff: small mammal-like reptiles, the lizardlike sphenodontids of which the New Zealand tuatara is a living descendant, foot-long ancestral crocodiles and small, bird-hipped dinosaurs. The dinosaurs of the early Jurassic were characterized by many small forms, turkey- to ostrich-sized; fleet and efficient predators, they were the forerunners of the towering terrors of the late Cretaceous. They shared a world that in all other respects was like the modern world in embryo, for the fishes, frogs, salamanders, turtles and crocodilians were already present by then.

The world of dinosaurs has been a lifelong passion for Olsen, so much so that Stephen Jay Gould's description of a palaeontologist as "one of those oddballs who parlayed his childhood fascination with dinosaurs into a career" almost seems to have been coined with him in mind. Olsen's interest in dinosaurs began in his early teens, when he and a high-school friend excavated a large number of dinosaur foot-

prints from an abandoned quarry near their home in industrial New Jersey. Their efforts to preserve their discoveries from industrial developers led to the establishment of Riker Hill Dinosaur Park and, for Olsen, a career in palaeontology.

The New Jersey fossil-hunting ground of Olsen's childhood and the Bay of Fundy both belong to a geological structure known as the Newark Supergroup, which was deposited 200 million years ago and extends from Nova Scotia to South Carolina. The Supergroup consists of a series of sedimentary basins that formed as the continental plates of Africa and North America pulled apart to create the Atlantic Ocean. The plates ruptured along fault lines roughly parallel to the contemporary continental margin. Rift valleys, or graben, similar to East Africa's Great Rift Valley, formed as blocks of land subsided along fault lines. Eventually, these blocks sank

The Fundy sediments, from the Carboniferous to the Jurassic, have yielded a rich variety of fossil footprints, such as the four-toed amphibian prints, above. The Fundy basin has well-exposed sediments, thanks to the erosive action of the tides, which have literally opened a window in time, as demonstrated by the neat hole augered through Long Island, facing page.

several thousand feet and were infilled with sediments from surrounding highlands. Today, several major sedimentary basins are identifiable, of which the Fundy basin is the most northerly.

Of all the basins, the sediments of Fundy are the best exposed, thanks to the erosive action of the Bay's great tides. Their ebb and flow have literally opened a window in time. Olsen was first attracted to the area by the fact that exposures were better there than anywhere else in the Newark Supergroup but also by the example of his early mentor, the Princeton palaeontologist Donald Baird. One of the world's leading ichnologists (experts in fossil footprints), Baird had worked throughout the 1950s and 1960s along the south shore of the Minas Basin, where he had uncovered large numbers of footprints and some bones of Triassic creatures. Olsen, who was still in high school when he first visited the Bay of Fundy, decided to look on the north shore of the Minas Basin, an area Baird had left largely untouched.

The Newark Supergroup had long been known as a rich source of fossil footprints. The first recorded discovery had been made in 1802 in the Connecticut River Valley by a young boy named Pliny Moody. In keeping with the then unassailable biblical version of Earth history, the tracks were described as having been made by "Noah's raven." Subsequently, many other tracks were reported in the Triassic trough, which extends from Northfield, Massachusetts, to New Haven Bay.

Sir Charles Lyell had been impressed by the Connecticut Valley fossil tracks when he made his tour of North America in the 1840s and noted the similarity between them and fresh bird tracks he had seen when reconnoitring the shores of the Minas Basin. In his *Travels*, he wrote: "On the surface of the dried beds of red mud at Wolfville on the Bay of Fundy . . . I observed . . . the distinct footmarks of birds in regular sequence, faithfully representing in their general appearance the smaller class of Or-

nithichnites of high antiquity in the valley of the Connecticut before described."

The sunbaked footprints had been made by sandpipers, which Lyell had seen scurrying along the Fundy mud flats. He salvaged a slab of dried mud flat for the British Museum, hoping that skeptical naturalists might "compare the fossil products of the month of July 1842 with those referable to feathered bipeds which preceded the era of the Ichthyosaurus, Iguanodon and Pterodactyl." With this wry observation, he endeavoured to convince skeptical colleagues that ancient birdlike creatures, the ornithischian dinosaurs, could have left their footprints in muddy ground just as modern birds do and that these footprints could have been preserved by the natural process of baking by the sun. His analogy takes on particular historical resonance in light of the current theory held by many of the leading palaeontologists that birds are in fact the dinosaurs' direct descen-

dants, if not their contemporary survivors.

Lyell returned to Nova Scotia a decade later and, in the company of Sir William Dawson, who was later to become president of McGill University, discovered at Joggins the oldest terrestrial vertebrate bones then known to science, entombed in what Dawson called "strange repositories"—the inside of fossil tree trunks. In the past century and a half, since palaeontology was born, the Fundy sediments, ranging in age from the Carboniferous to the Jurassic, have yielded a rich variety of fossil footprints. In 1841, Sir William Logan found footprints made by a small amphibian in 300-million-year-old sandstone at Horton Bluff, which proved to be the first evidence of vertebrate creatures other than fishes in the coal age. In 1903, the National Museum erected scaffolding and made plaster casts of 108 amphibian footprints exposed on the rock layers that rise up like book pages at East Bay, near Parrsboro. In 1964, Dr.

David Mossman, now a professor of economic geology at Mount Allison University, in Sackville, uncovered 27 footprints spanning an 18-metre distance at Horton Bluff. Until recently, these tracks—at 30 centimetres long, uncommonly large for the time period—were, at 350 million years of age, also the oldest in the fossil record attributed to terrestrial vertebrates.

It was in this fossil-rich hunting ground that amateur palaeontologist Eldon George grew up. At the age of 8, Eldon fell from a barn rafter and fractured his right arm in several places, an accident that resulted in the atrophy of his biceps muscles and a drop wrist. Unable to play many boyhood games, George could wield a geologist's hammer, and he turned to collecting the rocks and minerals that abounded in the basaltic cliffs near Parrsboro. Eventually, he took up fossil hunting under the tutelage of the man who also inspired Olsen—Donald Baird. Baird credits George with a number

of important finds. Palaeontology is one of the few fields of science in which amateurs have always made important contributions. George has amassed an impressive array of fossilized amphibian and dinosaur footprints at his Parrsboro Rock and Mineral Shop, which was registered in 1948, making it the oldest such shop in Canada. Many are familiar Connecticut Valley types—the ichnotaxa of G rallator, a small dinosaur, and the crocodilians Batrachopus and Otozoum— the latter a 45-centimetre track perhaps made by a primitive crocodile that probably had a large dinosaurlike skull, walked on two legs and measured six metres in length. These ancient creatures roamed the margins of seasonal lakes that occupied the ancient rift valleys of the Eastern Seaboard, leaving behind their tracks in the sticky shoreline muds much as today the sandpipers leave their three-toed footprints on the tidal flats.

On April 10, 1984, a typically cold, windy Maritime spring day, George made what may prove to be his most lasting contribution to palaeontology. He was on his four-wheel all-terrain vehicle cruising the Minas Shore when he stopped in the lee of an intertidal outcropping to get out of the wind. As he stooped over the buggy to warm his hands, shallow imprints in the red sandstone caught his self-trained eye ("I can see through rocks," he claims). "My God, those look like tracks," he said to himself. He began quickly scraping away loose sand with his hand. Then, as the imprints took on a more suggestive shape, he went to work with a jackknife. Another three-toed track revealed itself. "All of a sudden, I wasn't cold anymore," he recalled, as he proudly showed me the historic slab in his Parrsboro shop.

The 41-by-36-centimetre block of pale sandstone is crisscrossed by five tiny trackways, as if the creature had been practising a dance step. The three-toed prints are so perfectly preserved that even the digits, footpads and claw marks are clearly visible. What is most remarkable is the footprints' size: they are no bigger than a penny and are now recognized as the world's smallest dinosaur footprints, probably made by a creature no bigger than a robin. It is not known what species made the footprint (*Coelophysis* and *Compsognathus* are candidates) or even whether the individuals were adults or juveniles. Even so, the find of such tiny fossil footprints scales down the traditional image of the dinosaur and, at the same time, adds fuel to the controversy over whether dinosaurs were cold- or warm-blooded.

One of the arguments for dinosaurs as cold-blooded creatures has always been their large size: the small surface-area-to-mass ratio of large dinosaurs would have allowed them to retain heat. A dinosaur as small as that discovered by George, however, would have had the same heat-maintenance problem as a small bird. This suggests that it was necessary for such a diminutive dinosaur to have a mammal-like, therefore warm-blooded, metabolic system.

It is rare to find footprints and bony remains (so-called hard fossils) together, since they are formed under different climatic conditions. In the Fundy basin 200 million years ago, the climate alternated between hot, dry spells and heavy rains. Seasonal lakes surrounded by vast, sticky, sunbaked mud flats (similar to those now exposed at low tide) were formed, thus creating conditions ideal for track preservation. Like George, Olsen has uncovered a variety of footprints. But in 15 field seasons, he had found very little bone, with the notable exception of a vertebra from a prosauropod dinosaur and two small skulls of lizardlike sphenodontids. He little suspected that not far from where George overturned the rock imprinted with the small dinosaur's dancing footsteps lay a rich fossil bone bed.

In 1983, Neil Shubin, then a graduate student in biology at Harvard, was working the traditional Triassic-Jurassic hunting ground in Arizona. For logistical reasons, Shubin wanted to identify a promising field site closer to Harvard. When he returned from

the field, he called the acknowledged Triassic-Jurassic boundary expert, Paul Olsen, and asked for some suggestions. Olsen referred him to the north shore of the Minas Basin and, in particular, to Wasson's Bluff where, the summer before, he had turned up the two sphenodontid skulls.

The following summer, Shubin took his advice but returned from Fundy thinking his first season had been a failure. Back in the laboratory, however, Harvard preparator Bill Amarol picked out of the red sandstone the complete jawbone of a trithelodont, an extremely rare mammal-like reptile. It was the first such specimen from North America. Buoyed by their unexpected good fortune, Shubin returned to Wasson's Bluff the

A red sandstone bluff, facing page, stands out against a background of volcanic basalt. The two formations demarcate a critical juncture in Earth history called the Triassic-Jurassic boundary, when nearly half of the world's creatures met their demise due to a mass-extinction event. Among the survivors was a tiny dinosaur, which left its penny-sized footprints, above — the smallest ever found.

next summer and was rewarded even more generously. This time, he climbed halfway up the cliff face to search in the basaltic rubble—actually the preserved face of a palaeocliff, down which, 200 million years before, boulders had rolled onto the surrounding sand dunes. In the fissures, Shubin found stones so splattered with bone, he remarked later, "It looked like Rocky Road ice cream."

The bluff yielded hundreds of thousands of fossils, from small, unrecognizable fragments to anatomically perfect skulls; 12 complete trithelodont skulls, for instance, were so well preserved that they add considerably to our understanding of the origin of mammals. There were also abundant remains of long-legged ancestral crocodiles (including a sabre-toothed variety), small dinosaurs and primitive fishes. Olsen and Shubin announced their discovery to the world from the National Geographic Society's press room in Washington, D.C., on January 29, 1986.

Olsen was as surprised as anyone at the richness of the find. "This sort of abundance and degree of preservation came as a total shock," he admits. "We looked over the same rocks for years without actually making the discovery."

For Olsen, it was the payoff of more than a decade of diligent fossil hunting. During the lean time, however, he had made a critical breakthrough in the dating of the Fundy rocks—no mean accomplishment, considering that the age of the Newark Supergroup, whether it was Triassic or early Jurassic, had been a matter of controversy for 150 years.

Palaeontologists have a variety of means, direct and indirect, to determine the relative ages of sediments. Universally, palaeontologists date rocks by biostratigraphy, a technique based on the repeated occurrences of specific groups of fossils. If similar faunal assemblages are found in two locations, palaeontologists assume that the rocks in both sites are of the same age. But the method presents problems when ap-

plied to rocks of supposed Jurassic age in the Newark Supergroup. These Jurassic sediments are continental, laid down at a time when the sedimentary basins were part of the supercontinent Pangaea. Unfortunately, the classic biostratigraphy for the Jurassic is based on marine sediments found in the Jura Mountains of Switzerland. So it is difficult to compare Newark terrestrial vertebrate fossils to the types of fossils for the Jurassic, which are mostly marine.

Some fossils are shared by the two locations, though, including pollen and spore types, some skeletal remains and vertebrate footprints. The abundance of spores of the conifer species *Corollina* suggested to Olsen a Jurassic age for the Newark sediments, as did the footprints, which

were dominated by dinosaurs. Geochemical analysis (called radiometry) of the North Mountain basalts gave an age of 200 million years, which is probably the best date for the Triassic-Jurassic boundary. All of these lines of evidence led Olsen to an inescapable conclusion: any sediments found above the basalts, or interfingered with them, had to be early Jurassic in age.

Learning that the rocks were Jurassic rather than Triassic, as had been believed for so long, was the critical information Olsen needed to interpret the trove of fossils at Wasson's Bluff. Their discovery filled a conspicuous gap in the fossil record, which had been referred to in the literature as the "case of the missing earliest Jurassic." The Fundy fossils represented the first definitive

earliest Jurassic fauna. For the understanding of terrestrial animals of that age, according to Shubin, the discovery of Wasson's Bluff was tantamount to finding a palaeontological Rosetta stone.

The Fundy basin had something besides trackways found in none of the other Newark Supergroup basins—bony remains for both the Triassic and Jurassic periods. This made it possible to examine for the first time whether there had been a great dying at the Triassic-Jurassic boundary.

A decade before, Olsen himself had been skeptical about a major extinction at the boundary, chalking the theory up to poor early Jurassic records. But well-dated fauna at Wasson's Bluff pointed strongly to a catastrophic event. Representatives of almost every Triassic group – from thecodonts to large mammal-like reptiles – were known from the Triassic side of the Bay. On the northern shore, in the Jurassic age, they were gone. Similarly, footprints of Triassic creatures also disappeared from the record in the Jurassic sediments.

But how close to the boundary did those extinctions occur? If they happened over millions of years, the gradualists, who believed that changes in sea level or climate brought about the gradual decline and extinction of less adaptable Triassic creatures, would have support.

Fortunately, there is a very sensitive record of climate change in the Newark Supergroup in the form of cyclical lake sediments. These so-called Van Houten cycles occur on a 21,000-year basis due to astronomical cycles that affect the amount of sunlight reaching the Earth. During each cycle, large, shallow lakes formed – some as large as Lake Tanganyika – then slowly dried up, leaving vast salt deposits that remain as the strong light-coloured bands clearly visible on the contemporary cliff faces at Blomidon and Moose Island. Olsen could simply count the number of light bands and quickly click through the geological ages at 21,000-year intervals. From a count of these bands on both sides of the boundary, he concluded that the extrusion of basalt occurred over a period of 400,000 years and that the creatures at Wasson's Bluff were living a mere 100,000 to 200,000 years after the extrusion – in geological time, "the day after." The cycles, by their uniformity on either side of the boundary, also told Olsen that climate did not change dramatically during that time. "You know you're dealing with faunal changes and not just ecological changes," he says.

The absence of major climatic change between the late Triassic and early Jurassic pointed to a sudden, catastrophic cause of the extinction, an argument strengthened by the fact that at least four ecological niches are represented at Wasson's Bluff. Olsen and Shubin have sampled each

of these palaeoenvironments: river channels wending their way to a lake; a shallow lake lapping up against the basalt cliff; dune sands; and the basalt fissures where so many little creatures met their demise.

In each of the palaeoenvironments sampled, there was no evidence of the survival of the Triassic creatures; neither were there examples of new groups of animals. "This pattern of only survivors after the boundary," Olsen has written, "is exactly the kind of transition that would be expected of a catastrophic extinction event such as that proposed for the Cretaceous-Tertiary boundary. One would not expect to find in the immediate aftermath . . . of a catastrophe the origination of new families. Rather, day-after communities should be composed of survivors."

According to Olsen, there are currently two plausible explanations for the extinction – the massive volcanism that would have accompanied the rifting process or a meteoritic impact. The existence of the impact crater at Manicouagan, dated roughly to the time of the boundary, makes the meteorite theory more plausible for the moment. It is the smoking gun, and the crater is certainly large enough to suggest an impact that would have precipitated a major assault on the biosphere.

Nova Scotia is close enough to Manicouagan for some evidence of the impact to be found there and the mystery solved once and for all. However, finding crystals of

Columnar basalt, formed by the cooling and shrinking of lava flows, throws up a vertical wall of buttresses and rock towers against the sea's battering at the tip of Brier Island. The volcanic basalt was extruded roughly 200 million years ago, when the Atlantic Ocean was forming. Massive volcanism may have accompanied the mass extinction that ushered in the age of dinosaurs.

shocked quartz – grains that bear parallel fracture planes from high-pressure shock waves – is more difficult than finding a needle in a haystack. The second line of attack, the analysis of Fundy sediments for an iridium anomaly, has not yielded results yet either. However, the search to tie together the extinctions recorded in the Fundy rocks and the impact crater at Manicouagan will continue, for it represents the best opportunity to test a theory that has excited the imagination of the public and of scientists for the past decade.

Olsen reserves judgement on the impact theory, noting that scientific hypotheses can often be related to "society's norms and common philosophy." For example, Cuvier's "global revolutions" were perhaps the product of a mind shaped by the events of the French Revolution. In the same way, the attractiveness of the impact theory might bear some relation to the current fear that we could be wiped out by a catastrophe of our own creation, such as a nuclear holocaust. Certainly, the theory of nuclear winter developed by Carl Sagan and others served as a useful model for what would happen after an asteroidal or cometary impact.

"The parallel and intertwined development of the impact theory and nuclear-winter scenarios is a striking demonstration of how comfortably the impact theory fits with popular concerns," says Olsen.

While he asserts that "the asteroid impact theory is symptomatic of society's current philosophical milieu," Olsen hopes that its correctness will be judged only by critical tests. So far, the most promising place for such tests to be carried out is on the shores of the Bay of Fundy. Each year, the tides – the most patient of palaeontologists – expose a new layer of sediments and, with them, new fossils. These exposures may contain the answers to some of our most perplexing questions about the rise and the fall of the dinosaurs and about the emergence of the next animal group to dominate Earth's history – the mammals.

Seasons of the Marsh

Yet will I stay my steps
and not go down to the marshland —
Muse and recall far off
rather remember than see —
Lest on too close sight
I miss the darling illusion,
Spy at their task even here
the hands of chance and change.

–Sir Charles G.D. Roberts
"The Tantramar Revisited"

From my vantage point atop the dyke, I look out over a drab maritime prairie of brown grasses. Tide pools, like dark eyes trained skyward, dot the level land, and at the farthest reaches of the marsh, the Cumberland Basin is a muddy, brown strip adhering to the horizon. At the foot of the dyke and scattered elsewhere across the salt marsh, where the tide has dropped them like so many glacial erratics, are chocolate-coloured cakes of ice, mud-laden and moulded by water and wind into the organic shapes of beached whales or giant jellyfish. I scan the middle ground for Canada geese, and there, a few hundred metres away, I can make out the black, elegant necks of a small flock busily cropping the rhizomes and emerging shoots of goose grass, their long necks and proud heads weaving back and forth like piano hammers beating out some inaudible sonata.

Hoping to get a closer look at the geese, I descend the face of the two-metre-high

A red-winged blackbird, above, proclaims its territory with the flair of a sergeant major. It is but one of 228 bird species known to frequent and nest in the Tantramar Marshes. Facing page: Fundy salt marshes, like the one at Marys Point, support a host of resident and migrant creatures and play a vital ecological role in the neighbouring marine system through the action of the tides.

dyke and follow an oily three-wheeler track (a disturbing reminder of the marsh's misuse) into the landscape. Their lonely honking, which speaks more eloquently than words of the changing seasons, echoes intermittently across the hushed marsh as I pick my way deliberately in their direction. However, I don't get very far before a sentinel goose spies my approaching figure and alerts the flock. Three dozen geese arise en masse and fly off in characteristic V formation, the slow, powerful beating of their wings carrying them to the other side of the Trans-Canada Highway that divides the Chignecto Isthmus, the narrow bridge of land by which Nova Scotia hangs tenuously onto New Brunswick.

Chignecto is a Micmac word meaning "great marsh district." Before the arrival of Europeans, there were 20,000 hectares of tidally nourished salt marsh at the head of the Cumberland Basin. Each spring and fall, untold thousands of waterfowl, plying the

Atlantic flyway between their northern breeding grounds and southern wintering grounds, stopped off on these rich sea meadows to feed for the last leg of their journey. There are no reliable estimates of waterfowl numbers for the settlement period, but the anecdotal accounts of "skies black with ducks and geese, and teeming marshes" suggest much greater populations than exist today—perhaps as many as 10 times the current population. A goodly number from those vast flocks must have stopped off in Chignecto, for the region's first settlers, the Acadians, called the marsh country *tintamarre*, meaning "din" or "racket" —the rough music made by the wings and cries of waterfowl. The name has stuck, for today the marshlands of the Chignecto area—comprising the Tantramar, the Missaguash, the LaPlanche and the Amherst marshes—are collectively referred to as the Tantramar Marshes. Several thousand waterfowl still cycle through the region, but the descriptive name no longer seems to apply with the same force.

Midway between tide and upland, I stand in the largest remaining salt marsh in the Bay of Fundy, the 600-hectare John Lusby Marsh near Amherst, Nova Scotia. As a measure of its importance, it was the first area to be acquired under the national land-acquisition programme of the Canadian Wildlife Service (CWS), initiated to protect important wetlands in Canada; and in the 1960s, it was a major staging area for Canada geese, with as many as 15,000 honkers stopping here to feed for a month before proceeding to their breeding grounds in

northern Quebec, Newfoundland and Labrador. The salt marsh was the first snow-free feeding ground the geese encountered as they funnelled up the Eastern Seaboard from wintering grounds in New Jersey and North Carolina. While the uplands were still blanketed in snow, high spring tides flooded the ribbons of marsh at the head of the Bay of Fundy, melting the snow cover and exposing the succulent roots of the goose grass.

Now, fewer than 1,500 geese stop off in Fundy each spring. Geese are opportunists, and the Bay's salt marshes no longer present as good an opportunity for a meal as the winter wheat and stubble fields of Prince Edward Island. So the geese fly over the Tantramar and the Northumberland Strait to greener pastures.

The sound of the departing geese fades, and I am left alone, seemingly the only living thing in the great empty space of land and sky that is the marsh awakening from winter. The scene before me not only defies the historic accounts of the Tantramar region but, in its deafening quiet, is a silent accusation of just how effectively humankind has altered the habitat, here as everywhere along the Eastern Seaboard, and in the process has wiped out wildlife that depended on the wetlands.

The story of the Tantramar region itself is primarily one of drastic alteration of the natural environment. Fully 90 percent of the original 357 square kilometres of salt-

Ice clogs the mouth of the tidal Tantramar River, above. Ice that becomes stranded on the marsh in winter will carry some 25 tonnes of marsh-grass detritus into the upper Bay annually, where it forms a nutrient pool. The 600-hectare John Lusby Marsh, facing page, is the largest remaining salt marsh in the Bay of Fundy and an important waterfowl staging area.

marsh shoreline in the upper Bay of Fundy was once dyked. The Lusby Marsh, for example, was dyked by the mid-1700s and for two centuries thereafter produced crops of English hay. Now it stands as a remnant— a reminder—of the once great salt marshes that rimmed much of the upper Bay and were nourished by its great tides. It is also a symbol of the seesaw struggle not only between land and sea but also between differing views of how the marshlands should be used.

Because of the natural fertility of the mineral soils, the marsh district has always been prized by farmers. But many others value the inherent productivity of salt-marsh wetlands as a wildlife resource, and for that reason, the CWS moved to save the Lusby Marsh in its natural state after the sea reclaimed it in the 1940s. In which state—opened or closed to the sea—the marshes are of greatest value is a matter of continuing controversy.

Either way, the marshes themselves are a gift of the sea. W.F. Ganong, scientist, writer, explorer and one of Fundy's most gifted native sons, explained the formation of the Fundy marshes at the head of the Bay in his landmark paper of descriptive ecology, "The Vegetation of the Bay of Fundy Salt and Diked Marshes: An Ecological Study," published in 1903. The marshes, wrote Ganong, "have been, and still are being, built in a subsiding basin out of inorganic mud brought in from the sea by the rush of tides, whose height is the determining factor in their height." In places, the store of rich marine muds extends 30 metres below the prairielike flatness of the Tantramar. The muds—so rich in minerals—have their source in the 300-million-year-old sandstones and shales that form the sides and bottoms of the Bay and are scoured by the inrushing tides. "Thus," concluded Ganong, "the sea bottom supplies the materials, the rush of the tidal currents the power to remove, carry and lift them, and the quiet of the waters at the turn of the tide the condition allowing them to be dropped. In

this way, the sea is building up the land."

The marsh-building process is made possible by the gradual subsiding of the Bay of Fundy basin in a slow, delayed response to the removal of the ice load of the Wisconsin glacier, which vacated the area 10,000 years ago. At first, the land rebounded in response to the removal of the ice burden, but then it began to subside. As the glacier melted, releasing waters into the sea, relative sea level rose and drowned coastlines and river valleys. Numerous fossil forests exhumed from the marsh muds around the Bay attest to this. Because the land is continuing to sink and the tidal amplitude to increase due to resonance, sea level is still on the rise—and the marshlands with it—at a rate of 30 centimetres per century.

For millennia, muddy waters from the Bay spilled over the banks of tidal rivers and spread out over the marshy plain, where their burden of silt was deposited millimetres at a time. The tender spikes of marsh grass helped in this process, acting like fingers, reaching up and gleaning the muddy bounty from the sea. By the time the first European settlers arrived on the scene, the marshes at the head of the Bay held 20,000 hectares of fertile soils. It was a pleasant prospect for the French colonizers: "[There are] many large and beautiful meadows extending farther than the eye can reach . . . the country was for the most part agreeable and . . . would be very fertile if it were cultivated." The Acadians soon set about doing just that.

It is no exaggeration to say that Acadia was a culture based on the technology of dyking and that the people's sense of identity and distinctness was derived largely from their dependence upon, and shared experience of, the Fundy marshlands. At the height of the Acadian settlement of the Bay, just prior to the Expulsion in 1755, as many as 10,000 Acadians were tucked into bayside settlements from Grand Pré in the Minas Basin to the riverbank of the tidal Petitcodiac in New Brunswick.

The first Acadians probably brought dyke-building technology from La Rochelle region of France, to which it had been brought by Dutch engineers. The Acadian dyke builders began their battle with the sea by embedding logs in the marsh mud.

Around this core, they compacted marsh mud, then faced it with uniform sod bricks, or *permangues*, selected for their tenacious root systems that knit the structure together organically and provided another line of defence against the battering tides. The result was a wedge-shaped wall, 5 metres at the base, 60 centimetres at the top and 2 metres high—just enough to exclude the highest spring tides.

They called their system of reclamation *les aboiteaux*, for the tide gate, known as an *aboiteau*, which was installed at the foot of

A giant hay bale balances precariously atop a dyke. Because of the natural fertility of the mineral soils, the marsh district has always been prized by farmers, and fully 90 percent of the original salt marsh was once dyked. Others, however, value the inherent productivity of salt-marsh wetlands as a wildlife resource.

the dyke. The *aboiteau* was a simple but ingenious device that prevented the sea from flooding the land and at the same time allowed fresh water to drain from the land to the sea. In its most elementary form, it consisted of a hollowed-out log sluice fitted with a hardwood flapper at one end. The flood tide forced the flapper shut, thereby preventing salt water from reaching the land, and when the tide ebbed away, pressure from standing fresh water forced the flapper open and allowed drainage in the other direction.

the marsh had been dyked. This was the heyday of the Tantramar. Horses were the prime mode of transportation, and hay was their fuel—and there was no better place to grow it than on the Tantramar, known as "the world's largest hayfield." There were then 400 salt-hay barns—vertical-planked warehouses—silhouetted against the horizon of the maritime prairie. The Tantramar supplied hay to local lumber camps and mines, and hay was bundled onto coastal schooners and shipped to markets in New England and Newfoundland.

Howard Trueman is a sixth-generation descendant of one of the Yorkshiremen who first settled the Tantramar near the Aulac River. His early-19th-century family home in Pont de Butte—appropriately called Prospect Farm—sits atop Aulac Ridge looking down upon the Aulac Marsh. From the farm, I count 12 hay barns today. Eva Trueman, a sprightly octogenarian like her husband, remembers counting 100 barns from the same yard in the 1940s. Once, the Truemans themselves had 15 barns; they now have 2.

Howard is just old enough to recall when the marsh country was enjoying boom times. For him, it meant summers on a hay rake, the beginning of a career in farming that continues to this day. "Dad got a foot-trip rake, and I got onto it when I was 9 years old [in 1908], and I wasn't let off it from July till fall," he recalls with satisfaction.

However, World War I ushered the combustion engine into everyday use and signalled the end of the horse-hay market. The Tantramar entered a period of slow, steady decline. Marshland that had sold for $200 an acre in 1918 could be had for as little as $5 an acre in the 1950s. With no ready market for its hay, the dyke land became uneconomical to farm. Furthermore, the land was crisscrossed with drainage ditches that made it impossible to cultivate by tractor. Gradually, the dykes fell into disrepair, and the sea began to claw back for its own what had taken men and women 300 years to secure from the tide.

Dyking was dirty and sometimes dangerous work, but the unmatched fertility of the marsh soils (some dyke land has produced a hay crop for more than 200 years without application of fertilizer) made the labours against the race of tides more rewarding than slashing and burning upland forests.

Tragically, many generations of Acadians never got to benefit from the fruits of their ancestors' labours. When the Acadians were expelled, the organic patrimony of the marshland fell to the victors. A human tide of immigrants poured into the vacated Fundy marshes and began repairing and gradually improving the Acadian dykes and lands. Yorkshiremen, who were well acquainted with the difficulties of poorly drained land, settled the Tantramar and prospered. On visiting the region in the 1820s, Thomas Haliburton observed that "vast stacks of hay covered the alluvial lands as far as the eye can reach, and the substantial farmhouses and numerous herds bespeak the wealth and independence of the Yeomanry."

By the turn of the century, 90 percent of

Dyke land has been called "a reserve of energy in the form of fertility." In 1949, the federal government passed the Maritime Marshlands Reclamation Act to spearhead an emergency programme aimed at rescuing the dyke land "out to sea." A major component of the programme involved the damming of the larger tidal rivers in the Fundy region—the Shepody, Annapolis, Tantramar and Petitcodiac, as well as the Avon River at Windsor (which had consequences for the marine system as well). Eventually, 33,000 hectares of valuable dyke land were protected. Despite the herculean effort and expense, the Tantramar heyday has not come back, and much reclaimed dyke land remains idle.

In the 1960s, wildlife managers sought to return the more marginal dyke lands to wetland habitat. The CWS created the 1,740-hectare Tintamarre Wildlife Area—a package of boglands, abandoned marshland and the Jolicure lakes—in the hope of increasing waterfowl production, which had been depleted by the intensive dyking and drainage of the previous two decades. Ducks Unlimited (DU) has been an active partner in developing the wetland habitat on the Tantramar, primarily by lending its technical expertise in building flood-control structures. Unlike *les aboiteaux*, the flood dams are designed to retain fresh water in an impoundment, thus creating better brooding habitat for waterfowl. In total, DU has developed 7,340 hectares of such freshwater habitat on former salt marsh in

the upper Bay of Fundy. The first such area, developed in cooperation with the Province of Nova Scotia, was the Missaguash Marsh Wildlife Area, some 2,550 hectares of bog and natural lakes that were once drained by the Missaguash Canal.

The canal stands as an impressive 19th-century engineering feat and a testament to just how highly farmers valued dyke land. Dug by horse and spoon dredge in 1897 by the Missaguash Marsh Company (headed by Howard Trueman's father), it measures 10.7 metres wide, 4.6 metres deep and 8 kilometres in length. The shareholders hoped that the canal would carry valuable marine silt to the land—a technique called "tiding"—and that the added fertility would bring the upper Missaguash into valuable hay production. However, the tides did not prove strong enough to carry sufficient quantities of silt several kilometres inland, and the ambitious project had to be abandoned. Today, the canal provides a convenient, vegetation-free highway for DU personnel, duck hunters and muskrat trappers on their forays into the heart of the wilderness marsh.

"Boy, it's a still day on the Missaguash," observes DU biologist John Wile, referring to the miasma of mosquitoes droning undisturbed around us as we launch the canoe. The harsh sound of the outboard puts up small flights of ducks: a petite blue-winged teal, a shoveller, some ringnecks and black ducks from the cattails surrounding the open channels of the marsh. Surprisingly, however, for the first week of June, there is not a brood in sight. Occasionally, we take a detour into the cattails, where we cut power to watch and listen to the life of the marsh: a chorus of frogs, the manic winnowing of a Wilson's snipe as it circles high overhead, the pumping of a stake driver or American bittern, the whistle of a wigeon—a whimsical, wheezy little sound. The latter, Wile tells me, was not heard on eastern marshes before the freshwater impoundments enticed this western species to try nesting here. Other western ducks have followed, including pintail, shoveller, gadwall, redhead and ruddy ducks.

But DU has had trouble maintaining these impoundments as good waterfowl habitat. Within a few years of flooding, the cattails become so thick, DU must open up the marsh with a "cookie-cutter," a type of floating dredge that chews its way through the vegetation mats. "We're dealing with the effects of the Bay of Fundy," says Wile. "We're dealing with succession. Part of the struggle stems from the richness of the underlying soils; they're almost too rich."

The cattail problem in freshwater impoundments can be traced to the way in which the marshes were originally formed. Heavier silt particles settled out first, and therefore, the marshes tended to slope away from the tide's edge. At the upper end of the Tantramar, where the elevation is lower relative to sea level, drainage is poorer and bog conditions have developed, with the deposition of organic peat on top of the marine silts. This organic layer leads to the formation of thick mats of cattail when such areas are impounded.

There is also a natural decline in the biological productivity of such areas over time. At first, flooding releases nutrients stored in the soil, leading to a proliferation of the invertebrates that are the main food supply for waterfowl. As the nutrient source is depleted, the invertebrate population decreases, and as a result, waterfowl use of the impoundment declines. A similar process takes place when a beaver builds a dam; in the wild, however, the beaver moves on when productivity declines, the dam falls into disrepair, and the area is drained, allowing for renewal of nutrients

Apair of black ducks, above, is silhouetted against a golden marsh dawn. The Canadian Wildlife Service and Ducks Unlimited have created thousands of hectares of freshwater impoundments in the Tantramar region, but black-duck populations continue to decline due to hunting and interbreeding with mallards. Wind-blown fireweed, facing page, spreads its colour across the maritime prairie.

in the soil. With the construction of permanent flood-control structures, such as those built by DU, waterfowl managers are battling nature to maintain waterfowl numbers.

All efforts have not been in vain, though. Aerial surveys indicate that brood numbers have doubled since 1960. Ironically, hunting, which has been virtually unrestricted in these wildlife areas, may be nullifying many of the potential gains. Radio-tagging studies indicate that as many as 50 percent of the year's brood are being harvested on opening day on managed marshes. The CWS and DU are just now beginning to grapple with the issues of long-term intensive management of cattails, water-regime control and hunting.

Al Smith of the CWS in Sackville says that in future, he would like to concentrate more effort closer to the coast, where the fertility of soils is higher and there is not the organic layer to contend with. He believes that the juxtaposition of wetland types, natural salt marsh, freshwater marsh and the mud flats—another source of invertebrate food—would result in much more sustained use by waterfowl. As well, by employing the old technique of tiding—allowing salt water to enter the impoundment on occasion—cattail growth could be controlled and soil fertility renewed. Such habitat is favoured by salt-tolerant species such as the black duck, whose population has been severely stressed by hunting pressure and competition from mallards. To me, such an approach underscores the wisdom of working with the Fundy tides rather than against them; fighting the tides inevitably sets into motion a sequence of unforeseen, and often intractable, ecological consequences.

Smith has lived in the marsh for many years and has adopted an accommodating attitude toward the competing demands made on the fertile wetlands. "Looking at the marsh from the point of view of a landscape ecologist more than just a wildlife person," he says, "I think I have an appreciation for the agricultural use of the land as well as the wildlife use. It seems to me that

we've got to look reasonably at the land base itself and what multiple use can be made of it. We need an integrative-land-use type of planning." For that reason, the brackish cells he envisions would be smaller than the freshwater impoundments of the past, in part to take into account the needs of agriculture.

"You can't just be focused on your own little specialty," he adds, "or look at the situation with blinders on. You've got to look at the wide sphere of activity. An overall ecological approach applies quite well to the Fundy wetlands because of the tremendous long-term alteration of habitat and the vying and competing land uses now."

Smith recognizes that for 300 years, the marsh has served multiple purposes—as farmland, wildlife habitat and hunting ground—and this fact of life on the Fundy marshes is not about to change. Although there have been gains for wildlife, especially in the past 20 years, in the long run, the scales have tipped heavily in favour of agriculture. Currently, only 15 percent of Fundy's original salt marsh remains open to the sea's influence.

I never really appreciated the magnitude of the area affected by dyking until I saw the marshes from the air. The sinuous lines of the dykes, snaking along beside tidal rivers and the coastline, are impressive earthworks—like calligraphic messages to the gods writ large—and they have drastically altered the coastal environment. In checking the flow of the tide and isolating the land from the sea, the dykes represent the biggest ecological assault on the Bay of Fundy in the historic period, and the gain for agriculture has meant a significant loss for the productivity of the coastal zone.

Where salt marsh and estuary are allowed to meet and intermingle, there is a mutually beneficial exchange of nutrients. The tide carries a supply of mineral salts to the marsh, and the marsh, functioning like a primary-production factory, uses these nutrients to fuel organic production that eventually returns to the sea in the form of

detritus. This, in turn, promotes the production of mollusks and crustaceans and enhances offshore fisheries.

The prime photosynthetic converters of inorganic materials into carbon-based food are the marsh grasses, in particular the *Spartina* species. These tough grasses, commonly called cord grasses after a Mediterranean variety used to weave heavy cord, have adapted to the rigorous environment of the marsh by evolving a system whereby they excrete excess salt through specialized glands, as seabirds do. In this way, they cope with the salty water that inundates their root systems on a regular basis and would otherwise be fatal.

Two species of *Spartina* dominate the marsh vegetation: S. *alterniflora* and S. *patens*. *Spartina alterniflora*, because of its greater salt tolerance, dominates the so-called low marsh, which is closest to the coast and is flooded almost daily. A less luxuriant species, S. *patens*, thrives on the landward side of the marsh, and in the upper Bay, it may be flooded only three or four times a month during the highest spring tides.

The *Spartina* species are highly efficient photosynthetic factories. Because of them, salt marsh can produce 10 tonnes of organic material per acre, compared with 7 tonnes per acre for the most productive wheatfields. And this productivity is accomplished without the aid of any fertilizer or cultivation except that provided by the tides themselves.

Even though a Fundy marsh, where the growth of *Spartina* is limited to five months, is less productive than a Georgia marsh, for example, it still produces a surfeit of food for animal consumption. A small portion is consumed as a standing crop—on the stalk, as it were—largely by insects. At least 400 insect species have been found living in marshes along the Boreal coast. Many are herbivorous and feed on the cord grass; others are predatory. A visit to the marsh in high summer convinces one of the profligate abundance of insects of the pesky kind—mosquitoes and various biting flies.

Mercifully, damselflies prey upon biting insects, reducing their numbers and weaving their blue magic through the green stalks.

In summer, people venture onto the Fundy salt marshes in search of a seasonal delicacy: samphire, an extremely salt-tolerant little plant that adds tang to salads. As one strolls through the marsh meadows in search of this green, one is likely to be shushed by the wheezy song of the sharp-tailed sparrow or surprised by black ducks or blue- or green-winged teal, which use the salt marshes as feeding areas, dining on the *Spartina* grasses and other marsh plants. Greater yellow legs, dandy-looking shorebirds, join the heron patrol for minnows in tide pools as they make their way south in

T he sinuous lines of the dyke snake along beside a tidal river, facing page, like a calligraphic message to the gods writ large. By checking the flow of the tide and isolating the land from the sea, dykes have made possible a significant gain for agriculture. In its heyday, the Tantramar was known as "the world's largest hayfield," but every year, there are fewer of the old salt-hay barns left standing, above.

a leisurely fashion. Perhaps my most vivid childhood memory of the marshes, as I grew up along the Chebogue River at Fundy's southern extreme, was of the frantic din the willet made as they whirled in noisy flocks above their marshland breeding ground. In fall, marsh-grass plants and seeds provide fuel for the southern migration of ducks and geese as they return along the Atlantic flyway.

By September, the marsh grass has ceased to grow and the marsh turns to a subtle carpet of autumnal hues, from maroon to tow. Before the growing season begins again, spring tides will crop and transport some of the dying grass to the estuary. And ice that becomes stranded on the marsh in winter will carry a cargo of grass with it when it is refloated and goes to sea again in March. Through the mediation of the tides, the marsh sheds some 25 tonnes of detritus into the upper Bay annually.

As one flies over the Cumberland Basin, the nutrient pool of detritus is a highly visible reddish clot of flotsam. It was not known until recently how this hard-to-digest cellulose was being assimilated into the marine environment. In the course of their tidal-power investigations, researchers in the Marine Ecology Laboratory (MEL) at the Bedford Institute of Oceanography in Dart-

mouth may have hit upon an answer when they discovered the enzyme cellulase in the guts of shrimplike mysids. "The hypothesis is that older detritus, a month to a year old, could be grazed and used by the mysids, which, of course, are supporting the shad," says former MEL director Don Gordon. Shad, which throng the inner reaches of the Bay in summer, are not only eating mysids, but in many cases, as the work of Michael Dadswell demonstrated, they are ingesting the detritus directly, a behaviour observed with other plankton-eating fish. Marsh detritus is also a foodstuff for the mud shrimp, which, of course, are the prime prey of the shorebirds. So a larger, more integrated picture of the marsh's role in the Fundy ecosystem has begun to emerge.

It now appears that salt marshes not only support a host of resident and migrant creatures but also play a vital ecological role in the neighbouring marine system through the action of the tides. This marine system, in turn, fuels two massive migrations of fish and shorebirds. So the marsh appears to be the critical link between the three earthly domains—air, land and water—where they converge in the upper reaches of Fundy.

Gordon's group at MEL analyzed the sources of primary productivity and found that the marsh contributes fully 50 percent of the usable carbon to the Cumberland Basin, even though the marshes make up only 15 percent of the present area of the upper Bay. Keeping in mind that barely 15 percent of the original marsh is now open to the sea,

one has to ask how much productivity has been lost to the marine system through dyking. Perhaps before the Acadians' dykes interrupted the nutrient cycling between land and sea, even greater schools of shad thronged the muddy waters of the Cumberland Basin and larger roosts of shorebirds gathered along its shores—just as the sound of waterfowl on their spring and fall stopovers created a memorable hubbub.

Taking into account the historic alterations of the environment due to dyking, one has to consider further what effect a tidal-power dam would have on the marshes and their export of organic energy to the marine ecosystem. Like the dykes, a tidal dam would isolate a portion of the marsh from the effects of the sea, and vice versa. A dam across the entrance to the Cumberland Basin would dampen tidal ranges in the headpond – high water would be lower and low water higher. Therefore, the tide would not reach areas of the marsh that are now regularly inundated. These low marsh areas are the very ones that export the most organic material to the marine system. A tidal dam would remove energy from the Bay's total budget by impairing the mutually beneficial tidal link between sea and marsh.

Today, beef cattle – terrestrial herbivores – are the prime beneficiaries of much of the productivity of the marsh, as they ruminate on the marsh hay and pasture protected by dyking; but the dyke land supports wildlife of its own as well. The Tantramar Marsh has the second highest nesting density of northern harriers in North America. I have often stopped along the High Marsh Road, which bisects the reclaimed land of the Tantramar, to watch this skilful hunter stalking meadow voles. It is not uncommon to see the flame of a red fox, which also finds the marsh territory a good hunting ground. Likewise, although the freshwater impoundments have yet to prove themselves efficient "duck factories," muskrat are thriving there, and the new marsh habitat has attracted a wide variety of hitherto exotic marsh birds to the Tantramar region.

The Amherst Point Bird Sanctuary is part of the Chignecto National Wildlife Area, which includes the John Lusby Salt Marsh. The area was acquired by the Canadian Wildlife Service in 1968, and freshwater impoundments were developed there by Ducks Unlimited in the early 1970s. It is unquestionably the most productive wetland in Nova Scotia. The diversity of habitat – wooded upland, wetland, gypsum sinkholes and abandoned farm fields – attracts a wide variety of bird species. In all, there have been 228 species sightings in the sanctuary, which ranks it second only to Brier Island, a migratory staging area at the outer end of the Bay.

No one is more familiar with the avifauna

of "The Glen," as local birders affectionately call the sanctuary, than Con Desplanque, a Dutch-born hydrologist who has been an avid birder since his youth. He has also been a man of the marshes all his life. In his native country, he studied land reclamation, then as a member of the Dutch underground, he worked to repair the dykes broken by the retreating Germans. After the war, having, as he says, "avoided Hitler's claws," he immigrated to Canada in 1950 and designed *aboiteaux* for the reclamation of Tantramar dyke lands. He has been coming to the Amherst Point Bird Sanctuary for 40 years and, in that time, has identified more than 200 species of bird. Now retired, Desplanque still walks The Glen ev-

Beef cattle, facing page, roam much of the marsh today and are the prime beneficiaries of the natural fertility of marsh soils. The pattern of plenty: Drainage ditches crisscross the hayfields, above, that at the turn of the century supplied New England with "fuel" for horses. The Tantramar still produces bumper crops of hay where it is properly dyked and drained.

ery decent day, from spring through fall.

It was June when I followed him along a fern-bordered trail that wound through a landscape moulded into whimsical hillocks by the erosion of the underlying gypsum – "a landscape for gnomes," Desplanque called it. We spied a lone green-winged teal at the edge of a large sinkhole and later stopped to admire a handsome clutch of ring-necked ducks cruising near the cattail margin of an impoundment.

In past years, Desplanque said, he has spotted a variety of exotic species, including snowy egret, glossy ibis and green heron, unexpected visitors to northern marshes. At least 100 species are also known to breed in the sanctuary, including ones that are very rare elsewhere in the Maritimes. The black tern has nested there, as have the least bittern and common moorhen. More common marsh birds abound. The highest nesting density in North America of pied-bill grebes, nearly two nests per hectare, has been documented. American coots once nested here in large numbers. In recent years, however, Desplanque has witnessed a steady decline in the numbers and variety of marsh birds using the sanctuary – a pattern repeated at Missaguash and Tintamarre.

At a dyke that separated two impoundments, we paused to watch a young osprey poke its head above its nest balanced on a power-line tower, and we listened to the sweet whistling of a sora, which had a clear quality, like the ringing of a glockenspiel in the soft summer air. Desplanque unshouldered his scope, searched the open water and gestured for me to have a look. A solitary wigeon came into focus. "It's rather dead," he said sadly. "In the early days, if I put my scope up at random, I could see a bird."

It struck me then that the original Acadian settlers might express the same sentiment if they could return to Tantramar today. They, too, might wonder aloud: Why is the air so still? Where have all the birds gone? What happened to *tintamarre*?

The French Shore

"Such features are typical of Acadian villages on the seaboard: a string of similar houses along the highway, near the sea, and a church tower standing not far away."

– Alexander H. Leighton *et al.*
"People of Cove and Woodlot"

The houses, many of them the century-old white clapboard type common to all of Nova Scotia, hug the curve of the coast with tenacity, standing shoulder to shoulder so that if not for the road signs, I would not realize I had left one community and entered another. Concession roads branch into the forested interior; other roads lead to wharves decorated with fleets of candy-coloured boats and to the blue waters of St. Marys Bay. Mavilette, Meteghan, Saulnierville, Petit Ruisseau, Pointe de l'Église, Grosses Coques, Belliveau Cove, St. Bernard: the unbroken necklace of houses blurs the boundaries and ties the communities together into the semblance of a whole. The sense that this cluster of communities is, in fact, one community is no illusion, for it is the District of Clare, an Acadian stronghold in Anglophone Nova Scotia. The residents themselves call it *la ville française* – one village, one culture.

The southern shore of St. Marys Bay is a

Fancy finials and geometric lattice of an Acadian home, above, reflect pride of place along the French Shore. The District of Clare on St. Marys Bay is now home to 7,000 Acadians, who settled here in the aftermath of the 1755 Expulsion. In the fruitful Annapolis Valley, St. Charles Memorial Chapel, facing page, at Grand Pré National Historic Park bears testament to that tragic event.

cultural remnant of Acadia, the nation-to-be that two centuries ago girdled the whole of the Bay of Fundy, which was then called La Baie Française. The 60-kilometre stretch of road along Fundy's remaining French Shore has been called "the longest main street in Canada." To me, it is the best-known road in the country. I have been driving along this stretch of coastline since I was a boy growing up in Yarmouth, the "English" seaport and service town at the southwestern tip of Nova Scotia, and the corridor of friendly houses and the skyline, here and there pricked by a church steeple, still has the power to make me feel at home, with all the comfort and security that the phrase implies.

I remember my first trip into Clare, for instance, at the age of 5. My feelings then were quite different, being those of a neophyte adventurer expanding the boundaries of his known world for the first time. Every mile of the way – and progress was

as slow then as it is now because of the residential nature of the communities—I took in new sights: I had never seen St. Marys Bay or the distant, rust-coloured cliffs of Digby Neck, which Samuel de Champlain mistakenly thought were sources of iron when he sailed into these waters on his first voyage to the New World in 1604. Still, the landscape of water, marsh and low-lying forest and the wooden-frame architecture were not so different from what I was already familiar with in Yarmouth, until we reached St. Bernard, the last in the string of French-speaking communities. There, reaching to the heavens in all its forbidding Gothic splendour, replete with parapets and buttresses, was the grey granite edifice of St. Bernard Church, a full-

scale replica of a French cathedral, set down in this bucolic, humble landscape as if by divine intervention. To my impressionable mind, it seemed unimaginably huge. And today, it still impresses me with its sheer bulk and, I suppose, because it is so out of place, so disproportionate to everything around it.

When I first saw it, its impact was not merely visual. It struck me with the full force of revelation: here was a community next door that was somehow different. How could it have produced such a monument? Yarmouth was an English-speaking bastion, a linguistic garrison surrounded by Francophone Acadian communities. This demographic fact became abundantly clear to me when I started school, where play-

ground buddies had names like Surette, LeBlanc, Doucet, Saulnier, d'Entremont. Sadly for me—even more so for them—at school, we never spoke the language my friends spoke at home. Linguistically, we lived in two worlds, separated by history and politics 300 years older than ourselves.

Today, one often hears French spoken on the streets of Yarmouth and in shopping malls. It is a kind of street French, or patois, that has evolved here, with a generous sprinkling of English words, enough for me sometimes to catch the drift of a conversation. But to me, it is the energetic flow of sound that lifts my spirits, regardless of sense, and tells me I am home again.

In a way that cannot be denied, however, the two cultures—the English of the town and the French of the bay—have remained separate except where commerce has brought them together. Even though the fraternal French houses on St. Marys Bay have always made me feel that I was on familiar and safe territory, I had to admit to myself that I had rarely stopped long enough to get to know my neighbours—*les Acadiens*—better. So, 33 years after my first eye-opening glimpse of their world, I set out along the French Shore to talk with the people who make their home by the bay, in the only language I know.

Now there are more than 7,000 Acadians living on the shores of St. Marys Bay, the narrow arm of the outer Bay of Fundy sheltered by Digby Neck, a projection of the Annapolis Valley's North Mountain. It was not the place of choice for its first French-speaking explorers. In his cursory fashion, Champlain declared "the land low and good" but decided that it was not suitable for settlement, "having found in St. Marys Bay no place where we might fortify ourselves." After a disastrous wintering experiment at St. Croix Island on the New Brunswick shore, he sailed farther up the coast into the Annapolis Basin. "This place was the most suitable and pleasant for a settlement that we had seen," he recorded. Consequently, in 1605, he founded the Habitation at Port Royal, the first permanent settlement in North America north of Florida. Champlain remarked on the "many meadows flooded at high tide." It was these salt marshes, reclaimed from the sea, that were to become the basis for the expansion of the French community at the head of the Bay. The Golden Age of Acadia, as it is sometimes called, ended abruptly in 1755 with the Expulsion.

When the Acadians were allowed to return from exile, they found their old farms occupied by English settlers in what was once "the Acadian land, on the shores of the Basin of Minas . . . in the fruitful valley," as the Annapolis Valley was described by the American poet Henry Wadsworth Longfellow in "Evangeline." In 1788, Governor Michael Franklin designated the District of Clare a future home for the Acadians in Nova Scotia. (Ironically, the district was named for its Irish surveyor.) In a sense, Clare constituted a second exile, this time from the fertile banks of the Minas Basin to the rocky shores of St. Marys Bay. The story is still told of the sense of desolation the Acadians felt when they first made landfall near Church Point. The men, exhausted from rowing, saw the barren shore and the uncleared forest, and they broke down and wept. However, there was a young woman among them, Madeleine LeBlanc, who, like many others, had walked from Boston to her old home in Grand Pré before being forced to continue to Church Point. While the men despaired of the job ahead, Madeleine picked up an axe and felled a tree, a symbolic first act in the rebuilding of the Acadian homeland. A real-life heroine was born (much less passive than Evangeline) and a community given birth. "Listen, fellows," her act seemed to say, "this is no time to cry. Let us get busy. We need shelter for the night, and tomorrow will be another day." This is what Madeleine LeBlanc might have said, according to Edith Comeau Tufts, a direct descendant of the heroine of Clare. Historically accurate or not, the story serves as an expression of the indomitable courage of the Acadians in general and of the women in particular.

At 71, Edith Tufts is herself the embodiment of vitality, a sprightly woman with the

L*a ville française* stretches out along a 60-kilometre piece of shore road that has been called "the longest main street in Canada." The southern shore of St. Marys Bay is a cultural remnant of Acadia, the nation-to-be that two centuries ago girdled the whole of the Bay of Fundy, then called La Grande Baie Françoise.

energy of someone half her age, and a member of the Order of Canada and Le Conseil de la Vie Française en Amérique, honours bestowed upon her for her work in promoting the role of Acadian women in society. She noticed in helping her children with their lessons that the official histories of L'Acadie almost entirely ignored the contribution made by women. So in 1975, International Women's Year, she set the record straight with her book *Acadiennes de Clare*.

In addition to working as secretary to the president of the Université Sainte-Anne, in Church Point, Tufts found time to raise 15 children. When I showed surprise at the size of her family (surprise that it has not slowed her down), she replied with a mischievous, conspiratorial smile: "That was typically Acadian, wasn't it? At least, it was typical in the olden days; it's not the fashion anymore. But I think large families spelled survival for the Acadian community."

Acadians did find strength in numbers. But women contributed in far subtler ways to community life as caretakers not only of the home but of Acadian culture as well. "Men were the hard workers who went to sea and out to the woods," says Tufts, "but women stayed with the children and were the ones who kept the flame alive—their faith, their language and their traditions, because many of the Acadian traditions are in their cooking and in the costumes they wear on special occasions."

In a practical sense, survival for Acadian men and women, deprived of their once fertile lands, meant learning how to harvest the sea. "Today, no matter where you see an Acadian community—no matter what province it's in—you always see a lighthouse, a little wharf and a little fishing fleet," Tufts says. "Acadian men came to be known as fishermen rather than farmers."

Fortunately, St. Marys Bay, as part of the biologically rich outer Bay of Fundy, yielded a variety of fish species—cod, pollack, haddock, hake, mackerel and herring—as well as lobsters and scallops. Sailing vessels could make day trips, departing

and returning on the high tides—and those who stayed ashore could dig for clams and quahaugs (the large bar clams, or *grosses coques*) between tides. Today, the fishery is still the engine of a very buoyant local economy. Historically, however, the sea was only one component of a subsistence economy that also depended on the thin soil and woodlot. "During the first century," writes local historian J. Alphonse Deveau in *Along the Shores of St. Marys Bay*, "the sea, the forest and the land were exploited by each family as a family enterprise for the needs of the family . . . . If we judge by the size of the families in those days and by the rapid rise of the population along the bay, this subsistence economy was highly adequate to maintain a good life in relation

to the standard of living of the period."

Ultimately, survival for these people meant more than successful management of the elements of pioneer life. Cultural survival was also vital, and in this regard, geography was less generous. The Acadian community of Clare was an island in an Anglophone sea. The cultural centre of this island was the Université Sainte-Anne, founded in 1890 by the Eudist Fathers of France as an academy for boys from the French districts of Nova Scotia.

At the time, the few Acadians who were able to pursue higher education had to do so at Anglophone universities. Now, 345 students (one-quarter from Clare) attend the university full-time, and 400 more take six-week French immersion courses annu-

ally. Although the university was not open to women until the early 1960s, they now make up two-thirds of the student body.

Architecturally, the university is a mixture of old and new, sacred and secular. The original cream and chocolate-brown seminary is flanked by the new brick Centre Acadien and by St. Mary's Church, the tallest wood-frame church in North America. Its grey steeple rises 55.5 metres and is ballasted by 40 tonnes of rock to dampen its motion as the church sways back and forth in the strong winds off the Bay.

On a December day, with a biting wind blustering off the water, I received a warm greeting from Neil Boucher, director of the Centre Acadien, which houses the largest Acadian archives in Nova Scotia, including newspapers, books, land grants, private documents and more than 300 hours of taped interviews with elderly Acadians. The archives are used primarily for academic research, but they also play an important role in the genealogical research of local residents. "It reflects people's desire to know their roots," Boucher explained.

Joseph Dugas was the first to bring his family to Clare in 1768 — and the names of the families who followed still fill the local telephone directory: Belliveau, LeBlanc, Doucet, Maillet, Gaudet, Comeau, Deveau, Amirault. The community grew in isolation, and today, it is both smaller and less powerful than its counterpart on the north shore of New Brunswick, where sheer numbers — 250,000 Francophones, or one-third of the province's population — translate into New Brunswick's current status as Canada's only officially bilingual province.

It is ironic that Nova Scotia is Canada's oldest French province, yet its 30,000 Francophones enjoy less than full linguistic rights. However, Boucher assured me that the historical neglect of the Nova Scotia Acadian community by outside political forces was now changing. The economic upsurge of the French Shore in the past two decades — largely built on fishing enterprises — had suddenly made the government aware of its Francophone citizens. In effect, Boucher was saying that money talks, regardless of the language.

"The government of Nova Scotia has come to recognize the Acadian fact as an established fact," said Boucher. "I know that we don't have the same rights Acadians in New Brunswick do — maybe numbers account for that. But governments are lending an ear to the Acadians in the area, evidenced by certain concrete manifestations over the past few years."

On my drive along the shore, I had noted new bilingual road signs, which now call attention to the French fact — Meteghan River/La Butte and Little Brook/Petit Ruisseau — if, locally speaking, in reverse order of priority. Other signs are less con-

crete but no less meaningful. For example, the premier now defers to mumble a few French words at local political rallies. "He's not bilingual, but, by God, he tries," allowed Boucher. The most important development for the community, however, has been the passage of Bill 65 in 1981, which officially recognized French as a medium of instruction in the province. For the first time, Acadian children could receive instruction in their own language. It was a vital step toward instilling a proper sense of pride among Acadian youth in their roots, according to Boucher. "There's nothing bad, or there's nothing wrong, or there's nothing to be ashamed of, in one's culture."

As a parent, nothing could please him more. "My daughter is presently going to have the first six years of her education in French, and that's normal, it's normal," Boucher insisted. "First of all, she carries the name Boucher; second of all, she's living in an Acadian area; thirdly, she's going to a school that's called Joseph Dugas; fourthly, all her teachers are Acadians and 95 percent of the student population is Acadian — so it's only normal that she take her education in French.

"I'm the one who went through the abnormal situation 20 years ago," Boucher told me, with a passion that was no longer impersonal and studied, "because I was a Boucher going to Sainte Anne de Ruisseau with professors whose names were Surette and d'Entremont and I took everything in

F og descends upon a scallop dragger, facing page, docked in Yarmouth, an "English" seaport surrounded by Acadian communities. Tidal turbulence at the mouth of the Bay creates fog but also fuels biological productivity; abundant fish have supported French and English alike for two centuries. A French Shore resident, above, is smoking mackerel, an art passed on from his ancestors.

English. I'm the one who experienced the irony of it all. When we were in recreation, we would speak French amongst ourselves and to our teachers, but as soon as that buzzer rang, it was just like a linguistic light switch that you turn on and off. When that buzzer rang and you went back to class, the whole thing switched to English."

This fundamental change came very slowly — the light was not turned on overnight. One of the fathers of this enlightenment was Father Leger Comeau, a member of the same Eudist Order that founded the college in the late 19th century. A handsome, silver-haired gentleman wearing a pale blue turtleneck under a dark suit — which gives him at once a clerical and a casual air — Father Comeau proudly displays on his office desk the medal of a chevalier de la Légion d'honneur, received in person from President Mitterand just two weeks before. This rare accolade was accorded him for knitting closer ties among Acadians in Canada and for the rapprochement with friends of Acadians in France.

The need for such ties takes on new meaning for me when Father Comeau points out that the dispersion of the Acadians — the Expulsion — is very much a contemporary fact of life, not just history. The Expulsion was a devastating demonstra-

tion of the divide-and-conquer principle, for although the people returned, they were never again one community as they had been when the Bay of Fundy was their common homeland. Acadia, the nation in embryo, was permanently lost. "The dispersion is something we're still living today—we're still dispersed," Comeau reiterates.

This condition of contemporary Acadian life, more than any other, has motivated Father Comeau's work, which has been to forge connections between the scattered Acadian people. "We live in isolation here. Not only here but all Acadian communities in Nova Scotia live in great isolation from one another. Our big problem is precisely that we are surrounded by English communities. So it's very important for us to be in touch with other Acadian or French communities, to be in touch with the stronger Acadian community of New Brunswick, with Quebec, with France, with all sources of French culture and civilization."

Father Comeau believes, fervently, that Acadians are enriched by their contacts with other "fountains of French life," as he calls them, and ultimately become better Acadians for it. His own journey of self-discovery supports that belief. He reflects how strange it was that he took so long to discover his Acadian identity. Growing up in Clare in the 1920s and 1930s, he was taught in English and admits that he didn't know what an Acadian was when he entered Université Sainte-Anne (where French was his worst academic subject). It was only after spending time in Quebec and later in the Acadian community in northern New Brunswick that he came to realize he was "different: I was Acadian, and we had to work to help our own."

After what he describes as a roundabout journey—to Quebec, New Brunswick, Rome and Halifax—he returned home to Clare 15 years ago and now serves as vice president of external affairs at the university, which, he believes, is offering an essential service to Acadian culture. "Education is the most important thing today, because education is done in great part by television. And television is mainly English, which means that our young people are inclined to speak English much more than French—and if you don't have strong French schools, I think, there's very little hope for the future."

The watering down of French culture can be disturbingly conspicuous. After talking to Father Comeau, I dropped into the Tide's Inn, which once had the trendy but respectable French name La Cave. I ordered rappie pie, the Anglicized term for the Acadian dish made from grated potato and chicken. (The French name, *pâté à la râpure*, is derived from the verb *râper*, "to grate.") As I tasted the local French cuisine, I was serenaded by taped Nashville Christmas carols.

The jarring ambience underscored the argument that promotion of the French language and contact with French culture—as Father Comeau discovered himself—are the only means by which Acadians can maintain their identity. However, the District of Clare has unique cultural qualities that set it apart from other Francophone communities. For example, the language of the Acadians of Clare has a distinct flavour, which is the product of geography as much as anything else.

The expert on local Acadian dialect is a self-styled linguist and raconteur, Felix Thibodeau. Monsieur Thibodeau, a gnomish, ebullient octogenarian with a shock of white hair and a walrus moustache, took time to talk to me between his twice-daily routine of checking his rabbit-snare line near his home in Church Point.

On retirement, Thibodeau, a former industrial arts teacher, educated in classics, began writing down local anecdotes that he remembered being told by his mother and father. These often humorous tales turn on human foibles and local events, which, he admits, he "decorates a little bit." He graciously agreed to tell me one of these tales in English.

"In olden days, they used to collect seaweeds from the beach for fertilizer, and

Lobster boats shelter in the lee of Cape St. Marys, above. "Today, no matter where you see an Acadian village, you always see a lighthouse, a little wharf and a little fishing fleet," according to Edith Tufts. "Acadian men came to be known as fishermen rather than farmers." But a snow-dappled pair of oxen, facing page, suggests that some Acadians remain farmers at heart.

they would bring it all the way from the coast to the corner of the field where they were going to use it in the spring. This feller, Simon, he had a field not too far from a house where they had hens. Well, he went to see his pile of fertilizer, and he found the birds had gone into his pile and they [had] raised hell. On the way back home, he stopped into the neighbours', and he gave them hell because the hens had gone over to his pile of seaweeds. And then the neighbour says, 'I give you permission to put out snares, and all the hens that you get, I will give them to you.' So Simon came over with a few traps, put them over the pile, and the next day, he went over there again—it's true, that's fact—and he had two crows."

Both of us broke into laughter before Thibodeau, who like all good storytellers knows the importance of timing, delivered the moral.

"And when Simon came back, he didn't even look at the neighbours' house."

At first, he wrote these stories "in good French." But, he said, "they didn't sound the same at all, at all. So I wrote them as they were said, and they sounded good."

Thibodeau says that the French spoken by the Clare Acadians is a *parlez*, a deformation of the French spoken 300 years ago in the Poitou region of northwest France. Clare's isolation has preserved many quaint elements of this 17th-century French. For example, Clare Acadians substitute an "on" sound for the "ai" sound that Parisians or Québecois would use. Thus they pronounce "*pain*," the French word for bread, so that it rhymes with the English word "son." Thibodeau has compiled a dictionary of 3,000 words and expressions which, he says, "are different from the real French." Sometimes the differences are so great that contemporary French people cannot understand the Clare Acadians, who perhaps widen the communication gap by their habit of speaking rapidly.

As well, many English words have crept into the local French dialect due to the influence of radio and television and the im-

pingement of the surrounding English communities. It is not uncommon to hear French and English combined in one word, such as "*breakez*." "The language," laments Thibodeau, "is not like my father and mother were speaking it."

When I ask him whether the loss of language necessarily means the loss of culture, he replies: "Culture?" His voice rises with rhetorical fervour: "That's a word I don't understand. They say we're going to lose our culture. I think that culture is the way people live at the present—that's my definition of culture. In other words, the culture is lost if we don't live now the way my mother and father lived. In that way, we're losing it, but everybody is losing it, as far as that goes."

Life styles have changed—in Clare as everywhere else. But one change that many of the older generation have had trouble accepting is the waning influence of the church on Acadian life, even though Clare is no different from any other community in North America in this regard. The great church at St. Bernard can seat 1,000 people, but today, there are barely enough

faithful parishioners to maintain the church, let alone fill it. It stands as a symbol of the unwavering faith of the past—a kind of anachronism. But in another sense, perhaps the church never did represent the will of the people, for it might not be there at all, except for the once-unquestioned authority of the clergy.

"We're twins," Monseigneur Nil Thériault says of St. Bernard Church. Figuratively speaking, this is true. Monseigneur Thériault was born in 1910, the year the church was begun, and ever since, their fates have been curiously intertwined. It was Monseigneur Thériault, a child of the parish, who preached the first sermon in the church when it was completed in 1942.

The edifice was the vision of a local priest, Father Edward LeBlanc, who couldn't have foreseen the troubles it would bring upon his people. The grey granite blocks had to be shipped by rail 195 kilometres from Shelburne, then hauled by ox cart the final few kilometres to the building site, where local masons hand-dressed the stone. In this way, the church took shape, a row of stones each year, 8,000 stones in all. "What you now see as St. Bernard Church, I would entitle the 'agony of St. Bernard' because of its history of toils, reverses and hardships," said Monseigneur Thériault, who allowed that architecturally, it is "a marvellous jewel."

It truly was the toil of the people that built the church, for the people had little enough money during the time it was taking shape. This is perhaps the most conspicuous change in Clare, even to the interested passerby like myself. "I would look upon ours as the highest standard of living in Nova Scotia," declared the well-travelled Monseigneur. "I don't know of anywhere else where people are better off."

This new affluence has been long overdue, it seemed to me. There is a third car in some driveways, satellite dishes on the lawns and evidence of an entrepreneurial spirit in the community. Saulnierville now boasts a mini-mall, which provides the services that Acadians once had to travel to an English town to find. Traditional industries such as the A.F. Thériault shipyard in Meteghan River are booming again. When I visited, wooden fish draggers were pulled up onto the slips for their off-season overhaul. Under the roof of a new steel building, I saw workers putting the finishing touches on three fibreglass luxury cruisers for clients in Vancouver. For its first half-century, A.F. Thériault built only wooden boats, but now, it is gearing up to build its first steel boat for the new fleet that will ply the Canadian portion of Georges Bank.

Much of the prosperity along the French Shore can be traced to the upswing in the fishery in the Bay of Fundy and on the Scotian Shelf. The influence of the fishery on the fortunes of the region is so visible that one might add a fish plant to complete Edith Tufts' portrait of a contemporary Acadian community.

One company, Comeau Seafoods, has capitalized on the fishery resource at its doorstep. Comeau Seafoods was founded in the late 1940s by two brothers, both lo-

cal lobster fishermen. In the off-season, they processed smoked herring for the West Indies market. In the 1950s, they shrewdly invested in an offshore scallop fleet (built at A.F. Thériault). Today, Comeau Seafoods processes a full range of fish products—groundfish, lobster, scallops and herring—and has annual sales in excess of $50 million, making it the third largest fish company in the province. It employs 1,300 people in its fish plants and another 450 fishermen in its fleet—making the company by far Clare's largest employer.

The onshore jobs add a vital second income to many families. Locally, Comeau Seafoods is called "Little Freddie's," and Herbert LeBlanc, a member of a Clare band, The Party Goers of the Bay, has even written a song that epitomizes the good times the company has brought to the shore: "Everybody's driving a Trans-Am at Chez Petit Freddie's," goes one verse.

Current prosperity is heady but vulnerable. As the fishery goes, so goes the economy—and as the prosperous 1980s come to an end, the fishery appears to be headed for another of its cyclical downturns. Much to my surprise, I found that many older Acadians viewed the recent boom as a mixed blessing, that the good times had brought an undesirable materialism. I felt I needed to hear from the younger generation, so I sought out a young fishing captain, Daniel LeBlanc.

Two years before, buoyed by the opti-

Symbols of the new economic might of the French Shore, fish draggers, facing page, await a winter refit at A.F. Thériault shipyard in Meteghan River. The region's newfound affluence, built upon the boom years in the fishery, is threatened by serious declines in groundfish stocks caused by overfishing in the Bay of Fundy and on the Scotian Shelf.

mism enjoyed by the industry in the mid-1980s, LeBlanc had an $800,000 fish dragger built by A.F. Thériault. I found his large new cedar home set amongst a landscaped grove of pine trees with two late-model cars in the yard. From the outside, at least, it appeared that life was treating this young Acadian well.

At 27, Captain LeBlanc has accomplished as much as many men twice his age. His youth masks his experience. He began fishing summers at the age of 12, and he has been fishing full-time since he finished high school—at first with his father and for the past three years by himself. A better-than-average athlete, he might have become a physical education teacher, he says, but he opted for the fishery because he liked "the challenge every day." These days, however, the biggest challenge is finding enough fish to catch, as groundfish stocks in the Bay of Fundy and on the Scotian Shelf are, according to the Department of Fisheries and Oceans scientists, in serious decline.

"For people like me, I'm not afraid we'll ever catch the last fish out there," LeBlanc told me. But even fishermen's groups now acknowledge that fish stocks are in trouble, in part because fishermen have been cheating—landing more fish than they are allowed under the quota system designed to conserve fish stocks. It is a complex problem for which fishermen, processors, bureaucrats and politicians must share blame. And it is a difficult problem to solve. Scientists are only beginning to understand the ecology of groundfish: their breeding and migratory behaviour, their abundance and distribution and the natural fluctuations within populations. But there is a growing consensus that fish draggers like LeBlanc's exacerbate the problem by disturbing the sea bottom where groundfish breed.

However, as I listened to LeBlanc's plight, I found myself torn between my sympathy for him personally and my conviction that restrictions on fish catches must now be imposed to conserve the resource. With reduced quotas, LeBlanc could not foresee being able to meet operating expenses (for which he needs 1.5 million pounds of fish), let alone make loan payments. His home and cars have all been used as collateral for his boat. "If I make or break, I'd like it to be because of myself, not because of the government," he says, reflecting the adamant independence of area fishermen, English and French.

LeBlanc pointed out that it is more difficult for fishermen of his generation to ride out rough periods because of the investment needed to get into the fishery in the first place. In his father's time, there wasn't a need for so much capital. At the same time, the rewards are much greater when there are fish to catch.

Some people think fishermen like him are getting rich quick, I told him. In response, he reminds me that everything he has was the result of careful planning and patience. He bought the land for his house when he was 16, cleared it the next year, built the basement the following year, and so on, in stages. The tragedy is that LeBlanc's gains could be lost all at once, and it would not only be him but the whole community that would suffer from a collapse in the fishery.

"Everyone in Clare has a fisherman in the family," observes Maria LeBlanc, who stays home and looks after their daughter, 20-month-old Lorian, while Daniel is at sea for weeks on end. Last summer, Daniel was home only three days in seven weeks as he ranged far from the Bay in search of fish. During such times, Maria looks to the support of friends and family, the enduring forces that still bind *la ville française* together, in good times and in bad.

The LeBlancs' story—just one in the rise of the French Shore—reminded me of the steady determination that built St. Bernard Church—a stone at a time, a row at a time. I wished them good luck and drove the couple of kilometres back to the coast road deep in thought.

On the sombre, wind-tossed waters of St. Marys Bay, I could see a few lobster boats that had braved the wind and December

cold. Most, however, were sheltered behind the breakwater, and I found some of their captains and crew at Le Club Social de Clare, in Petit Ruisseau. On a Friday afternoon, there were a dozen cars parked outside; inside there was pool, beer and conversation in the Acadian *parlez*. A few kilometres up the road, I turned in at a sign that said "Râpure Acadienne," to pick up a *râpure aux palourdes*, made from the bar clams —the large clams that sustained the Acadian settlers of this region during their first hard winter along the rocky shores. Before

I left the shore, I made one last stop—at St. Bernard Church. I found it locked, the tourist season being long past. I craned my neck to admire the Gothic parapets soaring up into the grey winter sky. It seemed that the edifice—jewel or agony—had lost none of its power to impress since the first time I had seen it more than 30 years ago. And, for me, at least, it remains a symbol of the perseverance of the people who call the French Shore home—a people whose aspirations for their culture and for the good life by the Bay I now feel I understand better.

THE LOWER BAY
Oasis and Sanctuary

Tides coil around the islands of the lower Bay, providing sanctuary for breeding seabirds, such as these razor-billed auks, and setting a marine banquet of microscopic plankton, shrimplike krill and herring—food for a variety of great whales, including the rare North Atlantic right whale. The Bay also supports a rich fishery of lobster, scallops, groundfish and the "salad of the sea," dulse.

Life at the Top

"... a thin layer of water, containing a great variety of substances in solution, lying between the air above with its various gaseous substances and the earth below with its various solid substances, and exposed to sunlight coming through the transparent air, seems an ideal location for the production of life. Shallow inlets from the ocean have such characters, and one of these is the Bay of Fundy."

—A.G. Huntsman
"The Production of Life in the Bay of Fundy"

The surface of the water vibrates and shimmers with life. Herring are flipping free of the water in their frenzy to consume red rivers of the shrimplike crustaceans, called krill, creating a din similar to hail on a tin roof. Gulls are stacked up 20 tiers high in a white, swirling cloud, hovering above the banquet of fish. They plunge into the silver masses below and fill the air with their piercing, hungry cries. Nearby, several whales are feeding, their great black backs arching and their bushy spouts erupting above the teeming waters as they, too, work the shoals of herring and krill. Life here, in its myriad marine forms, is compressed into a thin window near the surface. Just by looking over the side of the boat, I can see the entire pyramid of the marine food chain: shrimp, herring and seabirds and whales—a feast for the eyes.

I am aboard the *Kenny and Girls 5*, a Cape Island lobster boat operated out of Brier Island, the period below the exclamation

A humpback whale, above, surrounded by gulls and shearwaters, is gorging on shrimplike krill. The humpback whale is a gulper. Ventral plates in its throat region expand enormously with the water ingested on its feeding lunge, facing page, adding to the imposing dimensions of the head, which has a knobby appearance due to the presence of raised sensory follicles.

mark that is Digby Neck, itself an attenuation of basalt that points out into the mouth of the Bay of Fundy.

Former Maine fisherman Carl Haycock and local lobsterman Harold Graham operate Brier Island Whale and Seabird Cruises as a means of financing Brier Island Ocean Study—a nonprofit organization dedicated to studying the whales and seabirds that exploit the marine system around the tiny island. Haycock, an unassuming 31-year-old with a powerful build and easy manner, first became interested in whales when fishing eight months of the year on Georges Bank in the Gulf of Maine. He recorded "just about everything" he saw and even kept an aquarium on board ship to study the strange creatures from the sea bottom that he brought up in his drags. But his main pursuit was whales, and Steven Katona, director of Allied Whale at the College of Atlantic in Bar Harbor, Maine, remembers receiving four-page letters from Haycock describing his

whale encounters. In 1979, Haycock sent a photograph of a humpback whale to Katona, who coordinates the North Atlantic Humpback Whale Catalogue, a clearing-house for the identification of individual humpbacks. Haycock had seen the whale off Freeport, Maine, while fishing mackerel with his grandfather. It was a new whale, one that had not as yet been identified, and was given the name Marble. As fate would have it, Haycock has seen Marble every year since he first came to Brier Island in 1984 looking to satisfy his whale-research interest in an area that had not been studied.

Sightings of whales had been made around Brier in the early 1970s, but Haycock was surprised by "the incredible richness of the marine habitat" and in particular by the variety of cetaceans that exploited it. On a given day, he might see fins, humpbacks, minkes, harbour porpoises and white-sided dolphins and, on occasion, pilot whales, white-beaked dolphins and the rare North Atlantic right whale. However, Haycock has focused much of his attention on the humpback whale, which is the most acrobatic and conspicuous of the cetaceans common to the outer Bay of Fundy in summer.

As I cast my eyes around the horizon, I can see several fine bouquets of breath, silver in the sun, drifting in the still air—the exhalations of whales, no doubt many of them humpbacks. Haycock has been diligently identifying individual humpback whales in Fundy using the distinctive white patches on the underside of their flukes as photo-identification tags. To date, he has identified 140 individuals off Brier. At any one time, there may be 100 humpbacks in the lower Bay, of which perhaps 50 can be considered residents. This information, compiled over the long term, will help humpback researchers detail the life history, migratory patterns and population dynamics of the species, which was reduced to fewer than 4,000 animals worldwide by the mid-1960s, when it was finally given full protection.

Carl Haycock, founder of Brier Island Ocean Study, is still surprised by "the incredible richness of the marine habitat" around the tiny island that attracts a variety of cetaceans. The most acrobatic and conspicuous is the humpback, as evidenced by its tail-breaching antics, above. Weirmen "dry up" their weir, facing page, causing the masses of herring to dance free of the water.

So far today, we have sighted two easily recognizable individuals. The first, Cirrus, has a wispy cloud pattern on its tail and has been seen off Massachusetts for the past eight years. When the second whale raises its flukes for a deep dive, Haycock cries out, "That's Floppy." A deep gash in one of the whale's flukes, which causes the outside edge to hang limply, is clearly visible. Haycock explains that Floppy is a juvenile humpback, who probably suffered the injury from a collision with a ship's propeller.

Humpbacks are found the world over and comprise three isolated populations: the North Pacific, the southern hemisphere and the North Atlantic. In the western North Atlantic, there appear to be three substocks, each of which comes north during the summer to feed: one to the Gulf of Maine and Bay of Fundy, another to Newfoundland and Labrador and the third to Greenland and Iceland.

Since 1973, Allied Whale has catalogued 4,000 individuals (not all still living) from both sides of the Atlantic—a statistic that indicates an encouraging recovery of the species. Katona estimates that the Gulf of Maine population is perhaps 300 to 400 strong. In the Gulf, the whales concentrate on Stellwagen Bank and in the Great South Channel of Georges Bank, but some of the same humpbacks also come to Fundy. "They all mix back and forth," says Katona. "Genetically, they're the same population, just as, I think, the whole of the North Atlantic is one genetic population. And the Gulf of Maine forms what you might call one cultural population, or one substock, or what some people call a feeding aggregation. But they all know each other."

Even so, there is some segregation of individuals between the Gulf and the Bay. Some animals have been sighted only in the Bay of Fundy. The whale Bermuda, for instance, was first photographed by Katona in the humpback breeding grounds in the Caribbean in 1976 but ever since has been seen only in the Bay. Having seen Bermuda and her calves for six summers in a row,

Haycock considers her a resident Fundy whale. He has observed that nonresident females may come to the Bay of Fundy in years when they don't have calves, but they'll return to their traditional feeding or nursery area in the Gulf when they do.

As whales seem to know one another, so do whale watchers, and by exchanging information, they are able to track the movements of individual whales from year to year or from one area to another during the summer. In recent years, Haycock has noticed that there seem to be more whales from the Gulf of Maine coming north to feed on herring around Brier Island. The reason may be the population collapse of the sand lance—a small, eel-like fish—on Stellwagen Bank off Cape Cod, Massachusetts.

Humpbacks are opportunists; that is, they will eat pretty much whatever is available on their feeding grounds—sand lance in the Gulf of Maine, herring in the Bay of Fundy and capelin off Newfoundland. Those that return to Fundy do so in July and August, when herring stocks are gathering in the Bay to feed on krill, and they stay until late fall. Haycock thinks that humpbacks prefer the krill, but as often as not, they will be seen lunging through schools of herring. In Antarctic waters, humpbacks have been observed to consume 1.5 tonnes of krill each day, and it is thought they need about one million calories a day to put on sufficient fat reserves for the three-month fasting period they undergo each winter in their southern calving and breeding grounds. Haycock has observed that when the whales return to Fundy in summer from the Caribbean—where they winter off the north coast of the Dominican Republic—the backbones of some are clearly visible. When they leave, they are bulging with blubber.

Many whale watchers set out to sea hoping to witness humpback whales hurling their 40,000-kilogram bodies free of the waves—a puzzling behaviour known as breaching—and I am no different. However, I am even more eager to observe a humpback whale lunge feeding. Like other ror-

qual whales (baleen whales with throat grooves, including blue, fin, sei and minke whales), humpbacks are "gulpers." Living juggernauts, they rise through a school of fish, opening their mouths as they do so, and break spectacularly through the surface in a vortex of boiling foam.

It is an ideal day to observe such behaviour, as the herring and krill are thickly aggregated at the surface, bidding the great whales to rise. Harold Graham manoeuvres the *Kenny and Girls 5* within 18 metres of a school of herring, and suddenly, a great head erupts at the surface. Like an outsize accordion, the ventral plates of its throat region expand enormously with the mouthful of water ingested on its feeding lunge, adding to the imposing dimensions of the head; buckets of water pour under pressure through its baleen plates, whose hairy fringes retain the herring and krill. Riveted by this spectacle, I note that the humpback's head has a distinctly knobbly appearance due to the presence of raised sensory follicles (whalers called them "stove bolts") on the upper and lower jaws.

The head sinks below the waves, and all of us scan the water to see where the whale will strike next. Soon it announces its coming by blowing a bubble cloud. I see the mist of bubbles rising through the green layers of water, then the surface of the ocean starting to churn like a pot of water reaching the boiling point. Suddenly, the white underside of the charging whale appears, and finally, its great head bursts through the schools of herring. The so-called bubble-net feeding is unique to humpbacks. Some observers believe that the bubbles act as an illusory barrier, a net that concentrates the fish; others believe that they serve as a veil to hide the whale itself as it makes its feeding lunge. In any event, it is a highly effective and ingenious strategy, which further heightens our fascination with the great whales in general and humpbacks in particular.

From the wheelhouse, Graham points out that the humpbacks appear to lunge-feed when they are dining on herring and side-feed, with one 4.5-metre-long flipper exposed, when they are exploiting krill. What-

ever it's feeding on, Graham says, the humpback must have regard for the frantically feeding birds, or it might get more than it bargained for. On one occasion, he observed a humpback inadvertently gulp a gull, only to regurgitate it, but there is a historical account of a humpback actually choking on a cormorant swallowed in such a fashion.

What is not obvious to the whale watchers, including myself, is how the humpbacks—and other whales in the Bay of Fundy—use the tides to feed more efficiently. Over time, Haycock has observed a distinct pattern that helps him to locate the whales. "They use the tides a lot up here," he tells me. "At the full moon and the new moon, we tend to see the food concentrated here [around Brier Island], and whales concentrate here. On the half moons, the food and the whales disperse.

"They're making these circles with the tide. They go up with the flood and come down with the ebb," says Haycock. "They save energy that way, plus the food's moving with the tides. They are a very powerful influence in their lives, so they might as well work with them. You see whales swimming against the tide, but most of the time, you see them going in the direction the tide's going."

In a sense, it comes as no surprise to hear Haycock say that the tides are the dominant factor in determining the whereabouts of the whales, for it is a principle I have seen repeated throughout the Bay—with shad, sandpipers and mud shrimp. More often than not, the behaviour of creatures living in the Bay can be traced to that overriding feature of the environment—the tides. However, I feel an extraordinary sense of exhilaration at seeing what the tide has wrought around Brier Island. The tides show their life-enhancing force here in a more dramatic way than almost anywhere else in the Bay. I find myself surrounded by life in all dimensions: flurries of white seabirds above me, gorging whales beside me, thick schools of herring and swarms of krill under me—where usually, I am accustomed to seeing only barren wave tops.

Dedicated birders have long been coming to Brier Island, which is an important staging area for the fall and spring migrations of hawks and songbirds. But until the recent whale-watching boom, the island was best known as the birthplace of Joshua Slocum, the first man to sail around the world alone. Slocum's account of that voyage, entitled simply *Sailing Alone Around the World*, has been called "a nautical equivalent of *Walden*," and the author himself "a Thoreau of the sea." His sailing career, which would take him to the ends of the Earth, began inauspiciously in the treacherous Bay of Fundy, as Slocum reveals in the book's first chapter: "As for myself, the wonderful sea charmed me from the first. At the age of 8, I had already been afloat along with other boys on the bay, with chances greatly in favour of being drowned." Today, Brier Island, the starting point of Slocum's historic solo voyage in 1895, itself seems at the end of the world, and getting there can be half the fun.

The road is a switchback from the top of North Mountain to the sea, where the ferry—the *Joshua Slocum*—waits to cross Petit Passage. The tide runs with such force through this sea-breached fault in the North Mountain basalt that the tiny ferry seems to crawl crabwise across the water. After driving the length of Long Island, you board the *Spray* (the namesake of Slocum's tidy nine-metre sloop) to cross Grand Passage to Westport, on Brier Island. Each time I make this journey to land's end, I am reminded of Slocum's own respect for the waters that surge around the island: ". . . the *Spray* sailed directly over the southwest ledge through the worst tide-race in the Bay of Fundy. . . . I was delighted to reach Westport. Any port at all would have been delightful after the terrible thrashing I got in the fierce sou'west rip." Cutting his nautical teeth on such waters must have prepared Slocum for the famous exploits of later days, and he says as much himself:

"It is known that a Brier Islander, fish or no fish on his hook, never flinches from a sea."

The turbulence that characterizes the waters at the mouth of the Bay of Fundy—and that so vexed the *Spray*—is associated with an oceanographic phenomenon known as upwelling. Upwelling usually occurs near the coast, where prevailing offshore winds move surface waters away from the coast, and as a result, colder, deeper waters move upward to replace them. The phenomenon is most frequently observed on the west coasts of continental margins, notably off the coasts of Oregon and Washington, Peru and Chile, and Morocco and Southwest Africa. Wherever upwelling occurs, observed Rachel Carson in *The Sea Around Us*, it results in "a profusion of life." The reason for the richness is that the deep waters bring with them a load of natural fertilizer, in the form of nutrients from the seafloor. This, wrote Carson, ". . . sets off the old,

A Grand Manan fisherman sets the seine around the inside of a herring weir, facing page. The outer Bay of Fundy, typical of other areas of upwelling, is a primary fishing ground. Fishermen land more than $200 million worth of fish annually. One of the most important catches are scallops, which litter the heaving deck of a Georges Bank scallop dragger, above.

familiar biological chain: salts, diatoms, copepods, herring."

The outer Bay of Fundy is typical of other areas of upwelling in being an important fishing ground, a privileged place in the fisherman's universe. I remember an elderly fisherman from Grand Manan, the largest of the Fundy islands, telling me: "Around here, there's always something different. They go netting fish and line fishing—for cod, pollack, hake and haddock—and they got [herring] seiners and weirs, of course. Then there's lobsters and scallops. And if you get right up against it, you can go clamming. There's lots of places they only got one thing. When it goes down, you're out of luck. Here, there's always something to go to."

Fishermen land more than $200 million worth of fish annually in the region, making it the most affluent in the Atlantic Canada fishery. Strictly speaking, the two most valuable components of the Fundy fishery are not fish at all but bottom-dwelling invertebrates—lobsters (crustaceans) and scallops (mollusks), which feed on the rich mixture of plant and animal marine life stirred by the tides. A major stock of the northwest Atlantic herring spawns off southwest Nova Scotia, on Trinity and Lurcher Shoals at the mouth of the Bay; juvenile herring—sardines—from this stock and the Gulf of Maine stock congregate in silvery shoals along the New Brunswick shore in summer to feed; and adult herring from Long Island to Cape Breton come to the Bay to exploit the "shrimp feed." The abundant zooplankton and herring also attract the largest concentration of nonbreeding, surface-feeding seabirds in the northwest Atlantic, not to mention significant numbers of whales, porpoises and dolphins.

Most upwellings are wind-generated. However, in the Bay of Fundy, the prevailing winds shift with the season, from northwesterly in winter to southwesterly in summer, which suggests that upwelling is not primarily the result of wind action. It turns out that the Fundy upwellings are tidally

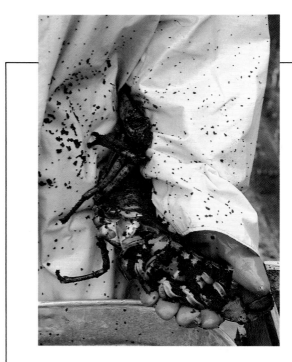

generated, as is the case with most phenomena in the Bay. The strong tidal currents as they pass around the corner of the coastline near Yarmouth – which is at right angles to the direction of the current – create an upwelling effect in the same way that turbulence is created when a river flows around a bend. Nutrient-rich cold water is stirred up with the predictable results: "a profusion of life" and fog, which hangs like a grey cowl over the region for much of the summer.

As the tide streams around the bend of southwestern Nova Scotia, it runs up against horseshoe-shaped ledges, producing the frightful rips near Brier Island that Slocum mentions. These are in fact miniature upwellings. I have noticed that the water around the island never seems to be corrugated by a regular array of waves. It is twisted into whirlpools, compressed into glassy streaks or thrown up into violent rips – constantly changing and impossibly complex. It is a testament to human ingenuity that local fishermen have learned by necessity to read the confusing patterns on the face of the water here as a means of navigating in the thick, seemingly eternal fog. One retired Long Island fisherman, Raymond Thurber, told me, "In some areas where you have streaks, we use them for

navigational purposes. We could tell by the looks of them to get bearings. This was before we had the electronics; we used them an awful lot for our navigating." The streaks – glassy ribbons of water surrounded by areas of ruffled water – are such permanent and predictable features of the seascape that Brier Island fishermen have even given them names such as "40 fathom" or "55 fathom" streak.

In the late 1970s, Thurber chartered his boat to scientists from Dalhousie University and the Bedford Institute of Oceanography, who were studying the tidal streaks and the marine life that seemed to be attracted to them. On a day when it was too rough for fishing, I hired Ray's son Jimmy to take me out to the tide streaks that run between Moores and Northwest ledges, five kilometres north of Brier Island.

At Freeport, Jimmy Thurber's new Cape Island boat, *The Bay Boy*, rested at low tide in a crib, a kind of boat cradle that prevents the boat from toppling against the wharf and tearing off the cabin. When enough tide had inched under the grey fibreglass hull to float it, Jimmy winched up the crib and we headed out through Grand Passage.

The passage on the flood tide flows like a powerful river between Brier and Long islands. Where this river of tide meets waves riding ashore from the open Bay, the clash sends whitecaps rearing. Harbour porpoises seem to delight in playing along the edge of this tide rip, which probably also

Lobster eggs, attached to the underside of the mother's tail for up to a year, stipple a fisherman's slicker, above. Lobsters reach the current legal catch size at 5 to 8 years of age, before they are sexually mature and able to replenish the stocks. Yet, lobster catches have doubled in the past decade, filling lobster pounds, such as the one in Grand Manan, facing page.

serves to deliver their food. Farther offshore, as we approached the area between the ledges, I began to notice small groups of little gull-like birds riding the chop and occasionally stabbing the water with precise pecks. These were phalaropes, which fishermen sometimes call gale birds for their habit of congregating near shore after a wind. They became more and more numerous, until the water was enlivened by continuous skimming flights along the line of the tide streaks, which were clearly marked by collections of rockweed. "See," Jimmy observed, "they pretty much stick to the rockweed streaks."

The scene reminded me of the flights of peeps in the upper Bay – there were thousands of birds on the wing – and in fact, it was a fair analogy. Phalaropes (grey and red-necked) are circumpolar shorebirds that breed in the Arctic and sub-Arctic as do the sandpipers. But phalaropes have a life history which is more like that of true seabirds. Except for their brief Arctic breeding period, they survive at sea, either wintering off the west coast of South America or, in the case of the phalaropes from eastern North America, off West Africa. The phalaropes come to Fundy's rich waters to fatten up in preparation for their autumn migration, just as the sandpipers do on the vast mud flats of the upper Bay. "It must be special, what they're eating," Jimmy said, "if they fly all that way. It must be powerful food."

The phalaropes are feeding selectively upon copepods, tiny flea-sized crustaceans that are the dominant members of the zooplankton community in temperate (or Boreal) waters. Copepods are grazers, which filter the water for microscopic plant life, the phytoplankton. The most common member of the copepod community in the Bay of Fundy (and most other waters, for that matter) is *Calanus finmarchius*. This organism spends most of the day at depths of 100 metres or more and comes to the surface only at night (called diurnal vertical migrations). But on the ledges off

Brier Island, the upwellings bring these weak swimmers bodily to the surface during the daylight hours. As phalaropes feed only at the surface and select individual prey by sight, they seem to depend on this food-delivery system, which brings otherwise inaccessible prey within their reach.

Examination of the feeding ecology of phalaropes in the Bay of Fundy has provided insights into the pelagic ecology of seabirds generally. Ironically, most of our knowledge of seabirds is based on observations during that brief interval in their annual cycle when they come ashore to breed—in other words, when these highly adapted sea creatures are on land. Seabird biologist Richard G.B. Brown of the Canadian Wildlife Service, writing in *Oceanus*,

points out, "The study of seabirds at sea is one of the last frontiers of field ornithology." Brown, an author and scientist, has been at the forefront of the renewed effort to understand why seabirds utilize certain areas of the ocean and not others. In particular, he has examined the direct links between the distributions of birds and oceanographic factors. The use of the Brier Island upwellings by phalaropes presents a perfect case study of this relationship.

Brown refers to the upwelling mechanism over Moores and Northwest ledges as a "tidal pump." Cool water and copepods are literally pumped to the surface as the advancing tide rides up the steep sides of the ledges. This produces divergence, or upwelling streaks. However, the up-

welled cold water sinks again—sliding under the warmer surface water downstream—in areas oceanographers call convergence zones. The convergence streaks are marked by accumulations of seaweed and flotsam. The phalaropes probably use these visual clues to find the best concentrations of copepods, as both divergence and convergence streaks usually contain higher copepod numbers than the surrounding area. It may be that to feed efficiently at sea, phalaropes and perhaps other seabirds require a food-concentrating mechanism such as the tidal pump off Brier Island.

During the breeding season in the Arctic, phalaropes rely on a diet of aquatic insects, which are extremely abundant in the shal-

low tundra pools. In fresh water, the birds employ a characteristic spinning or twirling motion that creates a tiny whirlpool under them. As they pirouette (about 60 revolutions a minute), the turbulence whips up bottom-dwelling larvae into reach. Obviously, however, this is an impractical strategy in the open seas.

Brown thinks that one of the advantages of the Bay of Fundy as a staging area may be that it allows inexperienced juvenile phalaropes to make a smooth transition from preying in shallow freshwater pools to feeding in the open ocean where marine zooplankton are usually found at depths too great to be influenced by the birds' conventional strategy. In Fundy, spinning is unnecessary—the tidal pump does the job for them. Field observations confirm that such oceanographic factors are important indicators of where phalaropes are likely to be found at sea. Phalaropes have been noted consistently at convergence fronts in Hudson Strait and the Labrador Current and in areas of upwelling off the coasts of Africa and Peru.

Between Moores and Northwest ledges, *The Bay Boy* cruised through continuous flights of grey phalaropes. The gale birds peeled off the water, circled and, after visually locating the streaks, settled again amidst the rockweed and copepods.

Copepods are not the only zooplankton brought to the surface by Fundy's tidal pump, nor are phalaropes the only birds attracted to the tide-delivered banquet. Euphausiids, or krill, also come to the surface in swarms near Brier Island, creating a colourful natural spectacle. Atlantic krill (*Meganyctiphanes norvegica*) are larger than the copepods but, like them, live in dense packs at considerable depths and normally do not come to the surface except during nocturnal migrations. However, in July and August, truly remarkable swarms of krill are observed at the surface over the Brier Island ledges.

I have seen red rivers of shrimp a few hundred metres long wending through the blue waters. Krill have bright red chromatophores, the pigment cells responsible for their colour. (They also possess luminescent photophores that flash electric blue.) Their eyes—in Gaelic, they are called *suil dhu*, or black eyes—are clearly visible as inch-long shrimp swim along in parallel fashion. Swarms can cover several hectares, or they can be concentrated into half a hectare, containing as many as 600,000 animals per cubic metre of water, stacked up in several layers. These "superswarms" result in an orgy of feeding, such as the one I witnessed from the *Kenny and Girls 5*, as all the higher marine predators—fish, seabirds and whales—jostle for a place at the table.

Several theories have been put forward

Gulls gather for a free lunch as fishermen clean their catch, above, at North Head, Grand Manan. A host of marine creatures—shrimp, herring, seabirds and whales, such as the finback, facing page, surging to the surface—gather in Fundy to take advantage of the food-delivery system of tidal upwellings, which blast zooplankton to the surface for the taking.

to explain why krill, which are much stronger swimmers than copepods and less susceptible to being transported passively, are found at the surface during daylight hours in the Bay of Fundy. It was suggested that they might simply be following their prey, the copepods, or that predators were pursuing them or that the swarms were actually spawning aggregations. Krill researcher Stephen Nicol put forward the latter theory when he found large numbers of newly laid krill eggs in surface waters when swarms were present off Brier Island. However, Brown has since shown that swarming tends to coincide with spring tides and with daily tidal maximums, which favours the idea that the krill, like the copepods, have no choice in the matter and are involuntarily blasted to the surface by the force of the tidal currents.

Once the krill come to the surface—for whatever reason—they are fair game. Shearwaters, both greater shearwaters and their darker counterparts, sooties, can often be seen planing across the waters in the uniquely graceful daredevil fashion that accounts for their name, dipping one wing tip and then the other to the water surface, anticipating each trough and crest with uncanny, effortless precision. Swarms are probably of particular importance to seabirds such as the shearwaters, which cannot dive to take krill at their normal depths. The shearwaters also take herring and squid, as do the herring gulls and great black-backed gulls that make up the bulk of the seabird cloud seen swirling above the swarms. Seabirds, in fact, are feeding at three levels of this short food chain founded on phytoplankton: phalaropes are feeding on copepods; shearwaters and gulls are feeding on krill; and the larger seabirds are taking herring and squid as well. As many as 10,000 shearwaters use the area around Brier Island as a summer feeding ground, and an equal number of grey phalaropes take advantage of what Brown has dubbed the "pump-copepod-euphausiid system."

A similar upwelling system exists across the Bay on the New Brunswick shore, where notorious tide rips career around the western isles of Passamaquoddy Bay. However, there is an interesting separation of species between these two oceanographically similar environments. On the New Brunswick side, Bonaparte's gulls take the place of shearwaters, and red-necked phalaropes replace the greys. The largest concentrations of both Bonaparte's gulls and red-necked phalaropes in eastern Canada occur in the passages at the head of Passamaquoddy Bay. As many as 10,000 elegant little Bonaparte's gulls, with their glacial plumage and jet-black heads, use the tidally turbulent waters as a staging area in early summer and in fall. As many as one million northern or red-necked phalaropes (which are darker than the greys) also use the Passamaquoddy area, where they sometimes congregate in impressive rafts of several thousand tightly packed birds.

Whales, too, seem to show some discrimination between the two sides of the outer Bay. Right whales are more common to the New Brunswick side of the Bay, particularly the Grand Manan Basin; humpback whales, on the other hand, show a preference for the area around Brier Island. Harbour porpoises are also concentrated in

and around Passamaquoddy Bay, which has been called a stronghold of the species in the western North Atlantic. It is common to see pods of harbour porpoises while taking the ferries that ply between Deer and Campobello islands in southwestern New Brunswick. Several thousand occur in these waters, although there seem to be only a few dozen around Brier Island and Digby Neck.

Why there is a clear separation of species on either side of the Bay is not yet fully understood, but it is surely some expression of feeding ecology. Brown has pointed out that the red-necked phalaropes have a thinner, more needlelike bill which may be adapted for catching the larger, more mobile copepods that predominate in Passamaquoddy. On the other hand, the grey phalaropes, with their deeper, broader bill equipped with tiny strainerlike papillae, may be better adapted to filter feeding on the smaller copepods that characterize the Brier Island zooplankton community. Similarly, the separation of cetaceans may relate to the fineness of their baleen fringes,

which are designed to sieve smaller or larger prey.

Either side of the Bay, naturalists are sure to find themselves in the midst of a great and diverse proliferation of marine life. A 21-metre fin whale, the stretch limousine of Fundy cetaceans, glides by, often accompanied by a frisky pod of white-sided dolphins whose speed and antics make up for their lack of size; Leach's storm petrels dance along the waves in the light-footed style they use to garner plankton, like a child picking wildflowers; juvenile gannets fold their great wings and plunge with headlong precision into swarms of krill; and if you're lucky, a humpback whale may hurl its boxcar-sized body free of the waters, perhaps for no other reason than to say, "Hello, here I am." Even in the fog, it's possible to hear the Vesuvian exhalations of whales surfacing. Such experiences connect us with the mysterious community of creatures so often concealed below the sea's seemingly barren waves, and they are the reasons I return to the Fundy isles year after year.

Dulse Tides at Dark Harbour

Dulse de dum
see it sun
sway in the warm salt pools

Dulse by gum
out you come
bend yer back and pull

—Song by Lutia and Paul Lauzon

At 4 a.m., we switchback down the narrow dirt road along the back of Grand Manan Island to Dark Harbour. Dark, indeed, as there is no hint of dawn yet in what islanders call "the Dulse Capital of the World." We have come at this predawn hour to take advantage of the dulse tides; that is, the ebb cycle of the spring tides. This twice-monthly occurrence, when the tidal range is greatest in concert with the new and full moons, exposes more of the intertidal zone for longer periods, allowing dulsers to find and pick more of the glassy, ruddy ribbons of the edible seaweed *Palmaria palmata*. The tides recede at 6 a.m. and 6 p.m., in accordance with the diurnal cycle of tides in the Bay of Fundy, so dulsers in summer can make two pickings per day. Unfortunately, or so I feel, having only recently left the comfort of my bed, one of these tides requires us to rise at an hour when the birds are not yet in voice.

We drive straight onto the gravel beach,

Burlap bags, above, bulge with Grand Manan's finest—Dark Harbour dulse, an edible seaweed sometimes called "the salad of the sea." Grand Manan is the prime producer of dulse, which can be eaten fresh or, more commonly, in dried form. Facing page: One of the island's irregular corps of a hundred dulsers bends to the rhythmic task of plucking ruddy ribbons of dulse from rocks exposed at low tide.

our headlights briefly illuminating the salt lagoon of the harbour before we douse them, and sit in the pitch-dark night, waiting for the small community of dulsers to rouse themselves from their ramshackle cottages that rim Dark Harbour. The lone settlement on the western shore of Grand Manan, Dark Harbour is occupied only during the dulsing months, April through October. The harbour is surrounded on three sides by sheer basalt cliffs (and is therefore nearly always shaded and dark) and bounded at its mouth by a great seawall of beach stone and driftwood. It is a salt lagoon connected to the sea by a narrow channel dredged in the 19th century to provide a safe anchorage for "the tempest-tossed mariner." This humanitarian public work was undertaken after Moses Perley successfully petitioned the New Brunswick government to enlarge the channel, making Dark Harbour "a place of refuge" along an otherwise ironbound coast.

Today, Dark Harbour serves as a refuge of another kind—for islanders seeking relief from the teetotalling atmosphere of the eastern shore, where there are 17 churches, one for every mile of road. The Marathon Inn, a survivor of the straw-hat and steamer-trunk days, earned the right to serve liquor only after battling the congregations of the Grand Manan Ministerial Association. A liquor store now dispenses wine, beer and spirits to islanders, but if they want to enjoy a drink in the open air, they repair to Dark Harbour, which has its own saturnalia of sorts—appropriately called Dark Harbour Days—during which the revellers elect their mayor and, just about any day, an islander can feel free to stroll the beach with a beer openly in hand. Tourists, too, come to Dark Harbour for its vista of splendid sunsets behind the wavy mauve line of Maine on the horizon. The lagoon shelters a herring weir and a successful Atlantic salmon aquaculture ranch, whose corrals

are now becoming visible as deeply etched charcoal lines against the first tentative pastels of dawn. With the light also comes the rumblings of a half-ton truck and stirrings from the dulsers' cottages.

Leroy Flagg, King of the Dulse Pickers, emerges from the half-ton and flashes an infectious smile. In defence of his title, Leroy claims to have picked more dulse than any man or woman on the island, and no one, it seems, disputes him. Now in his sixties, he has been dulsing since he was 12 years old, when he lived year-round in Dark Harbour with his parents; and even now, as one of the island's biggest buyers and sellers of dulse, he enjoys a day on the rocks. His son Gerald, who picks part-time when he is not tending his weir or fishing, accompanies his father this morning, as do three other dulsers of the island's irregular corps of a hundred or so.

We saunter down to the lagoon shore and load the meagre equipment of the

dulser's trade—burlap bags and wire baskets—aboard two cream-coloured Lunenburg dories. The channel to the sea is unnavigable at low tide, so we power across the narrow lagoon toward the seawall, waving to Vernon Bagley, the night watchman at the salmon ranch, as we go. Mr. Bagley, says Leroy, received a Carnegie Silver Medal for rappelling down precipitous cliffs to save two Maine boaters wrecked on the shore near Southern Head Light in February 1963.

With the aid of an outboard, it is a short trip from shore to shore. But now, we must negotiate the seawall, a steep, 122-metre-wide natural barrier rising up before us. I watch as Gerald attaches one end of a 15-metre rope to the high-raked bow of the dory, trudges up the incline and affixes the other end of the rope to a rusted winch at the top of the seawall. The ancient contraption backfires into action, then settles into a rhythmic racket as it slowly pulls the boat to the seawall's crest. With the satisfaction all older people seem to take in past hardship, Leroy points out that when he was young, the winching was accomplished by capstan and manpower. Even now, it is necessary to put one's back into the job. Gerry unties the dory, and everyone pitches in, grasping the gunwales on either side and sliding the boat gently down over the treacherously slippery beach stone and into the pearl-grey waters of the outer Bay. The whole operation seems to go smoothly. Gerry, however, notes with dissatisfaction that the bottom needs greasing.

"What do you use?" I ask.

"French-fry grease from local restaurants," he replies as if it should have been obvious.

Once at sea, we are suspended in a mercurial world of fog and water. The mist, in fact, has set in with such earnestness that the towering cliffs of Dark Harbour are now completely obscured. The lack of visibility does not deter Leroy, who seems to know precisely where he is going and just how to get there despite the absence of landmarks.

We cut a clean wake through the mysterious void. Only the herring weirs—ghostly houses for air and water—stand out against the grey background. The traditional heart-shaped weirs are a familiar feature of the Grand Manan seascape. At a distance, they have the grandeur of gossamer colosseums, and islanders reflect justifiable pride in their constructions by giving them dignified names. As we pass each one, Leroy calls out its name like an incantation: "Seawall . . . The Dream . . . North Air . . ."

Caramel fronds of horse kelp flutter at the surface as Gerry steers for shore. We pull the dory securely onto the rocks, where, as if by radar, we find a good patch of foot-long dulse just being exposed by the receding tide. I marvel at Leroy's knack of knowing where to bring us, even through fog of the pea-soup variety.

"You can't fool me on the dulse," he says. "I know every rock and curve on the coast. I suppose I've picked over every rock 5,000 times. I can always find good dulse because

I can keep it in my mind. I know where we picked six or eight weeks ago."

Dulse grows all around Grand Manan, but to Leroy Flagg, only one kind of dulse is worth picking—Dark Harbour dulse—and for that reason, you'll never find him pursuing his trade on the more civilized eastern shore of the island.

"Why is Dark Harbour dulse so much better?" I ask.

"Oh," Leroy begins slowly, "the high cliffs and strong tides, I guess."

The traditional heart-shaped herring weir, facing page, lends a mystical air to the Grand Manan seascape. Ghostly houses for air and water, they are effective fish-catching corrals. Weir herring are especially sought-after for smoking, and thus many are destined for smokehouses such as the ones at Woodwards Cove, above, on the eastern side of the island.

With prodding, Leroy explains that the high cliffs shade the dulse grounds at their feet, preventing the rockweed from getting sunburned. Also, the stronger tidal currents on the unprotected west side of the island seem to favour the growth of the seaweed and keep it clean of mussels and mud.

Leroy clutches a mittful of ruddy, glistening Dark Harbour dulse and holds it up pridefully. "This here is the only dulse in the world," he declares.

Although dulse grows all along the Boreal coast, from New Jersey to the Arctic, the conditions around Grand Manan and especially on the Dark Harbour side of the island favour the growth of the dark, thick-leaved variety of red algae, which is preferred to the bleached, thin-leaved variety native to other waters. Carolyn Bird, a phycologist at the National Research Council in Halifax (a phycologist specializes in the study of marine plants), confirms Leroy's firsthand observations as to why Dark Harbour dulse is of the finest quality. "The less bright light you have shining on the dulse, the darker it's going to be. These people who go over

to Dark Harbour know what they're doing. It's not called Dark Harbour for nothing, you know, because you've got this big cliff overhanging it, protecting it from the sun in the morning. And in the Bay of Fundy, the tidal cycle is such that you get your dulse tides early in the morning and early in the evening. So the sun is not really up then. And at more normal low tides, there's still apt to be a little water over the dulse, thereby sheltering it from sun even more. So, in essence, that stuff at Dark Harbour does not get exposed to very strong sunlight at any time."

Bird also confirms that because dulse throughout the Bay of Fundy is constantly exposed to strong tides, it is not as likely to become overgrown with such parasitic animals as hydroids or mussels—thus the esteem accorded Dark Harbour dulse by Leroy and his customers.

What we think of as the shore extends from the high tidemark to the low tidemark and, for this reason, is termed the intertidal zone. Due to the high tides in the Bay of Fundy, the intertidal zone is relatively great—1,052 square kilometres along a coastline of 2,745 kilometres. Tides, in fact, are the dominant force along the shore, and they ultimately determine the succession of living things. The rocky shore along the outer Bay of Fundy, as everywhere around the world's oceans, is divided into three distinct zones, each characterized by the types of dominant animals and plants that

A dulser's dory, facing page, rests in placid Dark Harbour, a saltwater lagoon connected to the sea by a narrow channel dredged in the 19th century to provide safe anchorage for "the tempest-tossed mariner." Often wrapped in fog and overshadowed by high basaltic cliffs, it provides a perfect environment for dulse, which grows best if it is shaded from strong sunlight.

live in it. Periwinkles are found with blue-green algae at the top of the shore, then barnacles in the midzone and, lower still, the brown and red algae.

Approaching the sea from the land, the first zone we meet is the black zone, so-called for its decidedly dark hue, caused primarily by the community of lichens and blue-green algae that thrives there. The most common animal of the black zone is the rough periwinkle. Its name, *Littorina saxitalis*, means "living among rocks," and its hard shell allows it to survive the battering waves that go with the territory. Periwinkles move about on a single foot, grazing on green algae, the most primitive and simplest of plants. In the Bay of Fundy, the bottom of the black zone is marked by a band of brown algae, and it is here that the periwinkle's domain ends and the barnacle zone begins.

In sharp contrast to the black zone, the barnacle zone is glaringly white due to the limestone shells of the barnacles. The barnacle is a crustacean; it glues its shell to the rocks and waits for the tide to deliver its meal of microscopic life. It lives head down in its volcano-shaped shell, the top of which is fitted with four trapdoors that shut at low tide to prevent the barnacle from drying out but open as soon as water covers the shell. Then six pairs of feathery appendages appear and begin to sweep the water, creating a vortex to draw food particles into the crater where the little animal passes its sheltered life. In Fundy, the barnacle zone is often blanketed by a slippery mat of brown algae—knotted wrack and rockweed, both of which possess air bladders to allow flotation at high tide.

Near the low-water mark, the brown algae give way to red algae, in the aptly named red algae, or Irish moss, zone. Here, where conditions are right, such as at Dark Harbour, dulse grows luxuriantly.

Dulse is sometimes called "the salad of the sea" and, as with many exotic natural foods, is an acquired taste. Foremost among its epicurean qualities is its saltiness, and many Maritimers eat the dried seaweed as a snack for much the same reason others eat potato chips. Dulse should be eaten in its dried form only, as fresh dulse is said to have the consistency of salted rubber bands. Commercial dulse is sun-dried, but some islanders—Leroy among them—like to cook fresh-from-the-sea dulse to a crackling crispiness on the stovetop. Dulse is also sold in powdered form as a condiment for soups, chowders and stews.

People of the Far East and Polynesia have long used marine algae as a staple, and the Hawaiians even cultivated royal marine gardens. The Icelandic sagas mention the eating of dulse as early as the 10th century, and it seems to have been a common foodstuff among coastal Europeans for centuries thereafter. The practice came to the southern part of North America with European settlement, and records show that dulse was being commercially harvested in Grand Manan in 1876. Forty years ago, Grand Manan supplied 75 percent of the North American market. It is still the prime producer, and each year, 34,000 kilograms of dried Grand Manan dulse are shipped to the mainland.

More and more, dulse is showing up on counters in health-food stores, because it is rich in potassium, chlorine and sodium and is a relatively good source of iron, magnesium and calcium, compared with terrestrial fruits and vegetables. Canada's Inuit recognized the dietary value of dulse, which by weight has 75 percent as much vitamin C as an orange. Dulse is 20 to 25 percent protein, comparing favourably with roast beef (25 percent) and canned salmon (20 percent). Fresh dulse is also a good source of vitamin A (in the form of the pigment carotene, which accounts for its auburn hue) and contains thiamine, riboflavin, niacin and pantothenic acid—the same substances virtuously listed on the packages of enriched breakfast cereals. Less than one gram of dulse supplies an adult's daily requirement of iodine. Dulse may have other medicinal qualities. In Ireland, where it is known as *dillisk*, dulse has a long-standing reputation as an effective vermifuge. This seems to be more than lore, as recent investigations carried out by the National Research Council's Atlantic Research Laboratory in Halifax detected an amino-acid constituent known to be a vermicidal agent. Although low in fats, dulse could serve as a commercial source of desmosterol, used in the synthesis of pharmacologically important steroids such as progesterone. More mundanely, dulse paste is used for body massages at a local Grand Manan spa.

Although humans have long found uses for dulse, its life history has been a mystery until recently. "For many years, phycologists were baffled by the apparent absence of females in this species," says Carolyn Bird. They therefore concluded that the plant had no sexual means of reproduction. However, Bird's colleagues at the Atlantic Research Laboratory exploded this myth when they discovered that female dulse plants were in fact microscopic. These little plantlets attain sexual maturity within days and are fertilized by the much older and larger male plants. The result of this union is that a new plant overgrows the female—obscuring it from scrutiny and masking the clandestine reproductive cycle between tiny females and giant, elderly males.

Dulse is considered an annual. The harvestable portion of the plant—the foot-long ruddy fronds that look like fingers, hence the scientific name *Palmaria palmata*—regenerates from a basal disc, the holdfast, which clings tenaciously to the rocks against the grinding forces of wind, tide and ice. During the dulsing season, dulse fronds can regenerate to a harvestable length within two weeks.

"I like the sound of dulse. I like that snap," Leroy says as another frond gives way just above the holdfast. Leroy's right arm is in a cast and sling, but he sets about picking with his good hand with the same unharnessed enthusiasm he has had for the task since he was 12 years old. "I like to pick dulse, and I have picked more dulse than anyone on this island."

I soon find myself acquiring a rhythm as handful after handful pulls away with ease. "Snap, snap." It is a contented, crisp sound. The dulse feels good too, slippery but not slimy, cool and comforting, as my fingers slide around another shiny bunch that has a surreal quality, like retouched ice cubes in a liquor advertisement. A good picker can gather enough dulse in a day to yield 45 kilograms after it is sun-dried on a field of beach stone. A 22-kilogram sack of wet dulse will yield 4.5 kilograms of finished product, for which Leroy pays $17.50. "If you've a mind to work, you can make pretty good money at it," Leroy says. But it is hard work—bent double, trying to keep your balance on the slippery rocks. The rhythm of the picking makes the two hours of dulse tide between the uncovering and covering of the dulse rocks pass quickly, though.

Leroy Flagg proudly shakes out a mittful of glistening Dark Harbour dulse, above. "This here is the only dulse in the world," he declares. Leroy has been dulsing since he was 12, and even now, as one of the island's biggest buyers and sellers of dulse, facing page, he enjoys a day on the rocks. "You can't fool me on the dulse," he says. "I know every rock and curve on the coast."

We load our half-dozen bags into the dory and slice our way back through the fog, feeling for the lagoon. On the way, we can hear the herring "running" along the shore. "Listen to those herring playin'. Hear that? It sounds like rainfall," Leroy says. He guides the dory in close to The Dream, where tiers of sardine-sized herring hang in the net twine, silver in the limpid light. He reaches up and plucks a handful from the twine mesh for his dinner. "They're lovely boiled with vinegar," he says. Nearby, the inquiring head of a harbour seal pops up above the waves. Like Leroy, it hopes to pick up a meal of herring from the weir-man's windfall.

At the seawall, we reverse the steps we took earlier that morning, winching the dory to the crest of the wall and sliding it down toward the lagoon. But before we do, we pause on the crest to survey the wreckage. Bone-coloured driftwood marks the storm-strewn remains of dulsers' shacks that used to perch precariously on this ridge above the waves. "The sea's got a lot of power. You come out here in the winter, and you wouldn't even know the seawall was there," Gerry observes.

Back at Leroy's house in Castalia, I watch the dulsers pick through their morning's harvest on sorting tables – removing barnacles and other extraneous material – then spread it on a field of beach stone covered with old fish netting. "This is one of the most beautiful drying grounds there ever was, right here," Leroy declares. "It's away from the water. Dark Harbour, you see, is all surrounded by water, so it's damp all the time."

If the fog lifts, the dulse can cure in a day. If it rains, the day's effort will be lost. "Rain just poisons the dulse," says Leroy.

Dark Harbour dulse, because it is thicker than that which comes from Cheney's Passage on the island's east side, takes longer to dry. But to Leroy, there are no shortcuts to producing high-quality dulse. First it must come from Dark Harbour, then it must dry properly under the Castalian sun. "I like to sell something good," he says.

Leroy's wife Angie, a silver-haired, energetic woman who has been listening to her husband with bemused interest, chimes in: "Ruined my dryer."

She explains that Leroy, losing patience with the Grand Manan weather, once experimented with drying dulse in her new clothes dryer, with dire consequences for the machine. "Yeah, but we got a half-pound of dried dulse," Leroy offers in his defence, closing his eyes and throwing his head back in laughter.

All this talk of dulse has given me a hankering for a taste. Angie disappears into the house and returns with a brown paper bag of the real thing: sun-dried Dark Harbour dulse. I reach in and tear off a piece, much as you might a plug of tobacco, and tuck it into my cheek. It dissolves, leaving a taste of the sea at the back of my throat.

Seabird Republic

"Next to the freedom of the open seas, the prime
fact of the seabird year is the island. Only the
island can give the seabird the refuge it needs
from a mainland teeming with enemies."

–Franklin Russell
"The Sea Has Wings"

The sound of a seabird colony is shrill aggression. Although the garbled vocalizations are a complicated discourse of defensive posturing, wooing and nurturing, the message to the interloper is clear enough: Keep away. It is this territorial declaration that filters through the woolly fog, off which the sound bounces like a ball against a wall, as we approach Machias Seal Island, two hours out of Seal Cove on Grand Manan Island at the mouth of the Bay of Fundy. I have been to Machias Seal once before, and like today, I heard it–the commingling cries of the breeding seabirds, the curling of breakers against its granite shores, the mulish foghorn–before I saw the red and white obelisk of the lighthouse with its bright eye on top revolving mystically in the suspended reality of grey fog, grey water and grey rock.

I note premonitory signs of the island's presence before it emerges from its fog shroud. An hour before, I saw the first

Speckled Arctic tern eggs,
above, rest in rudimentary nests
between outcroppings on Machias
Seal Island, where Arctic and common
terns, Atlantic puffins, razor-billed auks
and Leach's storm petrels breed each
spring. The island affords protection
from predators and access to rich
feeding grounds. An Atlantic puffin,
facing page, vigorously dries its wings
on its return to the island.

puffins, drifting in a turbulent upwelling where the tide had concentrated sea wrack. "Stemming an awful tide–28-footer, today," drawls Captain Preston Wilcox at the wheel of the *Seniorita*, a broad-beamed Cape Islander he uses to carry bird watchers like myself to the six-hectare islet. A while later, I see a puffin with a sardine-sized herring hanging limply like a silver moustache on either side of its parrot's beak. "Lot of feed off the ledges," observes Wilcox, a lantern-jawed man whose resonant baritone is famous in the churches of Grand Manan. "Lots of herring between here and Gannet Rock." The number of birds grows as we near the island. A flock of 15 terns hovers, with swallowtail feathers and sculpted, backswept wings spread out over the tide rips, before choosing the right moment to plunge into the bottle-green water; also, there are small rafts of puffins drifting with the tide as they rest between deep dives.

When we arrive, there is already another

boatload of bird watchers on the island. Anchored nearby is Barna Norton's new boat, *Chief*, its gleaming white hull and chrome rails dazzlingly bright in the fog-fractured light. "She's a beauty," allows Wilcox. "Of course, she's built just for this." For 20 years now, Norton, of Lubec, Maine, and Wilcox, of Seal Cove, New Brunswick, have been prime competitors in the lucrative enterprise of bringing bird watchers to this lonely island. Machias Seal Island is located 20 kilometres from Grand Manan and 16 kilometres from the Maine coast, in an area where the international marine boundary remains undrawn.

The island presents a unique opportunity for naturalists, as it is situated close to populous centres on the Eastern Seaboard and yet allows for close-up observation of a number of seabird species, including the Arctic and common terns, the common puffin, Leach's storm petrel and the razor-billed auk. Although Machias Seal Island

has been a migratory-bird sanctuary under the protection of the Canadian Wildlife Service (CWS) since 1944, people from both sides of the border traditionally came and went at will. However, human disturbance became a concern when tern populations declined precipitously at the same time as visitors to the island dramatically increased.

As a result, in 1985, the CWS decided to limit the number of daily visitors to 25 people. It was an unpopular and unworkable regulation for Wilcox. Because he had a slower boat and farther to go, he sometimes arrived at the island to find that the quota had been filled by American charter captains. Wilcox's Canadian customers were understandably unhappy when they found they couldn't go ashore. "I mean that was a hard thing for Canadians to take, not just me," Wilcox explained to me. "I mean it's their tax money as well as mine. It's been a Canadian island for 100 years and their island, and they can't land. They were say-

ing some pretty hostile things." Wilcox had to refund their money and go back to Seal Cove. Added to his financial loss was insult, for Wilcox had run the supply boat to the island's lighthouse twice a month for 21 years. The first-come, first-served system has since been revised by agreement among the charter captains to allow Wilcox to land 13 people a day, five days a week, but for Wilcox, the bitterness lingers.

Rather than go ashore immediately, I accept an offer from Preston's son Peter to row around the island in the punt we have towed behind the *Seniorita*. "It's hard to convince people that they'll see just as much if they go on the back of the island," says Peter, as he leans into the oars. For some bird watchers, this trip around the island might be satisfaction enough. For most, however, the snapshot has become the 20th-century tourist relic of their pilgrimage. They come to the island with cameras hanging about their necks to capture a souvenir – proof they were here – and to do that, they feel they must land.

"I love the ocean," Peter offers by way of explaining what he is doing here. He has a degree in education, but he left his mainland teaching job in Fredericton to return to his island birthright. By the way he negotiates the punt through the treacherous and confusing tidal rips that coil around the island, I can see he is a man born to the water.

The strong advance of the tide actually creates the illusion that we are rowing uphill. Peter pulls hard, and we round the point to the north side of the island, where a wall of smooth granite boulders forms a natural breakwater. Aligned on this sea fortress are the resident members of the auk family, both puffins and the larger and rarer razorbills. Peter spies a small group of razorbills inshore and ships the oars so that we can drift in close to them. These normally skittish birds, diminutive relatives of the extinct great auk, appear undisturbed by our presence, perhaps because the means of our approach seems to say to them, "We are something of the sea."

A razorbill soundlessly dips below the surface, and I marvel at its ability to fly underwater. Its wings rotate feverishly, like the whirring wings of whirligigs, as it sounds deeper until the black and white beating of the wings disappears into the green murk below. Recent research indicates that murres (close cousins of the larger razorbills) can make remarkable dives of 90 metres. No one knows how they find their prey in the lightless depths. Seeing these underwater fliers in action stamps in my mind the truth of the obvious: these are seabirds, marvellously adapted to the ocean's environment and congenitally out of place on land, to which they are obliged to go only during that hiatus of the breeding cycle. I realize as well that being on the water with the birds, in their element, is an experience unrepeatable on land, where their instincts make them irritable and aggressive to everything around them. It is this feeling

of oneness that the camera toter might well value more than a static close-up photograph of a bird perched on a rock.

I look up from where the razor-billed auk has disappeared, startled to see the downy corpse of a tern chick floating by. An adult tern hovers over the lifeless form, screeching what I interpret as a parental lament. It is only a matter of time before one of the great black-backed gulls congregated at the tip of the island, from which they make their predatory raids on tern nests, spots

Razor-billed auks preside over their guano-stained domain, facing page. Machias Seal Island is the most southerly breeding colony of this relative of the extinct great auk. Preston Wilcox rows a dory load of bird watchers ashore, above. Machias Seal presents a rare opportunity for naturalists to study a seabird breeding island. But human disturbance is an increasing concern.

the body and swoops down for the spoils.

The drama of the seabird's year comes to a climax on the breeding island. The Arctic terns travel the greatest distance, from as far south as the Antarctic ice cap, a round trip of nearly 30,000 kilometres. They arrive, predictably, on or about May 17 and circle the island in high-flying flocks. After several days of this type of social flight, they finally alight on the island to begin their breeding cycle. The puffins are the first to arrive in the chill waters off Machias Seal in late April. They have survived the winter months hundreds of kilometres offshore in the North Atlantic. Puffins spend this time individually or in small groups and only come together as a "seabird nation" for the purpose of breeding. The puffins do not immediately come ashore on their arrival at the breeding grounds but will wait for a foggy or rainy night before making their landward immigration en masse. Female puffins lay a single egg in simple nests secreted in burrows dug into the soft turf or improvised from the spaces under the granite boulders. The chicks hatch in mid-

June and are fed by their parents until the end of July, when they are abandoned. Again, under the cover of night to avoid predation by the ever watchful gulls, a new generation of puffins migrates back to the sea to renew the cycle. In good years, much life is renewed, but death in its many incarnations—starvation, foul weather, natural predators or careless humans—takes its toll while the seabirds are on the island.

We round the eastern tip of the island, and Peter pulls for the rusty slipway where I will disembark for my overnight stay. It is to be my rare privilege, granted by the CWS, to be with the breeding birds and the keepers of the light until the *Seniorita* returns tomorrow.

I step ashore onto a six-hectare crescent of granite, which rises a maximum of 8.5 metres above the turbulent waters of the outer Bay of Fundy. It is surprising, after only two hours on the water, how unfamiliar the earth feels under me. My unsteadiness is abetted by slippery footing on the sea-washed ramp. Immediately, a rapid-fire "che-che, che-che" turns my attention from the ground to the sky. I look up cautiously to see the back-lit swallow-tailed whiteness of an Arctic tern suspended elegantly but aggressively above me.

As I make my way along the boardwalks

toward the CWS residence, I feign ignorance of the parrying attacks of the terns, which seem to come out of nowhere in the atomized atmosphere of fog and sea air. Joe Kennedy, a CWS summer student, welcomes me at one of the three bungalows that once served as a lighthouse keeper's home. As the first order of business, I inquire about the rules of the island. "The only thing I tell people," he says, "is to watch where they walk, there are chicks everywhere."

It soon proves good advice. As I retrace my steps across the central, mowed portion of the island, around which the lighthouse, houses and outbuildings are grouped, a buff, spotted ball of down—a tern chick—hobbles under the protective covering of the walk.

Straight ahead, a queue of puffins lines the roof ridge of the shed that houses the diesel generator. I take one of the side paths leading through chest-high grass to a blind. I have the four-by-eight plywood structure to myself, now that the boatloads of visitors have shoved off. Through one of the six sliding observation windows, I look out to sea over the jumble of guano-stained boulders that constitutes the site of the puffin colony. Not four metres away are 50 or more puffins, assuming myriad deadpan poses.

It is not an idle claim to say that there is probably no better place in North America to observe puffins at close range than on Machias Seal Island. And most visitors come to Machias Seal for the express purpose of seeing this fellow, whom Franklin Russell once called "an evolutionary joke whose humour reaches the most dedicated bird hater." Although it is frowned upon in nature-writing circles these days, it is nearly impossible not to submit to anthropomorphism when trying to find words for the puffin. To me, this does not seem so unnatural, or undesirable, for the alternative is to be clinically descriptive. If metaphor is adopted to describe the effect of the puffin on your perception, without assuming it is descriptive of the true nature of the bird, no harm is done.

The white face patch, the theatrical eye markings and the exaggerated parrot's beak, so like a nose, combine to produce an illusion: when you look at a puffin's head, what you see, in fact, is a *face*, with all the expressive qualities that word implies. For myself, I see the tragicomic expression of Pierrot. This particular puffin persona is strengthened by the dapper little auk's costume of black back and pure white bib and underbelly.

The puffin pantomime is not exactly mute, though. In my notebook, I make the observation that the murmurings of the puffin colony are like the whirring of a chain saw. Later I discovered that this observation was not original. On his first visit to Machias Seal, Les Line, the editor of *Audubon*, came to the same conclusion. He, too, heard "chain saws" on the utterly treeless island. Puffin authority R.M. Lockley might well take issue with this metaphor, however; he characterizes the mechanical-sounding utterances of the puffins as "Aar-ha-ha!"

If I allow that puffins laugh, then the joke must be on me, the observer. After 15 minutes in the blind, I begin to have the feeling that it is I, not the puffins, under scrutiny. As I have remained quietly ensconced in the blind, the puffins have become less and less suspicious of my presence and now have begun to approach the window, hopping uncertainly from boulder to boulder and all the while beating their wings ineffectually. A small group is so close now that I can see one member is sequined with herring scales. I am literally surrounded by puffins, for I can hear the scratchings of their vermilion feet on the roof and have become aware that there must be a nesting burrow under the blind. After an hour, one puffin approaches within a metre of the blind, cocking its wedge-shaped head quizzically, first to one side then the other, as if pondering what kind of odd species I might be.

While this puffin has time to investigate its surroundings, others are busily feeding chicks. A puffin with a burrow close by comes in for a landing with still-twitching herring in its outrageously decorative beak. Anyone who has had the displeasure, as I have, of reaching into a puffin burrow and having its occupant latch onto his or her hand will know what a powerful tool is the puffin beak. It is also remarkably well designed for its job of carrying prey—as many as a dozen sardines at once. Although the mystery of this feat has never been fully uncovered, one theory is that the puffin catches its prey with the beak's sharp point, then uses its tongue to convey the fishes to the back of its mouth, where they are held in place by backward-pointing serrations—all this while the puffin "flies" many fathoms underwater.

The puffins' on-land histrionics are much less impressive. So ill-suited are their short legs to propelling and balancing their plump torsos and oversize heads that puffins appear to be walking on marbles, the loose earth about to slide out from underneath them. By comparison, the aloof razor-billed auks appear self-possessed. Perched atop the yellow lichen-encrusted boulders, they show a dignified posture accented by formal black colouring with only a hint of white on the beak and wings,

making them seem judgemental of the antics of the puffin colony.

After an hour, I, too, tire of puffin watching and become restless, anxious to move outside the confines of the blind. As I leave its protective shell, I am met almost immediately by an aggressive greeting party of Arctic terns. Their coral beaks fling a steady stream of imprecations on my head. In sharp contrast to the passive curiosity of the benign puffins, the terns' sole thought is to repel, to drive you off their island.

Brit (young herring) hang like a limp silver moustache from a puffin's outsize and outrageously coloured "parrot's beak," facing page. The beak can accommodate a dozen or more small fish, which the puffin catches while "flying" underwater. A downy tern chick, above, runs for cover in a rock crevice. Island visitors are warned to watch for chicks underfoot, and access to nesting areas is restricted.

For better or worse, humans have lived on Machias Seal Island since 1831, when the first of four lighthouses was installed. The island has also been the frequent destination of naturalists, including those of a literary bent such as Frank Graham and Franklin Russell. One of the earliest accounts is that of Frank Brown, who chronicled his visit to the island in 1911 for the Audubon Society's magazine Bird-Lore: "A yacht, now and again, lost in the fog offshore, a stray fisherman from the local coast and the launch which brings the mail and supplies, each two weeks in summer and monthly in winter, comprise about all the visitors to these distant islands.

"Their greatest interest, however, is the abundant bird life that fairly teems there from April to October or November of each year."

People still come to Machias Seal to satisfy that ornithological interest, but ironically, they do so in such numbers now as to imperil the very bird life they so cherish. The puffins, at 900 pairs, and the rare razor-billed auks, at 50 pairs, have shown a slight increase in numbers during the past 100 years, even though on Machias Seal Island, both of these alcids are at the southern limit of their breeding ranges. However, the number of breeding pairs of Arctic terns declined dramatically to a low of 1,400 by the early 1980s, compared with a peak of 3,500 pairs 30 years before.

On my first visit to the island in 1985, I spoke with the CWS warden-caretaker Steven Daniel, who was then finishing his thesis on human disturbance of the terns. Having divided the island into a grid system, he observed from the lighthouse tower the effect on the birds as people passed through the nesting plots.

"What you see are the Arctic terns defending their territory, leaving the young exposed. When there are no people on the island, one parent stays with the chick while the other parent is feeding. So even under adverse weather conditions, the chick will still be fed, and it needs a fair amount of

energy to survive. But when people come ashore, the system of parental care breaks down. Both adults will start defending their territory to get the intruder out, human or not—if it moves, it's an intruder. And when this happens, the whole system of protection and feeding breaks down. So the chick is exposed."

The first two weeks of life are the most critical in the young bird's life. It has not yet established a thermoregulatory system and so is vulnerable to the less-than-equable marine climate. When the parents take wing to defend the nest, the chicks often run into the wet grass for protection, where they get chilled, become hypothermic and go into shock.

"So when the adult comes back, even after the people have passed—let's say they've stayed in the quadrant for five minutes—that's a long enough time for these chicks to become cold and stop begging for food because they just go into a torpor."

The vicissitudes of maritime climate often exacerbate the effects of human disturbance. Machias Seal Island is regularly bat-tered by a summer rainstorm at the end of June, when the week-old tern hatchlings are most vulnerable. When people come ashore during such periods, the results for the tern colony can be catastrophic. One year under such circumstances, Daniel collected 263 dead chicks; the following year, when no visitors came ashore, he found only six dead chicks, even though there had been an even more severe summer storm at that time.

Such statistics make a very prejudicial case against visitors to the island, at least during the critical first two weeks of life for the terns. But CWS biologists acknowledge that food supply, weather and gull predation are other important factors affecting the tern population. Overfishing of Fundy herring stocks in the late 1960s and early 1970s may have contributed to the tern decline; during periods when small herring, or brit, were not available, the terns often brought to their young the roundish dollar fish, which is hard for the nestlings to swallow. CWS biologists are faced with the knowledge that they can control only two of the above factors: gull predation, which is being addressed, and human disturbance, which is now minimized by the current regulations.

Critics of the policy to limit visitors point to the fact that people have coexisted with the birds since the first lighthouse was installed. However, history tells us that it has not always been a beneficial relationship for the breeding seabirds. In 1886-1887, people decimated Gulf of Maine terneries for their feathers, then fashionable in millinery. It is not known whether such harvests reached Machias Seal, but a reduced regional population would have had a negative effect on the island population. A change in fashion and a bill passed by the Maine legislature to protect terns brought an end to the wholesale destruction. Although the mainland threat was staunched, island malevolence toward the birds flourished at that time. The keepers of the lighthouse disliked the puffins and other birds nesting on the island and, according to one report, "shot every bird [they] saw."

Captain Harvey Benson, who became head lightkeeper in 1944, seems to have been much more sympathetic toward the breeding seabirds and took a keen interest in their behaviour and welfare. On one occasion, when a marauding duck hawk, one of the tern's few natural predators, prevented the terns from landing, Benson shot the falcon. Gull predation on the young has been a perennial problem. In 1944, CWS ornithologist Robie Tufts observed that no young were raised and the terns left in midsummer. He attributed the failure to gull predation and recommended that the island be made a migratory-bird sanctuary.

Domestic animals and pets have also exacted a toll over the years. In 1944, there were as many as 40 sheep on the island. They wreaked havoc on grassy areas, the terns' traditional nesting ground.

Human predators have been a factor in the population biology of the terns as well. The traditional practice of egging by lighthouse keepers and parties of eggers from Grand Manan Island has been a persistent threat to the breeding terns. Oscar Hawksley, who studied the ecology of the Machias Seal Island terns in the late 1940s, reported: "Egging has been conducted on Machias Seal Island for years in spite of the fact that it is a sanctuary. . . . The local 'rule' is that eggs may be collected until clutches of two are found. This simple rule is enforced by the condition of the eggs after that, so egging lasts for only about a week in the first part of June.

"I doubt that any harm comes from this early egging," he concluded. "If anything, it might tend to make the time of hatching come a bit later, and thus young chicks would be less likely to die in storms which seem to be frequent in late June and early July. At least, the Machias Seal Island colony has flourished in spite of egging."

Many local islanders still adhere to this view. Among them is Jack Russell, who was

lighthouse keeper from 1965 to 1975. According to Franklin Russell in his book *The Sea Has Wings*, Jack Russell was "a new breed of lighthouse keeper . . . a protector and observer and recorder of tern and puffin, and so has helped to make the tern world safer." Russell seems to have been the first keeper to limit the areas where visitors to the island could go before any formal regulations were enacted.

At the same time, he defends egging: "People from Grand Manan used to go down to Seal Island and pick the terns' eggs. Six eggs equals one hen's egg, and they was good for custard. And they used to go down there for a picnic until the first day of June, and there was no law. They just automatically leave off. And the terns keep on laying. After the first of June, they lay their eggs, and they would hatch out [after 22 days' incubation] in nice warm weather, and they'd all fly. But now as soon as the terns arrive, it's cold and foggy, and

they build their nests and lay their eggs, and it's so wet and cold, they [the chicks] die of pneumonia."

I was surprised to hear Russell espouse this traditionalist viewpoint. The question of egging is at best a moot one. Gull predation, human disturbance and wet weather all combine to cause chick mortality. And certainly, there are no guarantees of good

An elegant but aggressive Arctic tern, facing page, swoops low over its grassy nesting ground, which it defends by dive-bombing intruders. A Canadian flag proclaims Canada's sovereignty of Machias Seal Island, above, though the United States also lays claim to the island. Canada has maintained a light on the island since 1832 and made it a migratory-bird sanctuary in 1944.

weather in July. When I was on the island in mid-July, there were fledging tern chicks, downy chicks and unhatched eggs. A thick blanket of fog had also been thrown over the island for two weeks, and the lighthouse keepers were overstayed on their tour of duty by six days because it had been impossible for the helicopter to land in the zero visibility. The foghorn had been their constant companion.

The presence of lighthouse keepers on the island provided continuity to the Canadian claim of sovereignty. Canada's claim to the island is based largely on the fact that it has maintained a lighthouse there since 1832; the United States' claim is based on an interpretation of the 1783 Treaty of Paris. Plans to automate the island's lighthouse in the early 1970s were abandoned when a dispute regarding ownership flared up because of confrontations between Canadian and American fishermen over lobster grounds around the island. Traditionally, there were two families on the island to keep each other company, but now, the keepers must leave their families ashore. The personal price of national sovereignty is loneliness.

On my first trip out to Machias Seal, I talked with then lighthouse keeper 27-year-old Brian Cossaboom and his 22-year-old wife Susan. They were returning to their post after a two-week vacation on their home island of Grand Manan. The young couple had taken the position to save money to build a home. Of their three years in isolation, Brian said: "It's kind of nice for the first year and a half. There's no one to bother you, neighbours dropping in or the phone ringing. But after that . . ."

"It gets pretty lonesome," Susan finished her husband's thought. It was August then, and I couldn't help noticing her pensiveness at the prospect of being on the island until Christmas. The previous Christmas, the helicopter had brought them a small artificial Christmas tree—a natural tree was too large to carry. The other couple had left the island in November, and after that, they had been alone.

Time passes slowly on this fogbound hunk of granite. Today, I find veteran keeper Allan Stuart busy at his newfound hobby of engraving pictures with an electric needle. His companion on this stint is Darrell Hussey, who worked at the Letite Central Monitoring Station, which monitors the lighthouses in the outer Bay of Fundy region. He is visiting each lighthouse in turn to familiarize himself with its workings—and with its signal. By now, the Machias Seal signal of 3 blows, 3 seconds' silence, 3 blows and 51 seconds' silence blaring to the grey world around the island once every minute has become maddeningly familiar. The round of maintenance duties—painting, lawn mowing and checking on the diesel engines—lessens the tedium. But during the breeding season, the keepers are unable to take a leisurely walk on the island because of the constant aggression of the terns, which on occasion draw blood when vigor-

ously defending their territory. Hung inside the door of the lightkeeper's residence, I find what they call the mowing hat: a fluorescent orange hard hat with a coat hanger attached like a radio antenna. On top of the hanger is a tiny Canadian flag, which serves as a decoy for the attacking terns. For me, it serves as an ironic reminder of whose island this really is.

In the evening, the four of us get together for supper and a game of pool. As I return to the CWS residence to bed down, I linger in the dark hoping to hear or see, in the lighthouse beacon, Leach's storm petrels returning from their day at sea. On the water, these swallow-sized, dark, graceful birds, known to sailors as Mother Carey's chickens, literally seem to dance across the ocean waves as they garner oil-rich crustaceans. They return to land only at night to attend to a single chick. As I stand in the salt-charged dark, I remember the evening, a year before, when I was on Baccalieu Island, off Newfoundland's northeast coast. There I had witnessed the spectacle of this mass landward immigration on a grand scale. The chirring of the little birds enlivened the air as they swooped around my head like bats and swirled around the lighthouse like moths about a lantern. Several even blundered into the lighthouse keeper's kitchen through an open window and were gently retrieved by the dog for release unharmed. But on Baccalieu, the petrels number in the several millions, ranking it as

A congress of puffins, facing page, strikes deadpan poses and engages in histrionics, while the razorbills remain aloof, their gaze directed toward the sea, their natural element. The Canadian Wildlife Service has undertaken several measures to protect the welfare of the seabird nations that frequent Machias Seal, including restricting visitors to 25 people daily.

the world's largest colony, whereas on Machias Seal, there were only 57 active nesting burrows at last count. This represents a drastic decrease in the size of the population from the early years of the century, when Brown reported that "the air seemed fairly alive with them . . . [and] in walking over the grassland of the island, it is almost impossible in many places to step without treading into the entrances of the burrows of the petrels." Pets and the spring grass burning carried out by lighthouse keepers in the past had decimated the petrels. On this evening, there are none in sight, nor can I detect their high-pitched staccato clicking in the dark, between the interminable blasts from the foghorn.

In the morning, I arrange to meet with Barna Norton of Lubec, Maine. His son John rows ashore to pick me up at the tramway, greeting me with the chiding, if erroneous, epithet: "Another bureaucrat?" With his gold earring and long hair, John Norton looks the piratical part often attributed to his father. The Nortons have a family tradition of single-handedly defending the island in the name of the United States. Legend has it that Barna's great-grandfather, Tall Barney Beal, once fended off a dozen Grand Manan fishermen with a boat oar. Norton himself has been characterized in the press as an obstreperous, swashbuckling character, so I am surprised to meet a frail-looking man in his seventies who speaks with a soft Yankee drawl.

In the past, Norton has claimed that the supply helicopter has caused tern deaths and that CWS biologists have literally studied the birds to death. On a number of occasions, he has defied regulations forbidding him to land on the north side of the island. His passengers, to their own dismay, have had to walk through the midst of the tern colony.

At all times, Norton carries with him a letter from the U.S. State Department claiming that the island "is part of the U.S. and has been since the founding of the Republic" and that he has every right to ignore the regulations set by the Canadian authorities. Norton's flagrant disregard for those regulations has won him little sympathy from naturalists and scientists, even in his own country. William Drury, for one, a tern biologist at the College of the Atlantic in Bar Harbor, Maine, has spoken out in support of his colleagues in the CWS, who, he says, "are clearly acting in the best interests of the seabirds."

It seemed that Norton had taken some of the criticism to heart, for I find him more conciliatory than I expected on the issue of his claim to the island. "The primary thing," he tells me, "is we have to protect the birds, and whom am I going to turn to to protect the birds but the Canadian Wildlife Service? It's as simple as that. If I claim the island, whom am I going to hire and pay to stay on the island and take care of the birds?"

I go ashore again to bid good-bye to the keepers and my CWS host. As I await the return of the *Seniorita*, I contemplate the long-standing sovereignty dispute, which seems no closer to resolution now than it ever has been. Neither country appears willing to make the investment required to secure its claim.

When I disembarked on the island 24 hours before, I met a couple from Iowa. We fell into a conversation that turned from birds to sovereignty. "I'm sure the birds don't care," observed the woman. "Wouldn't it be nice if neither side cared? Then the birds would be free."

I agree with her sentiment, but a human presence seems critical to maintaining the island for the good of the birds. The freedom once afforded by the isolation of the island has been lost forever. The best that can be done now is to try to maintain conditions on the island that resemble its natural state as closely as possible. The Canadian Wildlife Service has recognized the importance of stopping the decline of the Arctic terns, the natural police force of the island. In fact, Arctic tern numbers have rebounded to 1,800 pairs in recent years, making it the largest colony of Arctics in

eastern North America. Ultimately, the terns will help to protect the more passive, phlegmatic puffins and razorbills from gull predation and human ignorance.

The management of the island for the benefit of the birds is a balancing act between allowing access for education and limiting access in accordance with conservation. By being with the birds, naturalists or naturalists-to-be are brought into contact with one of nature's most vital places: the seabird island. It is hoped that this contact will translate into an urge to protect the sea-

birds and the vital nexus of their existence. The fundamental lesson to be learned from this fleeting contact is just how sensitive to disturbance a breeding colony is. After all, that is what the shrill terns are trying to tell us, wheeling and parrying about our heads. We must realize that as terrestrial creatures on this seabird island, we are the enemy—difficult as that may be to accept. At the very least, such a revelation should engender deference to our hosts. In time, we may even choose to view their world from a more polite distance.

Right's Last Refuge

"But still another inquiry remains . . .
whether Leviathan can long endure so wide a
chase, and so remorseless a havoc; whether he
must not at last be exterminated from the waters,
and the last whale, like the last man, smoke his last
pipe, and then himself evaporate in the final puff."

—Herman Melville, "Moby-Dick"

On a morning only September could manufacture—clear, hard light, the pastels of sunrise dappling the water with pointillist precision—we depart the harbour at Ingall's Head on Grand Manan Island under the watchful eye of a bald eagle perched on a nearby islet. Our intention is to rendezvous with the rarest of the great whales that frequent these waters from late July until October. We do seemingly endless transects—spying seabirds, porpoises and finback whales as we crisscross the waters —for six hours before the unmistakable head of a North Atlantic right whale finally breaks the blue waves like a sea-worn, barnacle-festooned boulder.

The whale announces itself with a diffuse, sputtering jet of vapour, expelled from its two blowholes in a tell-tale V shape. It moves forward ponderously, parting the waves, the arch of its great jaws bowed above the surface like the handles of a plough. Soon, another adult surfaces

A humpback whale sends flukes up, above, as it prepares to dive. The great whales, in particular the North Atlantic right whale, were hunted nearly to extinction. Just over 50 years ago, the rights were offered protection. A surface-active group of right whales, facing page, engage in sexual activity, providing hope that this severely depleted population of 300 individuals might yet recover.

nearby, and the ship's two-way radio relays the message that there is a mother and calf alongside the schooner belonging to Ocean Search—the whale-watching arm of the Grand Manan Whale and Seabird Research Station—whose white sail shows like the wing of a great bird on the horizon more than a kilometre away. I make a quick calculation and realize that here, in these four animals, is nearly 2 percent of the population of the world's most endangered cetacean.

More than any other cetacean in the Bay of Fundy, the right whale conforms to the mental image of what a whale should be. Its great head fuses imperceptibly with its bulging body, so it has none of the streamlined grace of the finback, for instance, that greyhound of the sea; nor does it have the knobby appearance of the humpback. Its sheer bulk bespeaks "whaleness." The smiling arch of its jaw hung with fringes of two-metre-long baleen completes the picture of a whale that a child might con-

ceive: fat and friendly, bobbing and spouting at the surface.

As I stand watching the whales' slow progress, there is a spate of activity behind me on the deck of the 35-foot Cape Islander. The tagging crew—Jeff Goodyear and Kaaren Lewis—are getting ready to go over the side in a Zodiac and a kayak, in pursuit of the whales. Goodyear loads two crossbows with feathered arrows tipped with radio tags. One of the tags has a suction cup on its business end; the other is an invasive tag that will actually lodge in the thick skin of the whale. The Zodiac is outfitted with a ready-made platform that will serve as a "harpooner's nest" to allow Goodyear the necessary elevated angle from which to fire his tags. He is one of the few people to tag whales successfully, although this is only his second effort to affix a tag to the fat back of a right whale (the first ended with the suction tag falling off after an hour). Right whales were the target of deadly harpoons for centuries. Now they are on the receiving end of the more blunt and innocuous instruments of science in a last-ditch effort to save them. The tags, if they hold, will help to track the movements of the right whales in the Bay, and an on-board computer will record the amount of time the whale spends submerged and at the sur-

face. Such data about the behaviour of right whales could be important to their survival in an area where marine traffic is a constant threat.

With this knowledge, I put aside my ambivalence and help lower the light pursuit craft into the Bay. As I return to the opposite side of the boat to check on the whales' whereabouts, the great barnacled heads submerge one after the other and, in apparent slow motion, the thick black stocks of the tails send flukes up. The smooth, jet-black flukes arch 90 degrees, point straight up, then sink, leaving behind a slick area on the surface that whale watchers refer to as "the footprint"—an ephemeral afterimage of the whales' presence.

Whale watchers on the Ocean Search schooner, above, encounter a pair of North Atlantic right whales engaged in courtship. Right whale mothers bring their calves to the Grand Manan Basin where food—copepods—is abundant and there are few predators. Tourists also come to Grand Manan to enjoy the scenery, like the smokehouses on stilts above the tide at Seal Cove, facing page.

The North Atlantic right whale was twice thought to have disappeared entirely, hunted to extinction—once in the early 1700s and again in the 1850s. Today, it ranks as the most endangered cetacean in the world and is the only great whale still threatened by extinction. Right whales were first reported in the Bay of Fundy in the 1960s by passengers aboard the ferry *Bluenose*, which plies regularly between Yarmouth, Nova Scotia, and Bar Harbor, Maine. However, the reports were rejected by a skeptical scientific community. Then in 1971, a team of scientists from the University of Guelph, Ontario, under the direction of Dr. David Gaskin, sighted several right whales in Passamaquoddy Bay, where they were conducting an ecological study of the harbour porpoise. Gaskin, who subsequently founded the Grand Manan Whale and Seabird Research Station, recorded the encounter:

"On August 22, 1971, we sighted a large whale which brought its flukes clear of the water when diving deeply. This was subsequently identified as a right whale by its strongly arched jaw with characteristic 'bonnet' of lightened, rough, epidermal outgrowths, V-shaped spout, absence of dorsal fin, and distinctive tapered flukes with smooth posterior margin."

A few days later, they observed a lone right whale breaching, and a week after their first encounter, they saw five more right whales near Deer Island, one of them a calf that appeared to be nursing. In 1980, scientists from the New England Aquarium, while doing aerial surveys for an environmental-impact study related to the Pittston Oil Company's proposed Eastport refinery, spotted 26 right whales in the lower Bay, including four cow-calf pairs.

Whale watching has since become a prime tourist attraction in Grand Manan—tourism being the island's main industry after fishing. Since the time of John James Audubon (who sketched here), the island has been a hot spot for birders, who have listed no fewer than 275 species. Similarly, painters and photographers have found their sought-after subjects in its steep sea-walls, spruce-clad capes, smokehouses built on stilts above the tide and its fog-wrapped, heart-shaped weirs. Willa Cather wrote novels here in artistic hermitage, but most people simply come for slow days of idle solitude on the many beaches or along wooded trails that thread the interior. For Grand Mananers themselves, their island home of prosperous, placid little villages curving with mathematical neatness around busy harbours is as much a place of refuge from mainland concerns as it is for a first-time visitor.

I had seen my first right whale aboard an Ocean Search whale-watching vessel in 1985, near the Bulkhead Rips, a tidal river within the sea where currents and marine life converge. On that occasion, a six-metre calf had repeatedly passed under the vessel, displaying a disarming curiosity; and later, we watched as a group of four whales splashed about on the surface in a sensual mating game, rolling and nudging their glistening black, 50-tonne bodies.

The presence of right whale calves and obvious frequent sexual activity among the adult mammals in the Bay of Fundy revised upward the fortunes of the right whale since it was protected from hunting in 1937. Until then, it had been the most harassed of the great whales—it got its name by being the "right whale" to kill. Whalers working from small boats could overtake the slow-moving whale, which travels at a maximum of five knots. Its uncommonly thick layer of blubber yielded great volumes of oil, and its generous supply of baleen (or whale-bone) was highly prized for corset stays, umbrella ribs, riding crops and clock springs. And conveniently, it floated when killed. Its preference for inshore habitat for breeding and rearing its young made it particularly vulnerable to primitive shore-based whaling operations. The Basques were the first to hunt it from small boats in the Bay of Biscay beginning in the 10th century. By the 16th century, the northeastern

Atlantic population had been destroyed, and the seafaring Basques switched their attention to the northwestern Atlantic, where they had ventured at first in search of cod. Archaeologist James Tuck of Memorial University of Newfoundland, in St. John's, has excavated one of North America's first industrial complexes—a Basque whaling station at Red Bay, Labrador. Such shore-based whaling stations were strung along the Strait of Belle Isle to intercept the right and bowhead whales that once migrated through this passage. In the last four decades of the 16th century, the Basques probably killed 40,000 whales, thus extirpating the local population.

I well remember my sense of desolation as I stood amidst a great collection of right whale bones warehoused at Red Bay. The pattern of wholesale slaughter of the whale was repeated elsewhere as the Eastern Seaboard of North America was settled. Subsequently, the Pacific right whale populations were completely decimated. Wherever right whales were found, they were relentlessly pursued, to the point

where recovery of the species in the 20th century, despite a total ban on hunting for the past 53 years, remains in serious doubt.

Unfortunately, because the animal became rare before it had been much studied, scientists know a lot less about its life history than they would like to. Dr. Roger Payne of the New York Zoological Society was, until recently, one of the few zoologists to have made long-term observations of the right whale. For several years, he returned to the Golfo San José off the coast of Patagonia, where each winter, the southern right whales (which number 1,500) go to mate, calve and rear their young. Payne remarked on the peacefulness of the right whale, which rarely engaged in any aggressive behaviour toward its own kind, even among males vying for the favours of a female. He delighted in the apparent playfulness of his mammalian companions. When the wind was up, they appeared to sail, using their tails. He also speculated that right whales used their tails to communicate during storms, when the underwater noise interfered with their low-frequency "voices,"

less flatteringly referred to as belches. On such occasions, they smacked the water repeatedly, a behaviour known as "lobtailing," or they would hurl their bodies free of the water in a dramatic effort, Payne felt, to show other whales where they were.

Right whales have a unique physical characteristic: thickened portions of skin called callosities. Payne noted that hair follicles were present in the callosities and that this facial hair grew in the same places as it does on humans, so the whales appeared to have "moustaches, as well as eyebrows, beards and even sideburns." Cyamids, or whale lice, inhabit the callosities, feeding off sloughed bits of whale skin and food spilled from the right whale's baleen plates, which act like a leaky sieve. The parasitic cyamids are thought to be responsible for the yellowish waxy appearance of the callosities. Barnacles also attach themselves to the protrusions, adding to their abrasiveness. The most prominent of the callosities is

found on top of the whale's head and was called a bonnet by early whalers. The function of the thickened skin is unknown. One early natural historian recounted a story in which a tormented right whale stove in a boat with its head, suggesting to him that it uses its bonnet in the same way a rhinoceros does its horn. Payne acknowledged that, on occasion, a whale might use the callosities in aggressive situations to rub up against a competitor's flanks. But he suggested a much more utilitarian function, speculating that they may act as a splash guard to prevent water from entering the whale's blowhole. Whatever function the callosities serve for the whales themselves, they have proven an indispensable diagnostic tool for people studying them. Every whale exhibits a unique pattern of callosities that forms "islands" and "peninsulas," thus allowing for clear identification of individuals.

Much of what we now know about the life

history of the western Atlantic population has been learned from photo-identification work spearheaded by the New England Aquarium. Photo-ID tags have made it possible to monitor the movements of individuals. In February and March of 1984, Scott Kraus of the New England Aquarium sighted 15 right whales in a coastal area extending from Savannah, Georgia, to Key Largo, Florida, including four cows with newborn calves. Each of these cows had been seen the previous summer in the Bay of Fundy, and two of the other adults were seen later in the North Atlantic on the Scotian Shelf, near Brown's and Baccaro banks, indicating that right whales observed at various locations in Canadian and U.S. waters form a single stock.

It now appears that the coastal area of the southeastern United States is a major calving ground. In spring, the right whales make a 2,900-kilometre seasonal migration northward, during which they stop off at traditional feeding areas along the coast. An average of 35 whales gather in Cape Cod Bay in late March and April; a similar number, including some cow-calf pairs, are seen in the Great South Channel, between Cape Cod and Georges Bank, in May. By mid- to late June, the whales begin to show up in the lower Bay of Fundy and on the southern Scotian Shelf, where they spend the summer laying on fat. By mid-October, the whales move out of these northernmost habitats, the pregnant females returning to the waters off the southeastern United States to bear their calves and the others dispersing over the continental shelf.

Still, there are many fundamental gaps in our knowledge of the right whale's life history. It is not known, for instance, how long its gestation period is. It was presumed to be 12 months, but some researchers now place it at 14 or even 16 months. Cows are rarely seen in the three-year intervals between calving, suggesting that somewhere in the world, there is an undiscovered summer feeding ground. Neither is it known where the majority of right whales, including juveniles, males and nonpregnant females, go during the winter months from November to March.

However, there is no question that the Bay of Fundy is the primary right whale nursery, where the majority of newborn calves are brought during their first year of life. Gaskin, the principal researcher of the right whale in the Bay, began his work on whale biology in the early 1960s as an observer and scientist aboard whaling vessels in the Antarctic Ocean, a distasteful experience he recalls as "six months of sheer butchery." At the same time, Gaskin is wary of too anthropomorphic an interpretation of the nature of whales—he disparages what he calls the "yellow press" that ascribes humanlike communication to cetaceans—but this more scientific approach has not diminished his concern for the future of the right whale, which he considers to be in serious jeopardy.

Gaskin is the author of a definitive study

on the ecology of whales, and he has focused his research on the feeding ecology of the rights in the outer Bay of Fundy. "I don't think you can protect an animal without knowing as much as possible about its life cycle," he says.

Fundy, Gaskin believes, is a dual-purpose area, serving as a nursing or training ground for young calves and as an important feeding ground for calves and mothers. Normally, right whales are skim feeders: they simply swim along the surface through marine meadows of copepods, or "brit," straining the tiny zooplankton through their baleen plates. The whale uses its great tongue to force water through the baleen filtering system, where the frayed, hairlike tips of the baleen plates retain the copepods and krill.

In Fundy, however, the whales exhibit an uncharacteristic feeding strategy by making deep dives in the Grand Manan Basin. Oceanographic factors account for this novel strategy, for in the Bay, copepod masses are concentrated near the bottom by a combination of ocean fronts and a local gyre that roughly follows the edges of the figure-8 shape of the Grand Manan Basin. Downwelling occurs at the edge of the basin, where well-mixed and less-well-mixed water masses meet. At this transition zone, the copepods settle out—in effect, sliding down the face of the transition zone as down a pane of glass—producing a high concentration of the energy-rich

The Grand Manan fishing fleet, facing page, finds protection within the sheltering arm of the North Head wharf. A 50-tonne right whale breaches, hurling its bulk from the Bay, which may prove to be its last refuge. Widespread pollution of the right's traditional feeding grounds elsewhere along the Eastern Seaboard and mortality from marine traffic threaten the species.

zooplankton below 100 fathoms. Because of the whale's great bulk, the small size of its prey and the filter-feeding method it employs, Gaskin speculates that for feeding to be energetically efficient, a right whale needs concentrations "equivalent to a coal seam of copepods, 1 to 2½ feet deep." Fundy, it appears, is one of the few areas in the world that offer this critical concentration of food.

Valerie Murison studied the feeding ecology of whales in the Bay of Fundy in the mid-1980s and is now chief field scientist at the Grand Manan Whale and Seabird Research Station. Murison showed that the right whales begin arriving from their southern spring feeding grounds off Cape Cod in August and September, just as the richest assembly of zooplankton occurs in the Bay. It is more than coincidence, according to Murison, that their arrival is timed to the peak pulses of biomass of the calanoid copepods. In fact, Murison was able to show a direct relationship between copepod concentration and the presence of right whales: wherever her plankton tows assayed sufficient food, she was sure to find whales.

To exploit these patches of plankton, the right whales make prolonged, deep dives. Murison estimates that they spend as much

as 18 hours a day feeding, with only short periods of rest between dives. An average dive is 10 to 15 minutes in length, and upon surfacing, the whale was observed to breathe heavily, catching its breath while continuing to move forward for the first minute after coming up. The whale would then spend several minutes "logging" at or just below the surface, during which it would breathe less frequently. Shortly before diving again, it would be seen to breathe more often and to begin moving forward. A high, arching back and up flukes would initiate another deep dive. Murison found that the whales always fed with the tide, never against it, presumably because the tidal currents carry the weak-swimming zooplankton along in their paths.

Recent research has debunked the notion that right whales are lethargic animals. In 1988, Jeff Goodyear was successful in tagging several of them, and he tracked one for three weeks. He was amazed by just how active the whales were. He estimates that they spent less than 10 percent of their time resting. Most of the time, they were either socializing vigorously or feeding intensively, even at night. In fact, Goodyear feels that there may be some inherent advantages to nighttime feeding because of the diurnal migrations of zooplankton: "The fact that the plankton are near the surface at night may mean that the whales spend less energy feeding because they don't have to dive as deeply. So there's an energy saving for them on a 24-hour basis."

There seems to be plenty of food available to them, even at the time that they be-

A whale researcher has a head-to-head meeting with a curious right whale calf. The white patches of thickened skin, called callosities, on the right's head serve as "fingerprints" for identification of individuals. Facing page: Swallowtail Light beams its warning to passing boats but attracts painters, photographers and those simply seeking solitude and a prospect of the sea.

gin to move out of the Bay in October en route to their wintering grounds in the south. Paul Brodie of the Bedford Institute of Oceanography has shown that fin whales migrate south to warmer waters, despite the fact that those waters may be relatively sterile when the ratio between heat loss and input of kilocalories as food becomes unfavourable. It appears that this behaviour evolved because it is more energy-efficient. Heat loss would not seem to be as acute a problem for the fatter, better-insulated right whales, at least for the adults. However, it may be a problem for younger animals whose surface-area-to-body-weight ratio is not as advantageous. They will lose proportionately more heat than adults, and this negative energy balance may be a significant factor in the southward movement of right whales out of the Bay.

Much of the right whale's natural history can be interpreted in terms of its energetics —what a large animal in cold waters must do not only to stay alive but to attain peak condition in order to reproduce. "You have an animal that lives in very cold waters feeding on very minute organisms," explains Scott Kraus, "so you get a lot of them when you can get them. But they need to have a lot of blubber. They need to have fat storage to do two things: to be able to insulate themselves and to buffer times when they're swimming between these heavy patches of copepods. So basically, the evolutionary strategy is to get fat."

The energy requirements also drive the reproductive cycles of the females. Females, especially, require a very high-energy diet to provide for their calves, which grow faster than any other whale species—with the possible exception of the blue whale—essentially doubling in length from four to eight metres in their first year. The mother provides all the energy for her calf in its first nine months, losing so much of her fat in the process that, in the whaling days, nursing cows were called "dry skins" by the Long Island whalers. Consequently, the females replenish their own fat stores by exploiting areas with high densities of copepods, such as the Bay of Fundy. A calf, before it can begin feeding on its own, must also acquire a thick insulation of blubber as well as an effective surface-area-to-body-weight ratio so that it is relatively heat-efficient. The physiological drain on the female makes it an "insane decision," according to Kraus, for her to have another calf the next year. The female is automatically driven into a resting period, which varies from three to five years, depending on the size of the calf and how much of an energy toll it has exacted on the mother.

"You can see that the ecological choices evolution has made for these animals drive the physiological requirements, which then drive this calving interval—and the calving intervals mean that the effective sex ratio of available reproductively active females is very low relative to the number of males."

This ratio—four males to one receptive female—accounts for the fierce competition for females observed by researchers in the Bay of Fundy and on the Scotian Shelf, a second area of summer concentration of right whales. The deep-water area between Brown's and Baccaro banks seems to be the prime location for courtship activity. Whales are often seen there in what are dubbed "surface-active groups," or SAGs. The whales in such groups are observed rolling together at the surface, stroking each other with their flippers or lying belly to belly. The average size of such groups is 4 or 5 animals, but as many as 13 have been seen in a single SAG.

The ostensible purpose of these groups is mating, but often, the female in the SAG is seen on her back with her genital area out of the water in a decidedly unreceptive position. When that happens, two or more males will rub and bump the larger female in an effort to roll her over, while another suitor waits underneath, belly-up, in what is referred to as the alpha position. Sometimes, the female appears to succumb to

her suitors, but it is still not known whether such mating activity results in conception. In fact, copulation has been observed on only one occasion. To make matters more mystifying, researchers have yet to identify a right whale from a SAG on Brown's Bank with a calf.

One explanation for such "promiscuous" mating activity may be what evolutionary biologists term sperm competition. Researchers have demonstrated a direct correlation between testes size and promiscuous behaviour in primate species such as chimpanzees and gorillas. Where sperm competition exists, the males try to copulate with as many females as they can and as often as possible to ensure their own reproductive success. The right whale not only exhibits such behaviour but also boasts the largest testes, at half a tonne each, of any species.

Despite its seeming titanic and persistent reproductive efforts, the right whale population is growing at a discouragingly slow rate—if it is growing at all. It is puzzling and troubling to all scientists currently

studying the animal that this population has not made as dramatic a recovery as has the grey whale, which was protected at the same time and which now has attained preexploitation levels of 15,000. Current estimates, primarily through the results of the New England Aquarium's photo-identification programme, put the population of North Atlantic right whales at a mere 300 animals, of which 265 have been positively identified.

One factor in their slow climb back may be that right whales have a relatively low reproductive rate for cetaceans. They mature sexually at seven years and give birth to a single calf every three or four years. (No one yet knows how long right whales live, though one female called Stripes was spotted off Florida with a calf 20 years ago and was identified again in 1981 with another calf.) If, as many researchers believe, the population was reduced to 20 or fewer animals by the time the hunting ban was imposed, then the population may be increasing at a maximum net output of 4 percent—or 7 to 12 animals—per year.

Such an increase, however, is barely perceptible using current census methods.

The worst-case scenario is that the population was reduced to such a critical level that the North Atlantic right whale went through what biologists call a genetic window—the number of individuals at which the continued survival of the species is threatened. In 1988, Moira Brown, then director of East Coast Ecosystems, collected skin samples from 51 right whales on Brown's Bank, using a crossbow and a retrievable tag that excised a tiny biopsy. Biochemically analyzed, these samples will yield DNA fingerprints from which Brown will be able to establish a pedigree for the population. This sophisticated biochemical detective work will establish maternal lines

and possibly, in some cases, paternal lines. "A pretty good trick," says Brown, "because that's something the right whales themselves don't know."

Currently, nobody knows how many females were left in the breeding population when the whaling was finally stopped. If, as some suspect, there were as few as 12, it could be that inbreeding has had a negative impact on the right whale's ability to rebound. Often, when closely related individuals mate with each other, recessive traits, manifested by reduced productivity, either through a failure to conceive or to bring to term, may result. Such a discovery would be alarming, although it would not necessarily spell doom for the right whale. Other populations, such as the elephant

seal, have recovered after being reduced to critically low numbers. In practical terms, it might mean that measures would have to be taken to reduce all sources of mortality. With the population hovering at barely sustainable levels, the loss of a single individual is a cause for grave concern.

The right whale's preference for coastal waters, its slow swimming speed and its habit of feeding at the surface—the same qualities that exposed it to harm in the past—make it particularly vulnerable to ship collisions, which appear to be a major cause of mortality today. In 1984, a calf from the Bay of Fundy was killed off Long Island when a tanker propeller severed its tail; in 1986, a dead adult, severely cut by propellers, was found floating in Cape Cod

Bay. Increasingly, whales are coming into contact with fishermen's gear and boats. Nets and ropes can become entangled at the gape of the mouth, around the flippers and, more commonly, around the tail stock, where 33 percent of all whales identified by photographs show evidence of scars or injuries. These injuries are not necessarily debilitating, but they can be fatal in rare instances. In 1988, a badly decomposed right whale carcass was found entangled in the rope of an offshore lobster trawl at the mouth of the Bay of Fundy.

A statistical analysis of mortality factors conducted by Kraus indicates that humans are probably holding back right whale revival. He found that shipping collisions and fishing entanglements have accounted for 30 percent of all the known deaths in right whales since 1970. In the first three years of life, 12 percent of the right whales disappear and are assumed to have died of natural causes. However, if 30 percent of these disappearances have anthropogenic causes, then humans may account for 4 percent mortality in a given year. Populations of southern right whales in Argentina and South Africa are experiencing a full growth rate of 4.5 to 6 percent per year, "which raises the possibility," Kraus concludes, "that the growth of the population is being inhibited simply by the mortality we're laying on the top of natural mortality, through shipping and fishing."

In recent years, North American coastal waters have become a less suitable habitat for cetaceans not only because of such crowded conditions but also because of the cumulative effects of ocean dumping of sewage and industrial wastes. Delaware, Chesapeake, Long Island and Cape Cod bays were all traditional areas for calving and mating, but now they are rarely visited by right whales, perhaps because pollution has significantly depleted plankton patches in these areas. This has made the relatively unpolluted, food-rich Bay of Fundy and Scotian Shelf even more vital to the right whale's long-term welfare.

The Bay of Fundy may have always been a natural refuge for the species. Historically, the ubiquitous fog and the treacherous tidal currents discouraged whaling in the Bay during that industry's heyday. The work done by Gaskin and Kraus during the past decade has made it very clear that Fundy will play a vital role in the right whale's precarious future. Cows with calves show a marked preference for the Bay over other areas, such as the Great South Channel and the Scotian Shelf, even though they also offer a rich copepod diet. There may be two reasons for this. Fundy is well protected from oceanic storms, and it enjoys a relative lack of predators such as the killer whale. (Six percent of right whales exhibit killer whale scars, although it has never been confirmed that killer whales are in fact successful in their attacks.) In Fundy, Murison has often observed calves alone on the surface for prolonged periods while

A right whale lobtails, facing page, smashing the water with its tail—a little-understood behaviour. Right whales may use their tails to communicate, especially when underwater noise interferes with their low-frequency voices; or they may use them as sails when the wind is up. Right whales need the continued attention of naturalists, above, and scientists to avoid extinction.

their mothers made feeding dives. Calves are obviously vulnerable during this time, and it appears that mothers feel they can risk leaving them untended. White sharks do prowl the Bay, but they seem to prefer harbour porpoises to large whales. Murison once observed a shark milling about in a group of seven right whales, including a calf, without eliciting any apparent panic in the pod.

The greatest threat to the right whale may stem from the crowding or outright destruction of its habitat. "I would consider this to be a stressed population," Gaskin says, "no matter what connotation you want to put on the word 'stressed.' It's a population that's always under some kind of threat. The animals may have adapted quite well to the continual presence of fishing boats, the continual noise of the tankers, the big-tanker traffic going to Saint John and the occasional appearance of whale-watching boats. But for some reason, these animals are just not increasing. And we simply won't know why for another 10 or 15 years. So we just keep plugging away."

In the meantime, it may be necessary to implement some tough-minded conservation regulations to stave off the threat of extinction that has stalked the species. Although the right whales' habit of aggregating in small areas makes them extremely vulnerable, it may offer an opportunity to implement some management options. In Fundy, the whales seem to confine their activities to the area of the Grand Manan Basin from July to October. Similar seasonal occupations occur on Brown's Bank and in the Great Southwest Channel. Shipping could be redirected or speed regulations imposed for these areas to minimize the possibility of collisions. Also, certain types of fishing—gill netting has proved deadly to right whales as well as to large numbers of Fundy harbour porpoises—could be restricted seasonally in the Grand Manan Basin. In the end, a seasonal sanctuary in this critical habitat for cows and calves may provide the last hope for the species.

RISE AND FALL
Tides of Time

Much of the Fundy coastline is as Samuel de Champlain found it four centuries ago. But increased industrialization and energy-related activities—transportation of oil, nuclear- and tidal-power development —threaten the future integrity of its environment. The great tides, through their erosive power, will eventually alter the Bay's shape and be their own undoing.

A Tide in the Affairs of Men

There is a tide in the affairs of men,
Which taken at the flood, leads on to fortune:
Omitted, all the voyage of their life
Is bound in shallows, and in miseries.

— William Shakespeare
"Julius Caesar"

Not long ago, I stopped by a fish shanty at Cape Forchu, at the entrance to Yarmouth harbour, the home of a family friend and former lobster fisherman. The fishery had been good to him, and although he was in his late sixties, he still ran his own fish business, buying and selling lobsters and salt fish. On that day, he was tapping together fish crates, a job he did not need to do but one he found therapeutic. "How's the fishing been?" I asked by way of initiating conversation. He stopped his work, raised his bushy eyebrows and fixed me with an ironic side-glance. "Man won't be happy until he's caught every fish in the sea," he declared with unexpected vehemence.

The recent history of the Fundy fishery tends to confirm my friend's disillusionment. Overfishing—the exploitation of a fish stock to the point of population collapse—has become an ill endemic to the fishery. As soon as one stock of fish is exploited to the point where it is uneconom-

Herring, above, is feedstock for marine mammals, seabirds and many other fish species in the Bay. Despite this, herring may be the best case study of a mismanaged species. In the 1980s, more than three-quarters of the herring caught had only the roe extracted; the rest of the fish was discarded. If such wasteful practices continue, herring may no longer blacken the waters, facing page.

ical to pursue it, the fleet directs its formidable fish-catching technology toward another, more numerous species without considering the consequences of its actions. Thus, haddock, the most desirable groundfish species, was severely depleted in the 1960s and has only made a tentative comeback. As we enter the 1990s, all groundfish species—including cod, pollack, flatfish and haddock—in the Bay of Fundy and on the Scotian Shelf off Nova Scotia's south shore appear to be at critically low levels because of overfishing.

The inshore fleet of vessels now has four times the fishing capacity it needs to take the fish available under quota. In the fall of 1988, the Groundfish Industry Capacity Advisory Committee made an unusually frank assessment of the situation: "The prospects for the fish resource under these conditions are not bright. Catch levels experienced in recent years are not sustainable. In the case of haddock, in particular,

yields have dropped substantially as a result of intense exploitation." It was a classic case of too many fishermen chasing too few fish. A sustainable harvest rate for most fish stocks is 20 percent. In recent years, 50 percent of the haddock stock, 35 percent of the cod stock and 30 percent of the pollack stock have been pulled from the seas. The committee put forward a series of recommendations to ease pressure on the stocks, and it placed the reduction of fleet capacity at the top of its list—a recommendation with profound implications for coastal communities where fishing is the economic mainstay.

It is a crisis that some saw coming. One of those is retired fisherman Raymond Thurber of Freeport, Nova Scotia, at the tip of Digby Neck, whom I met on one of my visits to Brier Island. Then 65, Thurber had retired from the fishery a decade earlier due to health problems. He had been fishing groundfish all his life, following the schools of bottom feeders as they cycled through the Bay of Fundy and the Gulf of Maine. He chased cod and pollack from May to June, hake until October, haddock until February and halibut during the rest of the winter.

He spoke despairingly—and prophetically, it now seems—of the dire condition of the resource. "I said five or six years ago, the day would come when you'd have to go to a museum to see a haddock, and the time is coming closer. The cod I see them bringing in now," he continued, "tons and tons of them, is the size we had to throw away. We couldn't keep them. They don't have a chance to grow up anymore."

"But some fishermen say the Bay is full of fish," I said.

Thurber remembered better times. "If you talk to some young person today, he might tell you there's an abundance of fish out there for the simple reason he's never seen it any different. He's never seen the abundance that someone like myself has seen.

So it would look like there were plenty."

Thurber lapsed into silence.

"I know one thing," he concluded gloomily, "I'm just satisfied that I've run the course, I don't have to do it over again."

Raymond's son Jimmy left university to return home and fish, despite his father's protests. On a day too stormy for fishing, Jimmy took me out to watch gale birds. The next day, the winds died down, the fog rolled out, and I went with him to bug for pollack in the fishing grounds near Brier Island. Bugging is a fussy technique. It requires hooks about the size of a crooked index finger covered with a sleeve of fluorescent orange plastic intended to imitate krill. A dozen or more of these hooks are attached to a weighted hand line which is thrown over into what the fishermen call a hole. On clear days, you can locate these holes quite easily without the aid of a depth sounder; they appear as slick upwelling areas surrounded by a ring of tide rips.

Once "inside" the 50-fathom hole, Jimmy checked his fish finder. "Fish got less chance all the time with all this electronic gear," he observed as he scanned the screen graded in colour from red, which indicated a concentration of fish or feed such as shrimp, through yellow, green, magenta, grey and blue – the last indicating water only. "It doesn't look very fishy," he said as he released the bugging line, which was raised and lowered on a small crank-operated drum. We drifted up the sides of the underwater crater that defined the perimeter of the hole, Jimmy winching the line up and down – bugging. To be successful, bugging requires perfect timing and a relative abundance of fish. That day, there were few fish to be had. Finding none in the hole, we motored 29 kilometres offshore, until Brier Island was the merest slip of land on the horizon. After six hours of bugging, Jimmy finally brought aboard two pollack, silvery green torpedo-shaped 10-pounders. It proved to be his day's catch, not enough to feed the shearwaters which had been vainly following the boat.

As groundfish decline, the herring have been making a slow recovery in the Bay of Fundy. Herring is the vital feedstock for marine mammals, seabirds and many other fish species in the Bay. Despite its cornerstone importance, herring may be the best case study of a mismanaged species. The wasteful policy of using herring, a source of high-quality protein, as the grist for fish meal continued unabated until the mid-1970s, when the federal government finally insisted that the industry use the resource for human consumption. It was a policy that added value to the fish, and although the prime motive seems to have been economic rather than conservational, it had the salutary effect of saving the badly ravaged stocks. However, in the mid-1980s, this policy took a strange twist when the Japanese aggressively entered the marketplace in search of herring roe. The total allowable catch doubled in the five years from 1984 to 1989 and now stands at 151,200 tonnes,

30,000 tonnes more than biologists had estimated to be the sustainable yield – that is, the number of fish that can be caught without damaging the reproductive capacity of the stock – a mere decade before.

More than three-quarters of the herring now caught is destined for the Japanese market, which means that just 5 percent of the usable protein – the roe only – is used. The rest of the fish is discarded. This has resulted in an abhorrent situation in which more than 100,000 tonnes of fresh fish are

A Brier Island fishing boat lies idle, facing page, as may many other Bay boats in the 1990s. The inshore fleet now has four times the fishing capacity needed to take the quota of fish permitted, prompting gloomy predictions for fish stocks and coastal communities. A worker, above, strings herring for hanging in a smokehouse on Grand Manan, once the world's leading exporter of smoked herring.

annually dumped into landfill sites or into the sea – a worse regime than that which prevailed under the wasteful fish-meal programme. The waste itself has become an environmental problem. Dumping on land has contaminated drinking water, while lobster fishermen fear that tonnes of herring waste are fouling or smothering traditional lobster grounds.

The roe fishery concentrates on one of the major North Atlantic herring stocks that spawn off southwest Nova Scotia in late summer and early fall. The ecological implications of fishing spawning stock are self-evident and disturbing. As Raymond Thurber puts it, "If you're going to take the seed, you're not going to have a crop." The point has not been totally lost on fisheries officials. In 1989, the Department of Fisheries and Oceans closed fishing on Trinity Ledge, the main spawning ground, a signal that the southwest Nova Scotia stock may be in trouble and that we are readying for another go-around in the cycle of overfishing, population collapse and tentative recovery.

Habitat destruction poses an even more fundamental threat to a resource than over-exploitation. Pollution in the Bay of Fundy is not as acute as in other Eastern Seaboard coastal areas closer to major population centres and industrial complexes, such as Chesapeake Bay and Delaware Bay, but the Bay of Fundy is far from pristine. Sources of marine pollution are often land-based and make their way from forests and farms to the sea in river runoffs.

During the 1950s and 1960s, large tracts of New Brunswick forest were sprayed with DDT, producing a "silent spring" in the province: the extirpation of the peregrine falcon from its Fundy breeding ground, as well as mass mortality of freshwater fish.

The Canadian Wildlife Service decided to monitor seabirds to determine whether the organochlorine chemicals were making their way into the marine environment. The most likely source of terrestrial-based pollution in Fundy is the Saint John River, the largest freshwater river flowing into the Bay. CWS analyzed the eggs of double-breasted cormorants from Manawagonish Island at the mouth of the Saint John River, those of Leach's storm petrels and Atlantic puffins from Kent Island and Machias Seal Island, respectively, at the mouth of the Bay, and herring gull eggs from both the river and the Bay. All species were found to contain traces of DDE, PCBs, oxychlordane and dieldrin. The surveys were made every four years between 1968 and 1984. The residues of the major organochlorines, originating from the extensive use of DDT and dieldrin in spruce budworm spray programmes in New Brunswick, have significantly declined since the early 1970s, when their use was curtailed. However, chemicals such as chlordane and HCB are as prevalent now as they were then. Alarmingly, the same trends were noted between the colonies at the mouth of the Saint John River and those at the mouth of the Bay, which shows the far-reaching effects of runoff.

The Bay of Fundy-Gulf of Maine oceanographic system is particularly vulnerable to pollution because of its so-called closed circulation. Water in the Bay is not regularly flushed out or replaced by inflowing deeper waters. Once pollutants are released into the Bay, they have a hard time finding their way out and therefore tend to accumulate through the food chain year after year. In his study of harbour porpoises in Passamaquoddy Bay, David Gaskin found ample and disconcerting evidence of the accumulation of pollutants. He detected DDT levels of more than 500 parts per million (ppm) and PCB levels of 200 ppm as well as significant quantities of HCBs and chlordanes. He recorded mercury levels of 90 ppm in liver tissue and 8 ppm in brain tissue, a concentration at which one might expect to see clinical signs of mercury poisoning.

Gaskin gathered his findings as part of a 13-year battle waged by environmental scientists against Pittston Company's proposal to site an oil refinery in Eastport,

A Fundy resident, above, contemplates the news, which has, in recent times, been mostly bad. Increasing industrialization, oil spills, pulp-and-paper effluent, agricultural and forestry runoff and the Point Lepreau nuclear-power plant all threaten the integrity of the Fundy habitat and the future of families, such as this one, facing page, enjoying a twilight stroll along Yarmouth harbour.

Maine, at the head of Passamaquoddy Bay. The risk of accidents is high there because of the strong tidal currents, extreme turbulence and thick fog that imperil navigation during summer months. He concluded that it was very important to keep such industrial development to a minimum in the Bay of Fundy region.

Currently, industrialization along the Bay is concentrated in the seaport of Saint John. Pulp manufacture, steel fabrication, shipbuilding, sugar refining, brewing and petrochemical refining are all potential sources of pollutants. If you stand overlooking the famous Reversing Falls at the mouth of the Saint John River, you cannot help noticing the globs of brownish foam floating toward the Bay from the Irving pulp mill just upstream.

Nicolys Denys, in his 17th-century *Description and Natural History of the Coast of North America*, witnessed quite a different picture at the mouth of the Saint John River: "Here the late Monsieur de la Tour had a weir built in which were caught a great number of Gaspereaux [alewives] which were salted for winter. Sometimes there was caught so great a quantity that he was obliged to break the weir and throw them into the sea, as otherwise they would have befouled the weir which thus would have been ruined. Sometimes there were also found salmon, shad and bass . . . which serves every spring as a grand manna for the people of the country." This once bountiful local resource has been lost to the people of Saint John. The fishery in the harbour has been closed because of local pollution and heavy shipping.

Saint John handles an average of 1,000 arrivals a year, not including the *Princess of Acadia* ferry, which accounts for an additional 700 arrivals. The port receives annually approximately 5 million tonnes of crude oil, 5 million tonnes of refined petroleum products and 60,000 tonnes of bulk chemicals, mainly caustic soda. A principal source of contamination may well be the Irving Canaport monobuoy, a crude-oil un-

loading system serving the world's largest supertankers. No fewer than 36 oil spills were recorded from this facility in the 1970s, during the time the Pittston proposal was being reviewed. In addition, there was an average of 35 mystery spills per month, many no doubt from ships flushing their tanks at sea.

The potential for a major spill such as that experienced in Chedabucto Bay in 1979, when the *Kurdistan* ran aground and broke up, spilling 8,000 tonnes of Bunker C oil, is ever present. The relatively small *Kurdistan* spill resulted in the contamination of lobster pounds and mussel and clam beds 170 kilometres from the site. Hydrocarbons persist in bottom sediments and therefore can have long-term effects as they are released slowly into the environment. Of particular concern in the Bay of Fundy is the impact on herring stocks. The Bay is a nursery for herring larvae, which have been shown to be susceptible to very small con-

centrations of oil—0.1 ppm oil in water gives a high incidence of deformed herring larvae. As well, any contamination of lobster would have a catastrophic effect on this $143 million industry.

Toxicity of oil is related to its solubility. Bunker C is a heavy oil and is considered less toxic than lighter, more refined oils such as diesel or gasoline because it is less soluble in water. However, when seabirds come into contact with Bunker C, it usually spells doom. "An increasing spiral of debilitation begins which usually ends in the bird's death," says seabird biologist Richard Brown. Oiled feathers and feather barbules lose their waterproofing and insulation value and absorb more water, adding as much as 10 percent to the body weight of the bird. Flying, swimming and diving become more difficult, so the bird is less able to collect food at the same time as its energy requirements are increasing.

Especially vulnerable are those species

which spend most of their time sitting on the water, including the divers such as the alcids (razorbills, puffins and dovekies); the diving ducks such as eiders; and the phalaropes, the only swimming shorebirds. Logically, birds such as phalaropes, which form dense flocks at sea, are at greatest risk from oil spills. Seabirds in the outer Bay, however, are also vulnerable because of the frenzied way in which they feed, concentrating in areas where the tidal-pump system brings food to the surface.

It has been estimated that a major oil spill in the Passamaquoddy Bay area would put at risk a minimum of 80,000 birds: 9,000 herring gulls, 3,000 great black-backed gulls, 10,000 to 50,000 northern phalaropes, 10,000 Bonaparte's gulls, 1,000 to 2,000 common and Arctic terns, hundreds of kittiwakes and several thousand double-breasted cormorants, eiders and black guillemots. Nearly the entire southern New Brunswick population of bald eagles and ospreys would also be threatened.

Various species of seabirds and ducks concentrate in the outer Bay during different seasons, so risk to a particular species varies according to the time of year. For example, the outer Bay near St. Andrews is the most important wintering area in the Maritimes for common eiders. The diving ducks—old-squaw, bufflehead, common goldeneye and greater scaup—also frequent the area from December through February. The shallows south of Grand Manan Island host thousands of dovekies during the winter and are also an important wintering area for razorbills. Perhaps the worst-case scenario would be a spill in August, a peak feeding time for seabirds in the outer Bay. A major spill at that time could devastate whole populations of Bonaparte's gulls, greater shearwaters and phalaropes.

Even small oil spills can have catastrophic effects, as was illustrated when the Irving Whale leaked a mere 27 tonnes of oil, which killed at least 5,500 birds along the south coast of Newfoundland. The potential for a spill on the scale of the Exxon Valdez always exists as supertankers carrying 1.5 million barrels of oil shuttle regularly to and from the Saint John refinery of Irving Oil.

In the event of disaster, containment and cleanup in the tidally energetic waters of the Bay of Fundy would be virtually impossible. As the slick was pushed and pulled by the flooding and ebbing tides, it could spread to the mud flats in the upper Bay, becoming a significant threat to the habitat of the migrating shorebirds. More likely, a spill would follow the counterclockwise gyre in the outer Bay and be directed along the New Brunswick shore toward Passamaquoddy Bay, where it would threaten some 40 fish farms that grow $40 million worth of Atlantic salmon annually.

On the evening of June 18, 1989, an oil spill was reported from the French supertanker Carmargue, which was taking on fuel at the Irving Canaport. Approximately 500 barrels (80 tonnes) of oil overflowed into the Bay, producing a slick three kilometres

long. The oil, a mixture of 90 percent Bunker C and 10 percent diesel oil, never did come ashore and was last reported south of Grand Manan, migrating into the Gulf of Maine. Ten days after the accident, Coast Guard trackers lost sight of the slick.

Yet another threat has loomed over the Bay since 1981, when the Point Lepreau nuclear plant went into operation. Not long after you leave Black's Harbour on the Grand Manan ferry, the white dome of the CANDU reactor comes into view, a reminder that this seemingly underdeveloped coast is not immune to technological threat. Lepreau is the only nuclear reactor sited on a coastline in Canada—and it so happens that it presides over one of the richest fishing and wildlife areas in the North Atlantic. The plant recycles seawater for its cooling systems. Researchers monitoring marine organisms in the area have detected elevated but acceptable levels of tritium, a relatively innocuous radioisotope. "My feeling is that in terms of chronic damage to the environment, we're not going to see any effect," says Dr. John Smith of the Bedford Institute

of Oceanography. But as Chernobyl and Three Mile Island have taught us, it is not the normal operation of nuclear plants that is at issue but the chance of an irremediable event of a meltdown due to human error—with, in the case of the Lepreau plant, massive releases of radiation into the marine environment and atmosphere.

The transit of oil to and from the Bay of Fundy and the generation of nuclear power at Point Lepreau are two aspects of the same issue: the supply of energy. Each presents its inherent risk to the environment, but convincing arguments against the use of foreign oil and nuclear power might be made on purely economic grounds. To those concerned about the environment, tidal power offers some advantages over conventional sources of energy. Foremost, it is nonpolluting in the traditional sense. Unlike coal generation, it does not despoil rivers, lakes and groundwater by contributing to acid rain. Neither does it abet the greenhouse effect. It does not carry the unacceptable risk of permanently polluting the marine environment with mutagenic molecules, as does nuclear power. It reduces our reliance on oil and thus the risk of oil spills with their catastrophic and long-lasting effects on marine organisms and the coastal environment. By displacing fossil fuels as a source of energy, it conserves those nonrenewable hydrocarbon stores for more vital purposes in the manufacture of a wide variety of useful substances. And, at least for all intents and purposes, it offers an endlessly renewable supply of energy—energy bequeathed by a fundamental force of the universe, gravity. Taking these relative virtues into account, one has to weigh in the balance the environmental consequences for society of *not* developing tidal power.

While pondering this question, however, it must be kept in mind that tidal power would not actually replace conventional electrical energy sources, such as nuclear or fossil fuels. Electrical utilities plan for peak demand, and from that viewpoint, tidal power has inherent problems, as the power must be generated in phase with the tides—whether high tide comes at 12 noon, when you need power, or at 12 midnight, when you don't. Therefore, utilities would continue to build nuclear and thermal plants to meet peak demand whether or not tidal power was on line.

Even so, the renewable, local, if not readily available, power source of the Fundy tides remains perenially attractive. However, the decade of intensive study of the environmental impact of large-scale Fundy tidal power has shown that there are significant environmental trade-offs. At the outset, it was recognized that all the environmental effects would flow from the basic changes to the tidal regime brought about by a barrage across a major basin. Mathematical modelling of the tides and the effects of a barrage have shown that these changes would not be confined to the Bay of Fundy but would extend far to the south.

A tidal barrage effectively shortens the length of the Bay and therefore brings it even closer to resonance. Seaward of a Minas Basin barrage, the tidal range might be expected to increase by as much as 15 centimetres 480 kilometres away in Boston Harbor. A suite of ecological effects can be anticipated due to an overall increase in tidal amplitudes and energies in the outer Bay of Fundy and Gulf of Maine. Scientists under the direction of Dr. Peter Larsen at the Bigelow Laboratory for Ocean Studies in West Booth Bay Harbor, Maine, have begun to compile a list of the "far-field effects" in the Gulf and along the coast of New England. Some of these effects are thought to be positive, others negative.

The socioeconomic impact of a tidal-power plant might indeed be very significant because of increased flooding and erosion: 1,700 to 4,000 hectares would be inundated by the higher water stand, and more coastal real estate would be lost through erosion due to higher current velocities. Municipal sewage systems, such as the low-head type used in Portland, Maine, might be impaired, resulting in considerable cost and inconvenience. Structures such as piers, decks, low-lying coastal roads and bridges would be further imperilled by the magnified effects of storm surges. Harbour navigation would also be adversely affected, especially at low tide, when safe navigation is already marginal. There would be cultural impacts as well. The Maine Historic Preservation Commission has estimated that 30 percent of the coastal archaeological sites would be lost.

Life on the Fundy shore is still firmly rooted in the traditional pursuits of lumbering, farming and fishing. Making silage, facing page, and picking apples, above, contribute to the livelihood of residents. Massive development of tidal power poses a threat to the marine and terrestrial habitats of basin, marsh and coastal forest that support the largely rural life style by the Bay.

The increased tidal amplitudes and currents would also have ecological consequences. Higher water levels would mean an increase in the size of the salt marsh and a corresponding increase in the area of the mud flat, which might have a beneficial effect on the shellfish industry. Estuaries would also be flushed to a greater extent, facilitating the removal of pollutants. But at the same time, greater flushing might remove fish larvae, whose nurseries are the estuarine backwaters, and this ultimately would affect offshore fisheries.

Even greater effects might stem from stronger tidal currents in the Gulf of Maine. Stronger currents would scour more nutrients from the seafloor and bring them into the photic zone, where they would fuel greater primary productivity. This is likely to have an overall positive influence on the fisheries in the region. One model predicts an increase in potential fish production of 7 to 12 percent in areas of the Gulf that are at present nutrient-poor.

On balance, Larsen believes that the changes to the overall ecology of the Gulf would not be that significant. In fact, tidal power would only hasten by about 30 years what is happening already. Sea level is now rising at the rate of 30 centimetres per century in the Gulf of Maine because of crus-

tal subsidence. "There will be changes that will be observed over time, but indeed, that's been the history of the ecology of the Gulf of Maine," Larsen reasons. "So, looking over historic time, let alone geologic time, these changes won't be especially dramatic."

Research on the effects of tidal power in the Gulf of Maine is at a very preliminary stage, perhaps where research in the Bay of Fundy proper was a decade ago. In the Bay of Fundy, much of the concern has centred, and still does, around the fate of the mud, which is sure to be stirred up, transported and set down elsewhere by the operation of a tidal-power plant.

The Windsor causeway has served as a focus of that concern. If it proves to be a good model for a tidal barrage, then massive siltation might be expected, along with the kind of wholesale mortality observed by Michael Risk on the Windsor Mudflat. Even if it is a poor paradigm, much of the productivity in the upper Bay depends on the intertidal zone—the mud flats at low tide—and the reduction by half of the area in the headpond would remove an important part of the feeding ground for shorebirds and fish. However, some have argued that the loss of benthic productivity (for example, among clams and mud shrimp) might be compensated for by increased phytoplankton growth in the water column. Currently, productivity in the upper Bay is severely light-limited. With the reduction of tidal turbulence in the headpond, mud normally suspended in the water is expected to settle out, resulting in clearer water and greater primary productivity in the form of phytoplankton blooms. Beneficial change might even present new economic opportunities in the form of aquaculture based on oyster production. To summarize, the more optimistic view is that although the types of creatures might change, with fewer creatures in the mud and more in the water, the overall productivity within the headpond would not be reduced, because phytoplankton blooms would compensate for the loss of benthic productivity.

The weakness in this quantitative approach to predicting the effects of tidal power on the ecology seems to be that it ignores the very special nature of the communities which have adapted to survival in this stressful area of high tides and strong currents as well as of those migratory species which depend on the endemic communities. Although the balance of the upper Bay's frugal carbon budget might not show a quantitative debit after the entry of a tidal-power barrage – the total biomass might remain the same – there could well be a qualitative red mark in the ecological ledger. Replacement of a food system based on detritus and benthic algae with a phytoplankton-based food system has acute implications for the fish and birds keyed to exploiting the upper Bay. They would arrive on their feeding ground looking for their favourite prey – mud shrimp, say – only to find that it was no longer there for the taking, at least not in sufficient numbers. In short, it appears that the trade-off might boil down to bartering shad for algae and shorebirds for zooplankton – to many, a dubious biological bargain.

Environmental changes from large-scale engineering projects on the coast are inevitable. However, some scientists, like Graham Daborn of the Acadia Centre for Estuarine Research, have pointed out that the upper Bay is a system that lives by change. Creatures who call the place home have to be robust enough to accommodate the "normal" perturbations such as ice scouring and storm surges that periodically wipe out benthic communities. These hardy communities of clams, mud shrimp and saltwater worms quickly reestablish themselves. "You rarely find a bare patch for long," Daborn says.

The major question with tidal power may revolve around how long it takes for the biological community to reach equilibrium after absorbing the shock that the project would inflict. The Windsor Mudflat may hold answers to this question. I have

watched it grow and change ever since I was an undergraduate at Acadia University, 20 years ago. I never drive the Avon River causeway without casting an inquisitive glance at this artificially constructed island. For more than a decade, there was nothing of note other than a bald, barren mound of purplish mud, and I sped on my way. But in the past few years, signs of life returning to the flat have caught my attention. There are now several tufts of green *Spartina* sprouting from the mud flat's formerly bald dome like the thin hairs atop a baby's head, indicating that some of the flat will eventually be transformed into a productive salt marsh.

Now, in July and August, a few dozen sandpipers can be seen skittering over the flats in their ceaseless search for food, confirming that the mud shrimp must be back. And last September, I brought the car to a full stop on the side of the causeway to observe a large flock of black ducks shovelling the mud for a meal of invertebrates.

It appears that some semblance of biological normality has reestablished itself at Windsor. This might be taken as a testament to the vitality and resiliency of Fundy. Yet I have to remind myself just how long it took for signs of health to return at Windsor. Twenty years is a very long time where shorebirds are concerned – more than a lifetime, in fact. While Fundy slowly rebuilt itself in its image before tidal power, a whole generation could be affected by the loss of critical feeding habitat. Shorebirds simply may not be able to adjust to a sudden major change to their traditional feeding habitat. Certainly, there appear to be no satisfactory alternatives to the major feeding stations found at Marys Point, Grande-Anse and Evangeline Beach, either within the Bay itself, on offshore islands or elsewhere along the Eastern Seaboard. And the return of vital signs at Windsor does nothing to mitigate the alarming arithmetic related to shad passage through turbines.

Operation of North America's first tidal-power plant at Annapolis Royal has established the technical efficiency of the straflo turbine. However, it has also confirmed the legitimacy of some environmental concerns associated with large-scale tidal power. Prime among them is the safe passage of fish through the turbine on the generating cycle. The radio-tagging work carried out by Michael Dadswell (now of Acadia University) is less than encouraging. The spawning shad population native to the Annapolis River has not fared well on its return to the sea. Dadswell has calculated a mortality rate of 20 to 50 percent. Larger fish such as striped bass and sturgeon – which, like the shad, use the Bay as a summer feeding ground – suffer even greater mortalities. Unless fish passageways can be improved or the fish redirected from the intake tube of the turbine (experimental work with sonic bangers has shown some promise), a large tidal-power plant would pose an unacceptable threat to the North Atlan-

I f the Windsor causeway is a good model for a tidal-power barrage, massive siltation and wholesale mortality like that on the Windsor Mudflat, facing page, might be expected. The tidal-power plant at Annapolis Royal, above, has proved the efficiency of the straflo turbine but has also legitimized some environmental concerns – in particular, high fish mortality.

tic shad population and other fishes using the Minas Basin.

"As far as environment is concerned, I don't think we're ready yet to accept the loss of a renewable resource like fisheries," says Daborn, who until now has remained equivocal about large-scale tidal power. "So in my own opinion, the large-scale tidal-power-development proposal is not likely to receive a much more favourable review in the next few years.

"A lot of migratory fish in Minas Basin and the populations of anadromous fish— salmon, striped bass, alewives, blueback herring, smelts and tomcod—in the Shubenacadie and all the other rivers upstream of the Economy Point barrage are very important to the region. I really find it hard to imagine that anyone is going to run the gauntlet that both the commercial fishermen and the sportsmen would force you to run in order to come through with the Minas Basin dam."

Some farmers on the Belleisle Marsh have claimed that the higher-than-average water levels maintained behind the dam at Annapolis have caused damage to marshland through impaired drainage and salt intrusion, although their claims have not been substantiated. Then there's the ubiquitous question of mud that always comes to mind when one is considering the ecology of the upper Bay. The operation of the plant appears to be shifting large volumes of mud about, either by eating away at the banks upriver or by scouring the sea bottom in front of the dam. Clam diggers in the Annapolis Basin charge that mud transported from the plant is ruining their clam beds, and they point to a precipitous decline in landings since the plant became operational.

The primary problem with tidal power from an environmental viewpoint, it now seems to me, stems from our approach to harnessing it. In the past, politicians, economists and engineers have pushed the biggest-is-best approach to development. Comparing tidal power to a vertical Churchill Falls, Gerald Regan, the premier of Nova Scotia in 1977, epitomized this attitude when he said, "One must consider a large development or nothing at all." This philosophy was reflected by the Tidal Power Review Board's choice of prospective development sites. The smallest site selected for serious consideration was the one at Cumberland Basin, which was by no means small: its installed capacity was 50 percent of the power demand in the province. The board's final recommendation in favour of the Minas Basin site—the largest one considered—underscored their bias.

Notwithstanding the economic arguments of scale, which are far from proven in this case, it is abundantly clear that the larger the project, the greater the environmental consequences. This applies particularly to the renewable resource of the fishery. A small project sited on a tidal-river estuary such as the one at Annapolis might have a significant but still localized effect on fish populations. However, blocking an entire embayment would endanger a whole population of migratory fish, not to mention put at risk the shorebird feeding grounds now protected as Hemispheric Shorebird Reserves. Obviously, such an action could not be initiated unilaterally but would require bilateral, if not international, agreement.

Two environmentally acceptable options remain open. The first and most significant is conservation, which would eliminate the need to undertake a massive project for the export of power. The second is development of tidal power on a small scale, thereby minimizing environmental effects.

Small-scale tidal-power plants employing alternative technologies may have a brighter future than megaprojects involving the building of barrages. Research and development are now being done on vertical-axis-type turbines that operate by extracting kinetic energy from tidal currents. The axis of the turbine is up-and-down, as opposed to the horizontal axis of the straight-flow type, and it operates much like a huge eggbeater. As the tidal current flows through, it causes the hydrodynamic blades to rotate. In much the same way that a wind-

mill captures a small part of the total wind energy flowing through at any one time, current generators capture only a small part of the kinetic energy of the tides.

The conventional approach to tidal power has been to apply 19th-century hydropower technology, which is what engineers know, to 20th-century megaproject mentality, which is what politicians like to promote in the name of economic progress. The design goal is to extract the maximum amount of potential energy from the system. To do this, immense dams must be built to interrupt the natural ebb and flow of the tide. However, we now know that by removing large amounts of tidal energy from the system to drive turbines, biological productivity, also tide-driven, is ultimately diminished. The alternative is to design for "inefficiency," as one engineer has noted, and extract only a small proportion of Fundy's total energy, which, after all, is very great.

That being the case, the most appropriate kind of tidal technology would be some variant on the current generator, which would produce power for a local market and have localized environmental effects. This design philosophy is a throwback to the prototype current generator developed by Clarkson and his associates in the Cape Split Development Corporation,

An elderly resident of the Bay touches up her Parrsboro home, facing page. Similarly, politicians and engineers renew the dream of tidal power for each new generation. The boy hightailing it from the general store in Great Village, Nova Scotia, above, may see large-scale tidal power become a reality. But it is now clear that the bigger the project, the greater the environmental consequences.

which brings the thinking about tidal power full circle.

Humanity's recurring dream of exploiting tidal power, of somehow joining forces with the great energy of the tides, has not died—and is not likely to in the future. Phoenix-like, it will rise again. Ironically, the most enduring legacy of tidal power may well prove to be our understanding of the ecology of the Bay. In that sense, it could be said that tidal power already has had a positive environmental impact. For the first time, we have been able to see beyond the hypnotic power of the tides as they rush, boil and eddy to and fro. We now see how those same tides, from their first tentative uprising where the Bay of Fundy meets the Gulf of Maine to the inlets where the tidal bore spends its energies far from sight of the sea, are the dominant forces that rule all living things in Fundy. The tides of Fundy, for all their formidable power, are first and foremost tides of life.

Epilogue

"Exposed to the fury of the sea, rendered still more boisterous by prevailing westerly winds, the majestic precipice has withstood its violence for many ages, or has retreated but slowly from the site where it formerly overshadowed the enormous whirlpools ever curling at its base. It is inaccessible at every point, and affords at high-water not a single broken pedestal where the tardy traveller might rest, had he neglected to retreat before the coming of the flood."

— Abraham Gesner
"Remarks on the Geology and Mineralogy
of Nova Scotia," 1836

On my first hiking trip to Cape Split nearly 20 years ago, I lay awake, my sleep stayed by the uproarious carryings-on of the tide ripping between the archipelago and the peninsula. Finally I drifted off to sleep, trying without much success to conjure up an image of the forcefulness of the chaotic sea change being played out in the darkness around me. Mass meeting mass. It was more akin to the metallic marshalling of railcars, more like steel against steel, than mere water in turmoil.

When I awoke the next morning, the tide was at rest, the Minas Channel a polished, sky-blue mirror for cumulus clouds. My wife and I ate our breakfast near the cliff's edge, watching the gulls and double-breasted cormorants as they made feeding forays from the towering sea stack. The abyss before us seemed to provide unassailable protection for the breeding seabirds, although geology pioneer Abraham Gesner once reported seeing a red fox trying to

The author, above, looks out over the tumultuous tide rips at the base of Cape Split. The promontory gives the best view of the changing of the Fundy tides and has also lent its name to the Bay—Fundy is derived from the French name Cap Fendu (Split Cape). The Pinnacle, facing page, the most seaward of the cape's archipelago, rises above the tide that pours through Minas Channel.

climb this natural fortress and being driven back by a parrying guard of the great black-backed gulls. And more than 200 years earlier, the French explorer Poutrincourt insisted on climbing the promontory in search of copper for Samuel de Champlain. He made it to the top, then nearly slipped to his death and had to be thrown a hawser to aid his safe descent to the beach.

Our plan was less ambitious than Poutrincourt's, but it turned out to be no less imprudent. We intended to climb the lesser peak of the Pinnacle—the most seaward in the Split archipelago—trusting that we had time to do so before the changing of the tides. It was a nearly fatal miscalculation, one that taught me an invaluable lesson: never venture into the intertidal zone of the inner Bay without a tide table.

We made our way down the headland's southern slope into Scots Bay and strolled in a leisurely fashion along the beach, taking time to read in the face of the sheer cliffs

the bold bands of successive lava flows that had formed the headland in late-Triassic times. Crossing the rocky reaches, where the tide had receded between the headland and its archipelago, we began our precarious ascent up the grassy, narrow ridge that led to the sharp peak of the Pinnacle, pitched 75 metres above the island's seaweed-draped pedestal. Reaching the top, we stretched out on the modest plot of turf to enjoy the view—and in my case, at least, to recover from a mild case of vertigo. We had rested no more than a few minutes when I looked down to see the tide making a muddy, swirling moat around our natural castle. Remembering the sound of the tide in the night, my gut tightened.

Our options were clear: either wait out the 12½-hour tidal cycle, or test the deepening waters below. We hastily descended the Pinnacle's spine, plunged into the waist-deep water and waded to the beach. As we beat a hasty retreat before the flood, I looked back to see another couple about to disappear around the Split. Amethyst hunters. As we had been minutes before, they were engrossed in the manifest beauty of the place and oblivious to its hidden dangers. I ran back to warn them. It was good for all of us that they agreed, albeit reluctantly, to accompany us. We met the incoming tide as it made its circuitous way around the hook of the Split and into the channel—in effect, doing an end run by first entering Scots Bay. We helped each other over the rocky reefs as the tide relentlessly ate up the beach. Within the hour, a torrent was flooding through the Split and pounding against the sheer cliffs that would have been our last resort had we been so luckless.

Between the ebb and the flow, when the tide is at full slack, the water off the Split is not unusually agitated. However, this resting state is short-lived. As the tide begins to flood over the submarine cape, the channel is almost instantly transformed into a zone of white-capped violence. Lines of breakers rise up and collapse upon themselves, producing a tumultuous commotion and whipping the channel into the semblance of marble. The conflicting currents streaming by the base of the Split converge in a V, which shoots like an arrow into the Minas Basin. The entire channel becomes a tortuous concatenation of gyres, eddies and whirlpools. Either side of the Split, a torrent of tide pours like a runaway river that has suddenly burst through the walls of a dam.

In the oral tradition of the Micmac Indians relating to the ebb and flow of tides into the Minas Basin, the Micmac man-god Glooscap, a figure of mythic proportions and strength, had his lodge high atop Blomidon, the red headland at the other end of the peninsula that terminates in the Split. The basin, it's said, was Glooscap's beaver pond, and the beaver dam was at Cape Split. Glooscap cut open the dam, allowing the waters to drain out—and, by implication, opening the basin to the sea and the tide. The Micmac name for Minas Channel —*Pleegum*—means "opening made in the beaver dam."

During the past decade, scientists have been piecing together a story of their own of how the highest tides in the world came to reside in the Bay of Fundy. It has been a challenging bit of detective work, as much of the evidence now lies buried under the rising waters of the Bay or under its accretion of marshes. The search has combined traditional and modern techniques—drilling cores into the sea bottom and the newest methods of computer modelling—with good luck, always necessary in solving any mystery.

Bay of Fundy tides are a relatively new phenomenon, geologically speaking, dating from only the end of the last Ice Age. When the mile-thick Wisconsin glacier covered the Maritimes 15,000 years ago, it acted like an enormous sponge, sucking up so much seawater that what are now the shallow fishing banks off Nova Scotia's shores were transformed into islands or, perhaps, peninsulas connected to the main-

land. Fossil evidence of the Pleistocene refugia has been inadvertently dredged up by fishing draggers working the northeastern peak of Georges Bank, 300 kilometres from today's shoreline. From depths as great as 120 metres, they have brought to the surface numerous mastodon and mammoth teeth. There is also living evidence of this Ice Age connection in the form of a unique coastal-plain flora, which is restricted in Maritime Canada to extreme southwestern Nova Scotia. The 30 species

Apinnacle of basalt at Red Head, Nova Scotia, facing page, is connected to the mainland at low tide but becomes an island when the tide floods into Minas Basin. A seawall of beach stone, above, thrown up by the action of the tide and the waves, protects the entrance to Advocate Harbour in Chignecto Bay.

in question, including the exquisite Plymouth gentian, do not occur again until the latitude of Cape Cod. The current theory is that this plant community survived the Ice Age on these once emergent offshore fishing banks and later transplanted themselves to the mainland tip of Nova Scotia as the ice retreated northward.

People, too, migrated north in the shadow of the glacier as the ice released its deadly grip on southern Canada. By 10,600 years ago, a community of Palaeo-Indians occupied a site near Debert, Nova Scotia, at the head of present-day Cobequid Bay. Discovered in 1948 by an amateur archaeologist who was picking blueberries, Debert remains the oldest Palaeo-Indian site known in eastern North America.

The hardy Ice Age colonists probably used Debert as a seasonal camp, having chosen the site to intercept the woodland caribou during their annual fall migration along the north shore of Minas Basin. (Caribou were extirpated from Maritime Canada by the 20th century.) Sea level 10,000 years ago was much lower than it is today, and the now shallow Cobequid Basin was a fertile plain and an attractive grazing area for the caribou. The Debert hunters used fluted stone spear points knapped from local volcanic chalcedony, or agate, to survive in a harsh environment where the mean annual temperature hovered near freezing and remnants of permanent snowfields shimmered like a low bank of pearly clouds on the Cobequid Mountains, eight kilometres away.

The sea reached its lowest level (80 metres below today's mean sea level) 7,000 years ago. During that time, the shelves and ledges at the mouth of the Bay of Fundy may have been exposed. Underwater archaeological evidence supports this idea.

In the 1970s, Digby scallop fisherman Dave Morrison dredged up two curious, half-moon-shaped objects similar to Inuit stone knives, or ulus, two nautical miles from Digby Neck in the outer Bay. Over the past 15 years, Dr. Stephen Davis, an anthropologist from Saint Mary's University, in Halifax, has documented the discovery of six such ulus from both sides of the Bay of Fundy. All were found at similar depths, which seems to rule out the possibility that the ulus might have accidentally fallen out of canoes. Davis is convinced that they belonged to a Maritime Archaic people who inhabited islands at the mouth of the Bay which have since been inundated by water.

Maritime Archaic Islanders (sometimes called Red Paint People for their use of red ochre in burial rites) probably occupied the former islands seasonally as part of an annual subsistence cycle based on maritime resources. Judging from their use by Stone Age Inuit, Davis feels that the ulus and a big slate spearhead, also recovered from a scallop drag, were most likely used for killing and processing sea mammals. Supporting his theory are fossilized walrus tusks—walrus no longer frequent the locale—found by fishermen throughout the Bay of Fundy.

From his excavations at a land site at Checoggin, near Yarmouth, Davis believes that the island-dwelling seafarers used heavy wooden working tools—axes, adzes and gouges—to make dugout canoes from which they hunted sea mammals and made journeys to and from their islands. As the sea level continued to rise, the islands were drowned, and with them went much of the archaeological record for the period in Maritime prehistory—8000 to 3000 B.C.—that has become known as the Great Hiatus.

It was during the latter part of this period that the high tides typical of the Bay of Fundy today began to develop. During the past decade, researchers Dr. Carl Amos and Dr. David Greenberg of the Bedford Institute of Oceanography and Dr. Dave Scott of Dalhousie University's geology department have shown that the critical factor in the amplification of Fundy's tides was the gradual inundation of Georges Bank.

Relative sea level reacted in an up-and-down seesaw fashion to the retreat of the

Tidal rips churn the water near Cape d'Or, above, where the Bay of Fundy divides into its two major embayments, Chignecto Bay and Minas Basin. Over time, the tides have created the perfect "bathtub" for their own propagation and have sculpted the coastline into whimsical shapes such as the "flowerpots" at Hopewell Rocks, facing page. In time, the tides will be their own undoing.

Wisconsin glacier. The land rose in response to the removal of the tremendous burden of ice, as did the sea level as the glacier melted. Later, the land began a slow subsidence that continues to this day.

As a result of these complicated processes, Georges Bank alternately rose above and sank beneath the waters of the Gulf of Maine. As an island, Georges Bank acted as a barrier at the entrance to the Bay, blocking the flow of the tide and dampening the resonance. When the obstruction sank beneath the waves for the final time, about 8,000 years ago, the ocean tide was able to flood freely into the Bay and ultimately engage its sympathetic shape. As a result, tidal amplitude increased rapidly between 7,000 and 4,000 years ago, drowning the islands of the vanished Red Paint People in the process.

At least, that appears to be the story for most of the Bay of Fundy, including Chignecto Bay in the upper reaches. The evolution of the Fundy tides may have been delayed for the Minas Basin, however. A dramatic episode in the making of the world's highest tides came to light in 1977, when a buried forest, in association with an ancient salt marsh and oyster bed, was discovered near Evangeline Beach in the Minas Basin by Dr. Sherman Bleakney of Acadia University. The time capsule of flora and fauna of 3,700 years ago indicated that the Minas Basin was then a brackish lagoon with very little wave action and a tidal amplitude of a mere 2 metres, compared with 15 metres today. Most intriguing were the perfectly preserved oysters that told a story of rapid environmental change. They were extremely elongated, not the standard basin shape. To account for this, Bleakney hypothesizes that the oysters were growing rapidly upward in a vain effort to avoid burial by accumulating sediments. The preservation of fragile surface details and the highly biodegradable periostacum also indicated rapid burial, as did the absence of spat, or oyster young, which cannot tolerate turbid conditions.

At first, Bleakney felt that only a catastrophe such as an earthquake would account for his observations. He now rejects that theory, believing that the massive erosion and sedimentation can be accounted for by the onset of greater tidal energies, coincident with a steady amplification of the range of the Fundy tides.

It is tantalizing to consider the Micmac story of the breaching of Minas Passage in relation to the sudden increase in tidal energies recorded in Bleakney's fossil oyster bed. The violent currents that now scour the Minas Channel make it impossible to take sediment samples or to undertake a seismic survey. However, bottom grabs taken in the area indicate that the 116-metre-deep trench is littered with bunga-low-sized boulders which are shifted about by the 8.8-knot currents. This may be all that is left of a glacial bar which partially or completely blocked the mouth of Minas Channel (the finer sediments having long since been swept away). Such a bar would have protected the Minas Basin from tidal action in the outer parts of the Bay and acted to keep the water clean and relatively warm for the oysters in the basin. As the tidal energies increased in the outer Bay because of the inundation of Georges Bank, increased tidal flow would have begun to eat away at the natural dam. Eventually, the dam would have been breached. As a result, the Bay would have been lengthened and brought even closer to resonance, further amplifying tidal energies and bringing about the demise of the oysters.

The dramatic shoreline of the Bay of Fundy bears the fluid moulding of the tireless onslaught of the tides. Tidal amplitudes are continuing to increase by 15 centimetres per century. The tides have been likened to a geological saw, and the shape of the Bay to the kerf. Over time, the tides have created, in effect, the perfect "bathtub" for their own propagation. Eventually, however, they will continue to cut away the present border until the ideal shape, therefore the resonance effect, is lost. Then the waters will no longer eddy and boil with such energy at the base of Cape Split.

In time, the tides of Fundy, which have been their own creator, will destroy themselves by their own surging power.

Further Reading

This book was conceived and written at a time when there was a renewed and intensive interest in the ecology of the Bay of Fundy, especially in the upper reaches of the Bay where a tidal-power barrage was proposed for the export of electrical energy. Scientists in the region responded by forming the Fundy Environmental Studies Committee of the Atlantic Provinces' Council on the Sciences. The work carried out by this interdisciplinary committee was the source of much of my research. A number of the more comprehensive technical reports are listed below.

Technical Reports

Daborn, G.R. (ed.), *Fundy Tidal Power and the Environment*. The Acadia University Institute, Wolfville, Nova Scotia, 1977.

Gordon, D.C. Jr., and M.J. Dadswell, *Update on the environmental consequences of tidal power development in the upper reaches of the Bay of Fundy*. Canadian Technical Report of Fisheries and Aquatic Sciences No. 1256, 1984.

Daborn, G.R. (ed.), *Effects of Changes in Sea Level and Tidal Range on the Gulf of Maine-Bay of Fundy System*. Acadia Centre for Estuarine Research, Wolfville. Publication No. 1, 1986.

Thomas, M.L.H. (ed.), *Marine and coastal systems of the Quoddy Region, New Brunswick*. Canadian Special Publication of Fisheries and Aquatic Sciences No. 64, 1983.

Plant, S. (compiler), *Bay of Fundy environmental and tidal power bibliography* (second edition). Canadian Technical Report of Fisheries and Aquatic Sciences No. 1339, 1985.

This updated bibliography contains 1,500 references on the environmental characteristics of the Bay of Fundy region, environmental impact studies of tidal-power projects and the engineering and economic aspects of tidal power.

Below is a selection of articles that address the major topics of the book and should be available to a lay reader.

Tides

David Greenberg discusses his modelling of the tides and tidal power in the November 1987 *Scientific American*. David Lynch explains the mechanics of tidal bores in the same publication.

Mud Flats

Mike Risk's "The Windsor Mudflats: Implications for Tidal Power," in the summer 1979 *Geos*, remains the best discussion of the importance and vulnerability of the Fundy mud flats.

Shad and Fish Migrations

Michael Dadswell summarizes his work on shad migration in *Common Strategies of Anadromous and Catadromous Fishes*, American Fisheries Society Symposium 1, 1987.

Migratory Shorebirds

A thorough article on "Mysteries of Bird Migration" appears in the August 1979 issue of *National Geographic*. Harrington and Morrison's article in *Studies in Avian Biology*, No.2:83-100, 1979, "Semipalmated Sandpiper Migration in North America," and Peter Hicklin's "The Migration of Shorebirds in the Bay of Fundy" in the December 1987 issue of *The Wilson Bulletin* provide an overview of shorebird exploitation of the Fundy mud flats. Also see "The Sandpiper and the Shrimp," by Adrian Forsyth, *Equinox*, November/December 1989 and Mary Majka's "Wings Over Fundy" in *Nature Canada* for two different views of the phenomenon at Marys Point. Finally, J.P. Myers and R.I.G. Morrison explain the rationale behind the Western Hemispheric Shorebird Network in "Conservation Strategy for Migratory Species," *American Scientist*, January/February 1987.

Dinosaurs and Mass Extinctions

Two articles in *Science*, "Extraterrestrial Cause for the Cretaceous-Tertiary Extinction" by Walter Alvarez, June 1980, and "New Early Jurassic Tetrapod Assemblages Constrain Triassic-Jurassic Tetrapod Extinction Event" by Paul Olsen, August 1987, put into perspective the Parrsboro dinosaur discovery.

Salt Marshes and Dyke Lands

David Green's article "Chignecto Marshes: Bird and Hay Country" in *Canadian Geographic* is a good introduction to the Tantramar region and the conflicts between wildlife and agricultural use of the marsh.

Seabirds and Shrimp

Richard Brown, seabird biologist and author, discusses what he calls "the last frontier of field ornithology," the study of seabirds at sea, in *Oceanus*, summer 1981, with special reference to the "tidal pump" system off Brier Island. "Suicidal Swarms" by Stephen Nicol, in *Nature Canada*, Winter 1990, presents another view of why shrimp swarm near Brier Island.

Whales

David Gaskin updates the status of the right whale in Volume 101 of *The Canadian Field Naturalist*, and Scott Kraus discusses his research on the North Atlantic right whale in the *Audubon Wildlife Report* 1988/1989. Also see "Right Whales, Courting for Survival Along the East Coast" by Charles Bergman in the April/May 1988 issue of *Canadian Geographic*.

Books, General

There are no books that deal in depth with the Bay of Fundy environment, but a number of books proved useful as background reading. Francis E. Wylie's *Tides and the Pull of the Moon* (New York: Berkley Books, 1979) is a lively, nonmathematical treatment of the mechanics and oceanography of the tides and tidal power. *Life and Death of a Salt Marsh* by John and Mildred Teal (New York: Ballantine Books, 1983) has firmly established itself as the best book on the subject. And, of course, Rachel Carson's classic, *The Sea Around Us* (New York: New American Library, 1961), is worth rereading. Added to this short list is David Gaskin's comprehensive *The Ecology of Whales and Dolphins* (London: Heinemann, 1982), which borrows from his own extensive research on whales and dolphins in the Bay of Fundy. A general book on whales, with an emphasis on descriptive anatomy and illustrations, is Richard Ellis' *The Book of Whales* (New York: Alfred A. Knopf, 1985). *The Sea Has Wings* by Franklin Russell (New York: Doubleday, 1973) is a beautiful evocation of the seabird's year, with photography of Machias Seal Island by Les Line.

Three books of a literary bent, set in Fundy, are: the collaborative portrait in words and pictures of a weirman, *Brown's Weir*, by Gwendolyn and Wayland Drew (Ottawa: Oberon Press, 1983); the wide-ranging work of natural history and philosophy, *Dancing On The Shore, A Celebration of Life at Annapolis Basin*, by Harold Horwood (Toronto: McClelland & Stewart, 1987); and Elizabeth Jones' *Gentlemen and Jesuits, Quests for Glory and Adventure in the Early Days of New France* (Toronto: University of Toronto, 1986), a historical account of the voyages of discovery in the Bay of Fundy.

Field Guides

Field guides are the naturalist's constant companion, and I found two of particular use in my Fundy rovings: A *Sierra Club Naturalist's Guide to the North Atlantic Coast, Cape Cod to Newfoundland* by Michael and Deborah Berrill (San Francisco: Sierra Club Books, 1981); and A *Field Guide to the Whales, Porpoises and Seals of the Gulf of Maine and Eastern Canada, Cape Cod to Newfoundland* by Steven Katona, Valerie Rough and David T. Richardson (New York: Charles Scribner's Sons, 1977). As always, *The Peterson Field Guide* series came in handy, as did *Guide to the Seabirds of eastern Canada* by A.J. Gaston (Ottawa, Environment Canada, 1984).

Books, Regional

Several books of regional interest deserve mention here: *The Birds of Nova Scotia* (Nova Scotia Museum, 1961) by the late dean of Maritime ornithologists, Robie W. Tufts, is still the regional bible on birds; *Summer Nature Notes for Nova Scotians, Seashores* by Acadia biology professor and naturalist Merritt Gibson (Hantsport: Lancelot Press, 1987) is crammed with curious tidbits on local creatures, large and small; two publications by the Nova Scotia Museum, *Geological Background and Physiography of Nova Scotia* by Albert E. Roland and *The Fossil Cliffs of Joggins* by Laing Ferguson provide insights into the geology and palaeontology of the Bay; two very different books about the marsh — *Maritime Dykelands, The 350 Year Struggle* (Province of Nova Scotia, 1987), a historical review of the effort to drain and dyke the marshes in the upper reaches of Fundy, and A *Naturalist's Notebook*, a memoir on the marshes of Yarmouth County by C.R.K. Allen (Nimbus Publishing Limited, 1987). Finally, an excellent booklet on the natural history of the Bay, *Fundy, Bay of Giant Tides*, published by the Fundy Guild, 1984.

Index

Credits

All photographs other than those listed below were taken by Stephen Homer.

Douglas T. Cheeseman Jr.: p.104, p.113; Carl Haycock: p.105, p.106; Brian Hoover/ New England Aquarium: p.133; Scott Kraus/ New England Aquarium: p.134; Greg Stone/ New England Aquarium: p.138; Laurie Murison: p.137, p.140; Margo Stahl: map p.167.

For permission to reprint copyrighted material, the following acknowledgments are gratefully made.

Reprinted with the permission of the Royal Society of Canada from the Transactions of the Royal Society of Canada, June 1952: p.8, p.104; reprinted with the permission of Peter Steinhart from *Audubon Magazine*, New York, July 1985: p.40; reprinted with the permission of Lancelot Press, Hansport, Nova Scotia: p.56; from *The Collected Poems of Sir Charles G.D. Roberts*, The Wombat Press, Wolfville, Nova Scotia, 1985: p.80; from *People of Cove and Woodlot*, Alexander H. Leighton *et al.*, Basic Books Inc., New York, 1960: p.92; reprinted with the permission of Curtis Brown, Ltd., copyright 1973 by Franklin Russell: p.122; from *The Sea Around Us*, Rachel Carson, Oxford University Press, New York: p.109; reprinted with the permission of Walter M. Teller, Princeton, New Jersey: p.109.

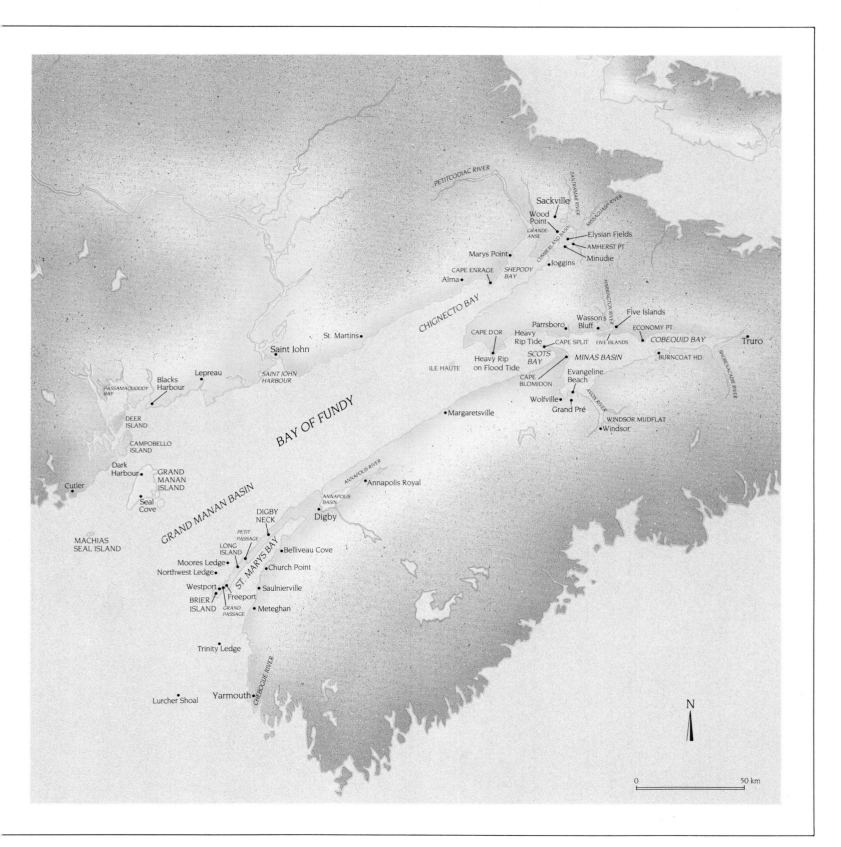

PETITCODIAC RIVER

Sackville

Wood
Point

*GRANDE
ANSE*

Marys Point

CAPE ENRAGE

Alma

*SHEPODY
BAY*

Elysian Fields
AMHERST PT
Minudie

•Joggins

JARTRAMAR RIVER

MOSAGUASH RIVER

CUMBERLAND BASIN

CHIGNECTO BAY

St. Martins •

Saint John

Lepreau

Blacks
Harbour

*PASSAMAQUODDY
BAY*

DEER
ISLAND

CAMPOBELLO
ISLAND

Dark
Harbour

GRAND
MANAN
ISLAND

Cutler

Seal
Cove

*SAINT JOHN
HARBOUR*

CAPE D'OR

Heavy
Rip Tide

ILE HAUTE

Heavy Rip
on Flood Tide

Parrsboro

Wasson's
Bluff

CAPE SPLIT

*SCOTS
BAY*

CAPE
BLOMIDON

Five Islands

FIVE ISLANDS

ECONOMY PT

MINAS BASIN

Evangeline
Beach

Wolfville

Grand Pré

HARRINGTON RIVER

COBEQUID BAY

BURNCOAT HD.

AVON RIVER

WINDSOR MUDFLAT

•Windsor

Truro

SHUBENACADE RIVER

BAY OF FUNDY

• Margaretsville

GRAND MANAN BASIN

MACHIAS
SEAL ISLAND

DIGBY
NECK

Digby

*PETIT
PASSAGE*

LONG
ISLAND

Moores Ledge •

Northwest Ledge •

Westport •

Freeport

BRIER
ISLAND

*GRAND
PASSAGE*

• Meteghan

Belliveau Cove

• Church Point

• Saulnierville

Annapolis Royal

ANNAPOLIS RIVER

*ANNAPOLIS
BASIN*

ST. MARYS BAY

Trinity Ledge

CHEBOGUE RIVER

Lurcher Shoal

Yarmouth •

N

0   50 km